"Fosters a refreshing educational discourse of possibility and offers some very useful classroom strategies that work with today's youth."

Peter P. Grimmett, PhD, Professor and Associate Dean
Director, Institute for Studies in Teacher Education
Faculty of Education, Simon Fraser University

"A wonderful guidebook for people moving toward constructivism and for many who are already there."

Geoffrey Caine, Director
Caine Learning
Idyllwild, CA

"The book's content emanates from a simple summary of research on natural learning processes. From this flows an array of exciting approaches for the classroom teacher of any subject. Various strategies, all shaped to kindle students' curiosity, involvement, and understanding, are tied to demonstration teaching units, which in themselves could be directly transferred to a classroom.

"'Handle with Care' should be on the front cover so that the eager teacher uses the book as an inspirational resource, gradually remolding practice and introducing change in appropriate increments. . . . This book might have immediate impact if used first as a discussion starter for small groups of teachers or as a study guide for staff development or 'retreats.' The message of the book, however, goes far beyond strategies for teachers. There are issues here for school administrators, for state-mandated goals and programs, and for teacher education programs. The book certainly deserves consideration by teacher education methods instructors. And as parental involvement is absolutely necessary if any constructive change is to take place, imagine how discussion of this text might perk up a PTA meeting!"

Roy Bentley, PhD, Professor Emeritus
University of British Columbia

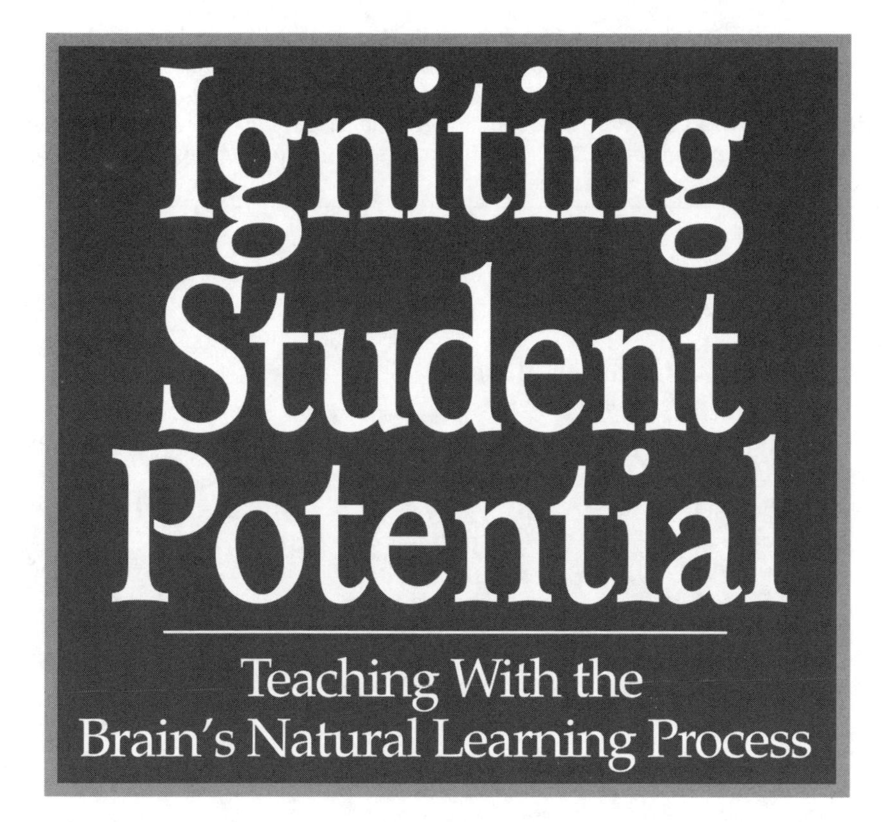

Angus M. Gunn
Robert W. Richburg
Rita Smilkstein

KH

For information:

Corwin Press
A Sage Publications Company
2455 Teller Road
Thousand Oaks, California 91320
www.corwinpress.com

Sage Publications Ltd.
1 Oliver's Yard
55 City Road
London EC1Y 1SP
United Kingdom

Sage Publications India Pvt. Ltd.
B-42, Panchsheel Enclave
Post Box 4109
New Delhi 110 017 India

Printed in the United States of America

Library of Congress Cataloging-in-Publication Data

Gunn, Angus M. (Angus Macleod)
Igniting student potential : teaching with the brain's natural learning process / Angus M. Gunn, Robert W. Richburg, Rita Smilkstein.
p. cm.
Includes bibliographical references and index.
ISBN 1-4129-1705-0 or 978-1-4129-1705-6 (cloth)
ISBN 1-4129-1706-9 or 978-1-4129-1706-3 (pbk.)
1. Learning, Psychology of. 2. Brain. 3. Motivation in education. I. Richburg, Robert W. (Robert Williams) II. Smilkstein, Rita. III. Title.
LB1060.G86 2007
370.15'23—dc22 2006021821

This book is printed on acid-free paper.

06 07 08 09 10 10 9 8 7 6 5 4 3 2 1

Acquisitions Editor: Faye Zucker
Editorial Assistant: Gem Rabanera
Production Editor: Libby Larson
Copy Editor: Jennifer Withers
Typesetter: C&M Digitals (P) Ltd.
Proofreader: Sally M. Scott
Indexer: Nara Wood
Cover Designer: Michael Dubowe
Graphic Designer: Lisa Riley

1/28/08

Contents

Acknowledgments ix

About the Authors xi

PART I. RESEARCH AND THEORY

Chapter 1. Why This Book? Why Now? 3
- The Moral of the Maginot Line 3
- Are Our Educational "Guns" Facing the Wrong Direction? 5
- A Bloated Curriculum 6
- A Testing Obsession 8
- Cultivating the Latent Ability of Every Student 10
- Life-Altering Teachers 12
- The Classroom as a Community 14
- Understanding Is a Key to Hope 15
- A Playful Classroom 15
- Notes 17

Chapter 2. How Learning Happens: The Natural Human Learning Process 19
- Students Are Natural Learners 19
- Trying to Find the Way 19
- Research on the Natural Human Learning Process (NHLP) 28
- Using the Missing Link in Math Education 33
- If All Students Learn the Same Way, Why Are Students' Fates Different? 34
- A Person's Fate: Nature or Nurture? 35
- Helping Students See Their Potential: Students' Self-Understanding 37
- The Benefits of the NHLP Research and Metacognitive Knowledge 38
- All Students Have an Innate Potential and Motivation to Learn 41

The NHLP Pedagogy 42
Notes 44
References 45

Chapter 3. How the Brain Learns: Student Empowerment and Potential **47**
The Seven Magic Words 48
Metacognition: Basic Facts About How the Brain Learns That Everyone Should Know 52
Motivation 58
Creativity 59
Emotions and the Brain: Fight or Flight 59
Constructivism 60
Reasons Students Are Not Motivated in School 63
Plasticity (Neuroplasticity) 70
No-Fail First-Stage Learning Tasks 71
Examples of No-Fail First-Stage Learning Tasks 72
Things That Can Make the Brain Go Wrong 74
Feeding the Brain 75
Opportunities to Fulfill Their Potential 75
Notes 76
References 78

PART II. CLASSROOM APPLICATIONS

Chapter 4. How Tall Am I? Real-World Math for Early Learners **83**
Transition From Home to School 84
A Math-Friendly Environment 85
Math Content for Early Grades 88
Multiple Intelligences and Student Potential 92
Exploring Outside the Classroom 93
Evaluation 95
References 95

Chapter 5. Can You Build an Igloo? Understanding the Past With Elementary Learners **97**
Discovering the Past 98
Beginning the Unit 99
Examining a Distant Place 101
Inuit Society Today 108
References 109

Chapter 6. Where Would You Locate Your Castle? Developing Potential in Early Adolescent Learners **111**
What Are the Relatively Normal Physical Changes That Occur With the Beginning of Puberty? 112

How Then Would We Teach? 114
Justin's Teacher 115
Building Relationships: The Key to Early Adolescents 116
Enriched Environments 118
Boredom Reduces the Adolescent Brain 121
The Importance of Play 123
The Opposite of Play Is Stress 123
Active Learning and Problem Solving 124
Connected Learning 125
Social Learning 126
The Importance of Emotion 127
Where Would You Put Your Castle? A Potential-Igniting Teaching Unit 128
An Acronym to Help Us Remember These Strategies 130
The Early Adolescent Needs a Uniquely Skilled, Compassionate Teacher 131
Notes 132

Chapter 7. What Keeps Satellites Above Earth? Scientific Investigations for Teenage Learners 133
Teenage Intellectual Abilities 133
Learning to Use Scientific Methods 134
Coral Atolls 136
Pendulum Clocks 138
Gravity 140
Satellites 143
Relativity 144
References 145

PART III. TEACHER SKILLS

Chapter 8. Learning Communities: Falling Empire and Rising Democracy 149
Learning Communities 149
Models of Learning Communities 150
The "Ask Them" Method for Assessment and Engaged Learning 154
Igniting Student Potential 160
Notes 161
References 161

Chapter 9. Assessment Strategies That Promote Learning and Ignite Student Potential 165
Instructional Sequence: Case 1 167
Instructional Sequence: Case 2 167

What Are the Differences Between Juan's and Mary's Approaches to Assessment? 169
Informal Feedback 172
Making Certain We Are Measuring What Our Students Are Learning 174
Test Considerations Versus Projects 177
Notes 179
Appendix A: Interest Inventory 180
Appendix B: Eporue 181
Appendix C: Juan's Classroom 182
Appendix D: Using Juan's Interest Inventory to Show Group Attitude Change 183

Chapter 10. Developing Teachers Who Inspire Their Students 185
What Is Different About Instruction That Allows the Brain to Learn in Its Most Natural Way? 186
Why Does This Approach Work? 190
How Do Teacher Skills Differ in Problem-Solving Instruction? 192
A Model Preservice Teacher Training Program: Training Teachers to Teach With the Brain's Natural Way of Learning 195
Candidate Selection Process 196
Program Structure 197
The Teacher Education Classroom as a Laboratory 198
A More Effective Approach to the Preservice Education of Teachers 199
The Ongoing Professional Development of Teachers 200
If the Resources Were Available, What Would a Model Professional Development Program Look Like? 201
Lesson Study: Another Professional Development Strategy 202
Educare 203
Conclusion 204
Notes 204

Index 207

Acknowledgments

Angus M. Gunn's acknowledgments: I am indebted to several colleagues at the University of British Columbia for their help in identifying the appropriate methods to employ with first and second graders. Primary teachers in two schools confirmed the appropriateness of their recommendations. Heather Bagshaw, who arranged a series of experiences with her own child, gave me new insights into the enormous potential of preschoolers if they are given freedom to learn in their own way.

Robert W. Richburg's acknowledgments: I want to thank Fran, my best friend and the love of my life, for her support and inspiration over the many years of our marriage. Also, I am more than grateful for my talented and caring sons, Matthew and Andrew, and to their wonderful spouses, Sara and Kristi. I am thrilled every day by the blessing of having Ellis, Blaise, Annie, Ben, and Emma as grandchildren. Finally, I am grateful to my students at Colorado State University, who have ignited my potential as a teacher.

Rita Smilkstein's acknowledgments: To my children, Jessica, Susanna, Diana, and Georgia, and my grandchildren, Laurel, Rome, Jesse, and Isabella, all of whom have inspired me to try to be the best I can be. To my friends, colleagues, and students, who have helped me see how everyone can be the best he or she can be. Also, a very appreciative thank you to the readers who provided invaluable suggestions for changes and improvements; to Faye Zucker, our editor, for her support throughout; and to Jennifer Withers for copyediting. And many thanks to Gem Rabanera for expertly and kindly keeping everything and everyone organized and on track.

Publisher's acknowledgments: Corwin Press thanks the following reviewers for their contributions to this book:

Roy Bentley
Professor Emeritus
University of British Columbia

Geoffrey Caine
Director
Caine Learning, LLC
Idyllwild, CA

Michael Dickmann
Professor
Department of Educational Leadership
Cardinal Stritch University
Milwaukee, WI

Peter P. Grimmett
Director
Institute for Studies in Teacher Education
Simon Fraser University

Marilee Sprenger
Professional Development Consultant
Peoria, IL

About the Authors

Angus M. Gunn, Emeritus Professor at the University of British Columbia, is author of numerous books, in addition to articles and media productions, on such topics as education, geography, and environmental science. A native of Scotland, he resides now in West Vancouver, Canada.

Robert W. Richburg, PhD, is University Distinguished Teaching Scholar at Colorado State University. A teacher of teachers, he resides in Ft. Collins, Colorado.

Rita Smilkstein, PhD, Faculty Emerita in English at North Seattle Community College and currently an invited lecturer at Western Washington University's Woodring College of Education, has authored textbooks and articles on brain-based, natural-learning education across disciplines. *We're Born to Learn: Using the Brain's Natural Learning Process to Create Today's Curriculum* (Corwin Press) won the Delta Kappa Gamma Society International Educator's Award, 2004. She is the recipient of many teaching awards and in 2006 was elected as a Fellow of the American Council of Developmental Education Associations.

PART I

Research and Theory

Why This Book? Why Now?

1

If you treat an individual as he is, he will stay as he is, but if you treat him as if he were what he ought to be and could be, he will become what he ought to be and could be.

—Goethe

This is a book about inspirational learning, the sort of learning that alters lives and enables children to be all they can be. We begin with an intriguing historical story. Though this is a story about Europe more than a half century ago, we think it has lessons for us today.

THE MORAL OF THE MAGINOT LINE*

The idea of building the Maginot Line was born out of a persistent and difficult problem. At the end of World War I, the French people had developed a venomous hatred and mistrust of Germany. The First World War had cost the French 1,500,000 men killed, literally an entire generation of its youth. Mourning had become the national dress of the women of France. The foundations of the idea for the Maginot Line were said to be in the cemeteries of France.

The French had been invaded by Germany 15 times in six centuries, and the French were determined that this would not happen again. The traditional route of German invasions had been down the Moselle Valley through the cities of Metz and Nancy into Lorraine and the northeastern corner of France. Led by Andre Maginot, himself a disabled veteran of World War I, the French were passionate to build a "defensive scheme in depth," unlike anything ever built in human history to keep the Germans out.

---

*Adapted from material in *The Great Wall of France* by Vivian Rowe. © 1961, 1959. by Putnam's Sons, New York.

The French invested half of their national income from 1920 to 1939 in building the "Great Wall of France." The most intelligent, energetic, and committed citizens set to work devising and building a network of fortresses and defensive structures from Belgium to the Alps Mountains along the Rhine River. The most talented young people graduating from the best French schools aspired to work on this great national project. It literally consumed France for a generation.

The wall they built was impressive. There were immense fortresses every one and a quarter miles. The fortresses held 1,200 to 1,500 men and had an array of guns with a 50-degree field of fire that overlapped so that every square inch from 5 feet to 50 miles to the northeast could be shelled with intense fire. Between these larger fortresses, every quarter mile, there were smaller artillery blocks with antitank weapons with a range up to 7 miles. The territory immediately in front of this line of fortifications looked like the back of a porcupine. For the entire length of the Maginot Line, steel girders imbedded in concrete were placed every 2 to 3 feet facing to the northeast to impale tanks or other mechanized forces that might attack. The entire line of fortresses was covered with 12 feet of concrete, and the entire structure, many hundreds of miles long, was connected by underground tunnels so the defenders would never be exposed to enemy fire.

There were huge armies behind this immense line of fortification as well. The British Expeditionary Force was amassed along the French-Belgium border. The French First, Second, Sixth, and Eighth armies were situated behind the Maginot Line from the Alps to the Ardennes forest, which was adjacent to Luxembourg.

The French designers had decided that there was no need to build their wall of fortifications next to the Ardennes because they judged it to be an impenetrable forest. Their military leader, Marshall Petain, had determined that if the Germans massed their troops near the Ardennes, the French and British would catch them in a pincerlike move and destroy them.

So, what happened in May 1940 when Germany invaded France for the 16th time?

The Germans did not do the predictable thing. They did not attack the Maginot Line from the northeast, the direction they had come so often before. They did not mass their troops opposite the Ardennes forest and give Petain time to anticipate an attack. They kept their mechanized forces well back in Germany and then rolled down their autobahn, cut narrow tracks through the Ardennes, and swept in behind the Great Wall of France. There was virtually no fighting, and the guns of the immense French fortresses were never fired. They were all facing the wrong direction.[1]

The story of the Maginot Line is a tragic one because for a generation, the talent, resources, and energies of an entire nation were absolutely wasted. The passion, hard work, creativity, and dedication of the French netted them nothing. That which they most wanted to avoid happened, and in their preoccupation to avoid this outcome, they undoubtedly lost opportunities for far more positive national outcomes.

We think this story from Europe in the last century may be a metaphor for today's educators in North America. We may be as absorbed with our concerns about our schools' performance as the French were with their scheme to defend their country. Is it possible that, like the Maginot Line, our "guns" in education are facing the wrong direction? Is there any chance that our resources, talents, and efforts are being directed in ways that will prove as unproductive as those of the French before World War II? Equally important, in our present all-consuming efforts, are we missing what our students and society need most? We fear that these are more than possibilities and that the costs of our mistakes may be similarly high.

ARE OUR EDUCATIONAL "GUNS" FACING THE WRONG DIRECTION?

There is no more conscientious and caring group of people in America than educators. With very few exceptions, their dedication and efforts are exemplary. Teachers, however, are being frustrated by well-meaning but naive policymakers and overseers who are steadily moving the direction of instruction away from authentic genuine learning, the sort of learning that brings out the best in students. Below are just a few of the many ways that the energies and efforts of these educators are being aimed in the wrong direction.

The most serious "misaim" in American education is barely on the radar screen of most educational reformers. The most certain way to elevate the level and quality of learning in our nation's classrooms is to provide more time in the teacher day for planning and professional growth. We mistakenly think of the teacher workday as the number of hours and minutes they are actually with children. The approaches to teaching that we are advocating and that inspire students require far more time to create and organize than the 20 to 50 minutes the typical American teacher is given for planning each day. Much of this allocated "planning time" turns out not to be available for lesson planning anyway. It often is spent contacting parents, dealing with discipline issues, and attending necessary meetings with other teachers.

Veteran teachers, who understand what it takes to prepare lessons that interest and excite learners, talk of a two-to-one ratio of time to prepare as compared with actual in-classroom time. They understand that creativity in developing their lessons takes time. The arguments against providing this time center on resources. Schools aren't given the money to provide for teacher planning time. Interestingly, the other nations in the developed world—whose students' achievement is being compared with ours—do provide this time. Whereas American teachers are with students an average of 25 to 30 hours a week, European and Japanese teachers average only 16 to 20. If our students are going to have lessons that captivate and energize them, schools will have to find the time and opportunities for their teachers to plan collaboratively together, observe and critique one another, and be genuine learners themselves. The research is clear that when teachers are excited learners, planners, and collaborators, their students are more effective and enthusiastic learners.[2]

A BLOATED CURRICULUM

A second, more subtle way our guns in American education are being misdirected is the result of the so-called knowledge explosion. Because the totality of human knowledge is doubling every few months, it becomes imperative that we accept the fact that a good education doesn't mean that students have mastered all or even a significant portion of that knowledge. Right now, the curriculum our teachers are given to teach contains too much content. It is overly broad and therefore superficial. We operate under fear that students will be missing some essential piece of knowledge, and ironically, in trying to cover so much, we end up with a less effective education.

The standards developed in the 1990s were put forth as an answer to this concern. They were intended to define the key ideas and skills from each subject so that the curriculum would focus on a more limited knowledge base and thereby be more manageable. Unfortunately, these standards have been of only limited value in reducing the amount of content teachers are expected to teach. In a study conducted by the Mid-Continent Regional Educational Laboratory in 1996, the essential standards from 15 subject areas were examined. Altogether, there were 245 standards. Reflecting on this number, the authors determined that it would take 21 years of intense instruction to teach these in any systematic way. Unless we plan to keep our K–12 students until they are 25 years old, we have far too much content in our curriculum.[3]

Two negative things happen when teachers feel the pressure to teach too much material. First, they lose sight of broader educational goals, such as preparing students to live effectively or helping them to become good citizens. Learning the major concepts of each discipline doesn't necessarily lead directly to these outcomes. Teachers must teach their subjects with a conscious eye on life preparation goals in order for these to be accomplished. The word *curriculum* reminds us of this. The term comes to us from a Latin verb meaning "to run a race." It conveys the idea that our curriculum should prepare students to run the race of life. In other words, what we learn in school should help us to live effectively in life. Unfortunately, when teachers feel inordinate pressure to cover burdensome amounts of content, they won't take the time to share messages that could provide insights about life and living. Let me relate a story that illustrates this.

A social studies teacher friend of mine found a news story about a triathlete, Jim McLaren, who at the height of his competitive career suffered a series of accidents that left him paralyzed. This teacher noticed the story because of the attitude this disabled athlete had toward his misfortune. He was certainly disappointed, but not in any way bitter or angry about what had happened to him. Rather, he had come to see his disabilities as a way to encourage others who had suffered disabilities. McLaren became a motivational speaker and shared his "10-90" rule with audiences around the country. He told his listeners that life is 10% what happens to you and 90% how you respond. What a great example of how to maintain a positive attitude while dealing with adversity. My friend planned to use this lesson in a unit on Theodore Roosevelt in an Advanced Placement U.S. History class. It would be appropriate there because Roosevelt had overcome several physical challenges himself. However, my history teacher friend never used the story of Jim McLaren. With all the topics on the syllabus—the muckrakers, the many social reforms of this period, and the events leading to World War I—there was no time to engage his students in a discussion about dealing positively with the challenges of life. A potentially valuable lesson was lost to the perception that the job of a teacher is simply to plow through the course content.

The processes of instruction or pedagogy are also negatively affected when there is too much content in the curriculum. Because most teachers are dutiful and try to do as they are directed, they fall into a mode of instruction that is lecture or teacher centered and that allows them to "cover" material. We now understand how difficult it is for the brain to process into memory material presented this way. There is simply too much, coming too fast. Many students see the futility in this and don't even try to learn. The highly motivated will work to retain the ideas their teacher has conveyed long enough to pass the usual weekly test, but then these "learnings" disappear quickly.

The reason that content coverage is a subtle problem is that students must be involved with rich content if the best they are capable of is to emerge. Focusing on rich content means that ideas and concepts can be explored with enough depth and integrity to promote wonderment or genuine insight. Raising the bar in education should not be construed to mean covering more content. Depth and understanding will serve our students better than simply getting through material, and until we are willing to acknowledge that we are purposefully leaving material uncovered, we will never have the quality of instruction our students need. There is little doubt that less is more when it comes to curriculum.

A TESTING OBSESSION

There is a related but even more destructive misdirection of American education. It involves our policy makers' obsession with standardized testing. Giving students tests in order to hold them, their teachers, and their schools accountable for learning seems like an unassailable way to improve education. If large amounts of public monies are going to be spent on education, the public has a right to know that students are learning. If the tests show that schools are performing below some norm, they should be restructured or closed. The way to improve the learning in our classrooms, so the argument goes, is to hold students, teachers, and schools to high performance standards through mandated yearly testing and to punish under-performance wherever it is exposed.

Unfortunately, like many things in education, meaningful accountability is more sophisticated than this, and oversimplifying the issue is causing more harm to children than good. First, even before the mandated testing of the No Child Left Behind Act, American children were the most tested in the entire world. As a nation, we have typically spent more than a half billion dollars annually on testing our children. Virtually all school districts have had their own procedures for testing their students and thereby providing needed feedback to teachers about areas of the curriculum that need more emphasis. What policy makers want instead are standardized tests that would enable the achievement in buildings and districts to be compared. In this way, those performing above the norm could be identified and praised, while those falling below could be compelled to improve. Again, this sounds like a good idea, but there are some major problems.

In order to do these large-scale comparative assessments, a significant additional amount of time must be allocated to the testing process. This testing time is in addition to the "levels" tests that schools already administer in order to provide specific feedback on the goals of the district. In schools I am familiar with, these state-mandated standardized tests require nearly two weeks of testing to be inserted in an already crowded school calendar. We certainly need tests and other assessments. The question is how they are used. Tests that are diagnostic provide feedback to the learner, the teacher, and parents and help focus and inform the learning process. These tools also help identify holes and weaknesses in school curricula and are therefore important for school improvement purposes. This whole process deserves special attention. That is the focus of Chapter 9.

What about the need to compare schools and districts so we know who is doing a good job and who is not? If all students and schools started their educational processes on an equal footing, such comparisons might make sense. The problem is that they do not. Because property taxes are the primary form of school funding and the disparities in property values in America are enormous, schools in some neighborhoods and communities have far greater resources to work with than others do.

Our students don't start on an equal footing either. There is a great deal of evidence about this. A study by David Berliner provides a sample of it. In 2001, David Berliner reviewed the test results from the Third International Math Science Study (TIMSS). In this study, U.S. eighth graders as a whole placed 18th in science achievement and 19th in mathematics compared with students from 37 other developed nations. In his review, Berliner disaggregated the national data and showed the remarkable influence of socioeconomic factors on our students' performance. As one example, he cites the comparison of two groups of students from the state of Illinois. Apparently, 20 of the most affluent school districts in suburban Chicago asked to be considered as a separate nation in the TIMSS competition. Their scores were higher in both mathematics and science than those of any of the other nations. On the other hand, Berliner examined the scores of the students of East St. Louis, Illinois, one of the poorest communities in our nation, and this community showed a completely different result. These students, who live in dire poverty, finished lower in math and science than any of the 37 nations.[4] As Kenneth Wesson writes, "It is widely acknowledged by test-development experts that a higher socio-economic background gives students a positive boost in standardized-test achievement."[5]

However unfair the results of these tests may be, they have a strong influence on how the public views its schools. Property values go up in neighborhoods served by so-called 'high-performing' schools and down in those where achievement results are lower, further intensifying the problem. In some parts of our nation, schools are ordered to close because their test scores are not high enough. Consider the pressure there must be on students as they face these exams! If they don't do well, their school will be punished by losing state resources or will even be closed. Is it any wonder this process is referred to as "high-stakes testing"? Predictably, the schools being closed are in the poorest urban areas. The students from these discontinued schools are then wrenched out of their familiar surroundings and reassigned to a supposedly "higher-functioning" school that simply has more resources or a more affluent clientele. How likely is it that such a reassignment will enable these students to be better learners?

There is still another issue with high-stakes standardized tests. Because they are designed to be given to large numbers of students, they must be able to be machine scored and thus have a multiple-choice or single-correct-answer format. This dictates the sorts of questions that can be asked and limits the level of sophistication of thinking that can be measured. There is virtually no way to use these tests to assess the complex higher-order abilities that students need in order to be effective participants in the world they will live in. We can foresee that, in the world, they will have to be able to evaluate ideas, think creatively, solve problems, work well in teams, and have a variety of other sophisticated skills—none of which are measurable with these standardized tests.

The accumulating effects of these high-stakes tests are overwhelmingly negative. Audry Amrein reports that students' intrinsic motivation to learn diminishes because of the influence of these tests. Teachers are using fewer hands-on and active learning strategies and more boring drill activities. Students are less likely to engage in critical thinking because so little is called for in these tests. Nationally, dropout rates are climbing, and researchers attribute this trend to these tests. There is evidence that these tests have led to a narrowing of the curriculum as art, music, creative writing, physical education, and even recess are reduced or eliminated in order to focus more on the subjects that are tested. Even within the areas of the curriculum that are tested, schools are not teaching subareas if they are unlikely to appear on the test. If, for example, quadratic equations are not anticipated on a state's math test, quadratics won't be taught as a part of the algebra curriculum.[6]

CULTIVATING THE LATENT ABILITY OF EVERY STUDENT

The intention of this book is not primarily to focus on the problems and failures of current educational practice. We only mention these issues because they have turned our attention and resources away from what our focus should be. While we have been caught up in trying to cover content and prepare for standardized tests, we have moved away from the development of the talent in each child. Cultivating the latent ability of every student is the central task of all education. The very meaning of the Latin verb *educare*, from which we derive our word *education*, conveys this ideal. *Educare* means "to draw out" as in drawing out talent or ability. The fortunes of our society depend on the degree to which educators are able to do this. Let's look at another story that illustrates how we might orient our energies, resources, and classrooms.

What follows is a story about a real 14-year-old student. As you read, consider how you would develop this student's latent ability if you were one of his teachers.

W.C. is an ugly child. His head is too large for his slight frame. His stomach protrudes. He's sickly, weak, and uncoordinated. He misses a lot of school and is bullied by other kids when he is there.

W.C. is a serious discipline problem. He is written up for some class disturbance every week. He is always late for class. When he does get there, he doesn't bring his texts or any materials.

Virtually every teacher despairs about having him in class. He hates math and is the lowest-performing student in foreign language class. He sees no point in studying English and usually sleeps in class. This is a remedial English class and he is failing because he doesn't turn in any work. He is thought to have some ability in history, but his teacher dislikes him intensely because W.C. contradicts him and argues with him about everything. W.C. even hates PE, although he would like martial arts, if that were offered, because he fights all the time.

He does have hobbies. He likes to read, especially about wars and famous people in history. He sometimes memorizes lines from plays. He is fairly artistic and draws well.

On campus, the most often used terms to describe this student are *hopeless* and *dismal.* Assuredly, he would have been kicked out of school except for the fact that it would bring a lot of negative publicity to the school because of his family. His father is a prominent political figure. Neither parent pays much attention to him.[7]

Make no mistake: W.C. is going to make your job more difficult. He will take your time and attention from other students who need your help, and no matter how hard you try, he is not going to pass the mandated achievement tests that will be given in the spring. If your school does not show the improvement on these tests that is prescribed by the No Child Left Behind legislation, the extra time you spent with W.C. might jeopardize your school. You must be realistic.

So, how did W.C.'s teachers deal with him?

Fortunately, W.C. lived in a time and place where there were no high-stakes standardized tests, but there was plenty of pressure on his teachers anyway because the school he attended was a prestigious school. After several years of disruptive behavior and failure, he was assigned to three teachers who, fortunately, had a life-changing influence on him.

The first teacher, whose name was Moriarity, taught W.C. fencing, but his instruction went far beyond the skills of handling a foil. W.C. exhibited few physical attributes to attract this teacher's attention. Moriarity wrote of W.C. that he was "weak, uncoordinated with the fragile hands of a girl." It was obvious to Moriarity that W.C. would never be much of a fencer no matter how hard he worked with him. Despite W.C.'s physical failings and lack of aptitude, Moriarity invited this 14-year-old to his home in the evenings, where the two of them talked about literature and history and practical things about life and living.

The second teacher to influence W.C. was C.H.P. Mayo, a math teacher. W.C. later said of Mayo, "No credit is too great for this man." W.C. believed that no matter how hard he would try, he would never succeed at math. Yet in the way that Mayo taught, W.C. came to see that "mathematics was not a hopeless bog of nonsense. There were meanings and rhythms behind the comical hieroglyphics." We know nothing about the techniques Mr. Mayo used, but he was able to make his subject comprehensible to a student who was certain he could not learn it. In doing so, he gave W.C. hope. Without hope, a student won't invest the effort to try to learn.

The third teacher who had a powerful influence on W.C. was a new teacher at his school, Robert Somervell. Probably because he was a new teacher, Somervell was given the assignment of teaching remedial English. W.C., who had already failed this course twice before, was taking it again because he was considered too much of a "dolt" to learn the regular curriculum of Latin or Greek. Remarkably, Somervell was enthusiastic about teaching a remedial course to learners who had already failed the subject. W.C. later wrote of Somervell, "His enthusiasm was infectious. He just knew how to do it. He taught as no one else has ever taught it." He apparently drilled them regularly, but he did so in a way that appealed to the "playful instinct of every boy." W.C. continued to be a student of Somervell's for three terms, and under this masterful teacher he developed a fascination with words and a deep interest in writing. Though it is not what he is most famous for, W.C. would later write more than 50 highly respected and influential books.[8]

LIFE-ALTERING TEACHERS

It would be difficult to overstate the importance of what these three teachers did for W.C. Certainly our world would be different today if they had not helped him see the person he was capable of becoming. At the time that they encountered him, he was exhibiting very little talent or motivation. According to his biographer, William Manchester, with the exception of these three instructors, the remainder of his masters described him as "unmotivated," "willfully troublesome," and "intellectually inept." Yet this "dismal" student, who attributes his turnaround to these three teachers, went on to become a brilliant orator, award-winning author, and arguably the finest statesman of the twentieth century. W.C. is none other than Winston Churchill, a dominant figure of his time.

Not every unmotivated, nonperforming student has the potential to be another Winston Churchill, but there have been countless students with remarkable talent whose teachers had no idea how to promote their talent. Albert Einstein's teachers described him as a "dull student." Walt Disney was described as "slow." He never experienced success in school. The list includes renowned anthropologist Dr. Mary Leakey, codiscoverer of the Zinjanthropus fossil remains in East Africa, and George Marshall, author of the Marshall Plan, which revived Europe after World War II. Film director Steven Spielberg was not considered a student with ability. The list of those who have been written off by their teachers includes astounding numbers of statesmen, astronauts, and college professors.

Churchill too was written off by the educators at Eton College. He graduated last in his class. The three special teachers he encountered there, however, gave him the greatest gift a teacher can give. They helped him develop a vision of his own greatness. Pulias explained this gift this way: "The individual cannot or will not take advantage of opportunity, however physically available it may be, unless he is brought to believe that he has possibilities for growth and that this opportunity is a door for him."[9] How does a teacher inspire the development of this vision? How, like Churchill's teachers, can we influence students to believe that they can grow and accomplish important things?

Teachers hold the power to unleash a psychological force that brings out the best in a child. The process apparently begins with the perceptions they have of their students. Arthur Combs and others have reported a quarter century of research about how the perceptions of individuals in the helping professions affected their clients. The results were the same across all helping professions—teachers, counselors, ministers, nurses, and the like. Those who were effective differed from those who were not effective in the degree to which they held positive perceptions of their clients.[10] Good teachers, as an example, may be clearly identified by the fact that they view their students as "able" rather than "unable," "worthy" rather than "unworthy," "dependable" rather than "undependable." Subtly or not so subtly, they give students messages that communicate these perceptions.

- "You have such a wonderful way with words, Justin. Look at the way you phrased this idea . . . Since the beginning of the year I've believed you could be a very good writer."
- "This is a very perceptive comment, Jen. You are showing a lot of maturity in your thinking. Let me explain why I think this is so good . . ."
- "This is an impressive part of your project, Kari! You are asking the kinds of questions a scientist would be concerned about. I hope you are considering taking more science courses."

Most students will respond with stronger efforts when they receive specific positive messages such as these from adults who they respect. These teachers are building on their students' strengths by making specific comments on elements of work that are strong or show promise. It doesn't mean that they can't find weakness as well, but correcting behavior must be done with extreme care. Students of any age, in fact virtually all human beings, are sensitive to criticism. Even gently offered suggestions can overshadow what a teacher wanted to be a positive affirmation to a student. Building on strengths may mean overlooking some errors or even needed improvements. These comments may be more appropriate at a later point. The message that so many students need to hear isn't that this or the other thing is wrong but rather, "You are capable and doing particular things really well."

THE CLASSROOM AS A COMMUNITY

Positive perceptions and affirming messages are certainly not the whole of the process of encouraging potential. Affirmations are rather a step in developing an atmosphere of community in a classroom. Part of the positive support system young people need must come from their peers, but it is up to the teacher to develop that peer support. Learning occurs more readily when students feel their classroom is a partnership.

They perceive "It's the teacher and us against the curriculum," rather than "It's me by myself against the teacher and the curriculum." This spirit of community is forwarded through strategies like cooperative or team learning where students study together and teach each other. The highest correlate with student achievement involves a methodology where students are explaining the material to be learned to fellow students.

In research done in the 1990s, a researcher described the teachers who get special results from their students as being "intuitive." They have an almost inexplicable ability to become one with their students.[11] They have a deeper sense of purpose and commitment to building positive relationships with their students than the norm. We see this with Churchill's fencing teacher, who took a personal interest in Winston by spending time with him and even inviting him to his home.

Relationship building is a delicate matter and will look different in every classroom. It might be as simple as making a point to remember birthdays or taking time to attend a student's extracurricular activity and making mention of their contribution. Some teachers make quick calls home when a child has accomplished something special. These efforts take time and thought because they are not mechanical or formulaic. They carry risks as well. It is easy to cross the line and try too hard to be a "buddy" with one's students. But as David Berliner commented, "the expert teacher's edge is caring," and caring will work magic. Students who perceive that their teachers genuinely care work hard to please them.[12]

We all need someone in our corner. We all need someone who genuinely believes in us. When we have someone who is a supporter and cheerleader and who demonstrates their support by investing in us, it becomes easier for us to believe in ourselves. A large percentage of young people come to school with no such support and no vision of who they could become. A conference speaker, whose name I have long since lost, put it this way: "So many children thrash through the dense jungles of life alone and with only a child's-sized machete." Who will come alongside and help them clear their path if not a teacher? Along with their parents, their teachers are in the best position to help them develop a vision for who they are capable of becoming.

UNDERSTANDING IS A KEY TO HOPE

Churchill's math teacher reminds us of another essential quality of teachers who maximize their students' potential. They know how to take abstract or difficult concepts understandable. Churchill came into Mayo's classroom believing that mathematics was nonsensical and that no matter how hard he tried, he would not be able to understand it. Yet he did succeed in that class. Mayo apparently invested the effort and creativity to find ways to connect the ideas from his curriculum to the lives of his students and in doing so made the incomprehensible comprehensible. It is easy to observe this happening in the classroom but so hard to actually do it. When it happens and the light of understanding goes on, hope replaces hopelessness, and hope enables students to persevere.

A PLAYFUL CLASSROOM

Somervell's playfulness and "infectious enthusiasm" uncover yet another key to unlocking potential. Though a new teacher, teaching a remedial subject, Somervell made it a joyful experience for Churchill. He was playful. He made learning fun. How does a teacher do that? We sometimes mistake playfulness as simply "fooling around." There are certainly moments for lighthearted behavior that might be described as fooling around, but playful classrooms can be wonderfully more purposeful and engaging than that. Dale Mann of Columbia University calls play "the engine of real learning."[13] My sixth grade teacher taught me the truth of this.

Mrs. Montgomery was my social studies teacher at Central School in Glencoe, Illinois. I owe my decision to become a teacher to her because we had so much fun in her classroom. When we studied the Ancient Egyptians, we built scale models of the pyramids with sugar cubes. We read stories about Egyptian mythology and investigated mysterious things about the Pharaohs. We wrote an original play about daily life in Egyptian society. We even got to share our play with other sixth-grade classes. We were totally absorbed in these projects and could hardly contain ourselves waiting for social studies time each day. We perceived them as serious activities because we knew we were learning so much, but we also felt like they were play. Though Mrs. Montgomery had little interest in compelling us to memorize things that we were studying, I remember so much about these projects decades later.

I completed many social studies classes after sixth grade where all I was called upon to do was sit, listen, and give back what I heard on tests. Sometimes these teachers tried to be entertaining, but my only memories of these classes are that I was painfully bored.

Somervell and Mrs. Montgomery understood a simple but profound dimension of awakening student potential. When students are invited by their teacher to be involved in inventive, expansive, self-directed activities, learning becomes play. Learners become motivated, absorbed, and even enthralled. When there is a sense of mystery or intrigue, the absorption is even better, and serious learning results.

This is a book for teachers, but it is important to note that teachers and other school personnel do not control all the variables that lead to the success of students in academic situations. Genetics and home environment are obvious in their role in this process. In a classic study of student achievement done over two decades, the Illinois Valedictorian Project identified the key factors that influenced the outstanding academic performance of high school valedictorians in the State of Illinois.[14] These most successful students knew from a young age that they were bright and gifted in school-related abilities. Usually, however, they did not perceive themselves to be the brightest in their age group. They knew how to earn good grades. They knew themselves to be "school smart."

Overwhelmingly, these valedictorians grew up in two-parent families. Out of 81 of these superior students in Terry Denny's study, only 3 lived with divorced or single parents. In virtually every case, there was at least one parent at home who paid close attention to school achievement, set high standards, and communicated the importance of being successful in school to the student.

Teachers have no control over either the inherent ability of the students who enter their classrooms or the degree of support and nurturance that they have received at home. Teachers also have little influence in another support factor that came out of the valedictorian study: the majority of these students had strong religious involvement, which was another source of support and which served as a buffer against negative extracurricular activities, including partying.

Terry Denny's study did bring to light the importance of teachers and the factors they do control. Every one of the valedictorians in his study identified one or a few teachers who were instrumental in their success. Many of these students remembered special attention and praise from elementary teachers. All identified high school teachers who challenged them, for whom they had worked hard, and whom they wanted especially to please. Most could name teachers who taught them to love their subject and made them excited to learn. Overwhelmingly, these inspirational teachers helped them know it was acceptable to be a good student and to be proud of their successes.

This is a book about this sort of teaching—teaching that inspires. It's a book about learning that brings the best out of learners by helping them see who they could become. It's a book about learning that motivates, absorbs, and sometimes even enthralls the learner. It's a book about joy—the joy of learning. In American education today, teachers are not being praised or rewarded for teaching that inspires students and helps them understand their capabilities. Sadly, teachers are only being commended for raising test scores. Like the French before World War II, our guns are pointed in the wrong direction.

In writing a book about inspirational, joyful learning, we have advantages today that haven't been available very long. Because of breakthroughs in neuroimaging technology in the past decade, we have a far better understanding of how the human brain learns and retains learning. If our instruction can utilize the tremendous power of the brain operating in its most natural and effective mode, learning tasks are dramatically easier. Chapter 2 investigates this natural learning process. Chapter 3 focuses on instruction that makes learning playful. We now understand the power of play in the classroom.

Part II has four chapters devoted to practical teaching strategies that work in concert with the brain's natural learning processes to provide teachers with the means to develop student potential. Each chapter focuses on a particular developmental level of learner from early elementary through postsecondary.

Part III asks two key questions. First, if our goal is to develop student potential, how might we use assessments skillfully and sensitively to promote that goal? Second, how might we educate teachers, both preservice and inservice, to have the unique skills to be promoters of student potential?

NOTES

1. Rowe, V. (1961). *The Great Wall of France*. New York: Putnam.

2. Raywid, M. A. (1993, September). Finding time for collaboration. *Educational Leadership*, *51*(1), 30–34.

3. Marzano, R. J., Kendal, R. J., & Cicchinelli, L. (1999). *What Americans believe students should know: A survey of U.S. adults*. Aurora, CO: Mid-continent Research for Education and Learning.

4. Berliner, D. C. (2001, January 28). Averages that hide the true extremes. *The Washington Post*, p. B3.

5. Wesson, K. (2002, August). "What everyone should know about the latest brain research." Retrieved April 4, 2002, from www.sciencemaster.com/columns/archieves/wesson

6. Amrein, A. L., & Berliner, D. C. (2003, February). The effects of high stakes testing on student motivation and learning. *Educational Leadership*, *60*(5), 32–38.

7. From *The Last Lion: Winston Spencer Churchill Alone* 1932–1940, Vol. 2, by William Manchester. Copyright © 1988 by William Manchester. By permission of Little, Brown and Co., Inc.

8. Manchester, W. R. (1983). *The Last Lion*.

9. Pulias, quoted in Purkey, W., & Novak, J. (1996). *Inviting school success*. Belmont, CA: Wadsworth, p. 36.

10. Combs, A. (1976). Fostering maximum development of the individual. In W. VanTil (Ed.), *Issues in secondary education* (pp. 65–87). Chicago: National Society for the Study of Education.

11. Purkey, W., & Novak, J. (1996). *Inviting school success*. Belmont, CA: Wadsworth.

12. Berliner, quoted in Agne, K. J. (1992, Spring). Caring: The expert teacher's edge. *Educational Horizons*, *71*(1), 120–124.

13. Mann, D. (1996, Spring). Serious play. *Teachers College Record*, *97*(3), 446–469.

14. Arnold, K. D. (1995). *Lives of promise*. San Francisco: Jossey-Bass.

How Learning Happens 2

The Natural Human Learning Process

STUDENTS ARE NATURAL LEARNERS

Is it true that students are natural learners and know how to learn? Apparently they are and do. After all, they have taught themselves to be computer experts; they know the statistics of not only their favorite team but also the other teams in the league and can compare and contrast the performances of various players; they know how to play incredibly complex video games, meeting challenges and problem solving for hours; they know what the latest "in" styles are and how to play the sports they spend hours practicing. If this is true, why are these same students not learning in school, resisting learning, or not learning as well or as much as they should?

If they are indeed natural learners, how do they naturally learn? Brain researchers can tell us how the brain learns, but how do people learn? What is their natural learning process? If we know that, we can teach the way they naturally learn, and then they will be as successful learning in school as out of school. Can that really happen?

TRYING TO FIND THE WAY

What is the reality for one high school English teacher? Let's go into her home this evening and watch her grading her students' papers.

Act 1, Scene 1. Homework

Anne, high-school English teacher

Mike, Anne's husband

In Anne and Mike's living room. Anne is at a table up center correcting papers. Mike is in an easy chair down left reading the newspaper.

Mike: (Eyes on his paper. Neutral tone.) Aren't you done yet?

Anne: (No response.)

Mike: (Eyes on paper, as before.) How much longer is it going to take?

Anne: (No response.)

Mike: (As before.) How much longer? One, two, ten hours?

Anne: (Looking up.) I don't know. (Goes back to the papers.)

Mike: (With an edge.) Don't you give them enough of your time all day at school?

Anne: (Looking at him, quietly.) I have to do this if I want them to learn.

Mike: (Coolly.) Well, that's some lousy job you've got.

Anne: It's not lousy. (Starts to pick up papers, preparing to leave the room.)

Mike: (Sarcastic.) Oh, there she goes again—all upset and hurt feelings.

Anne: (Getting her papers together. Calmly.) My feelings aren't hurt. I just can't talk to you.

Mike: (Mimics her.) I just can't talk to you. (Angrily.) But you can spend hours and hours writing notes to *them*!

Anne: (Calmly.) You're exaggerating.

Mike: Am I? (Anne starts to leave.)

Mike: And what good does it do? Do any of them ever get any better? (Anne stands at the door, back to him, head down.) Maybe, if you were teaching kids who want to learn and get ahead and have the brains for it, it'd make a difference. But these kids. They don't have it and they never will. Face it. So what's the point?

Anne: (Low voice.) I want to help them.

Mike: You can't help them. They can't be helped. You're wasting your life!

Anne: (Slips to floor, drops the papers, and starts to cry.) I want to help them. . . .

Mike: I don't understand! Why do you want to help these useless, stupid kids!?

Anne: (Crying.) They're not stupid . . . they're not useless . . . they want to learn . . . they have hopes and dreams . . . they want to have a good life. . . .

Mike: So why *don't* they?

Anne: (As before.) They don't know how. (Suddenly shakes papers and speaks loudly.) And I don't know how to help them!

Mike: (Taken aback. Calms down.) Then why not give it up? Why do you keep banging your head against the wall?

Anne: Because I know they can do it! I know they desperately want to do it! I just don't know how to help them, and it's driving me crazy! (Mike goes to her and starts to put his arms around her. Anne pushes him away.) I've tried everything! (Weeps.)

Mike: (After a moment, sympathetically, trying to be helpful.) Maybe it's the *way* you do it? Maybe if you . . . ?

Anne: (Interrupting. Turning to him, furious and desperate.) No! It's *not* the way I do it! I don't know *anybody* who knows how to do it! (Throws papers on the floor.)

Mike: (Taken aback.) You don't know anybody who knows how to teach?

Anne: No! No! How to teach *these* kids! They write them off, they think they're stupid—like you think! But they're not! I know they're not!

Mike: (Trying to be rational about it.) But what if they're right and you're wrong? I mean in the face of the facts.

Anne: What facts? That they're poor? That they live on the wrong side of the tracks? That they're failing their classes?

Mike: (Maintaining his rational approach.) Aren't those the facts?

Anne: What do *they* have to do with it!?

Mike: (Looks at her for a moment.) What's the matter with you? I've never seen you so out of control.

Anne: (Hands over face, crying.) . . . I don't know what to do—I don't know what to do! Why can't you help me instead of tearing me down?!

Mike: (Gently.) I don't want to tear you down. I'm trying to help you. (Puts his arms out to her.)

Anne: (Pushes him away.) You're not helping me! You're telling me I'm stupid and wrong and wasting my life!

Mike: (Weakly, afraid he's gone too far.) No, I'm not.

Anne: Yes, you are! (Weeps.) Maybe I *should* quit! Maybe I *am* stupid and wasting my life!

Mike: (Putting his hand out to her, worried, conciliatory.) . . . No . . .

Anne: (Looking up.) Yes, I will. I'll quit. I'll give up being stupid and banging my head against the wall. I'll . . . (Starts to laugh and cry.) But first I have to finish correcting these papers! (Kneels to collect them from the floor, where she'd dropped them earlier.)

Mike: (Kneels beside her, very worried.) Anne . . . Anne . . .

Anne: (Stands up with the papers and waves him away.) Forget it! Tomorrow I'm quitting! (Exit.)

Curtain

Just before I started as department chair, I had heard through the grapevine that the standardized test scores would never improve because the students weren't capable of higher achievement. . . . I discovered, however, that . . . our low scores did not necessarily reflect what our students knew or could do. The belief that the students could not handle the work became a self-fulfilling prophecy that teachers were all too willing to buy into. It was easier for them to believe that it was the students' fault or the sum of all the negatives they faced than to rework lesson plans. . . .[1]

Act 1, Scene 2. Students Pay Attention

Anne's classroom the next day. Twenty-five students of different races, black, Hispanic, Asian, white, are in class; most are lounging in their tab-arm chairs, paying no attention. Their clothing indicates their low socioeconomic status. Tia is in the front row; Gabe is in the back row.

Anne: (At the front of the room, next to her desk, wringing her hands, unfocused.) Okay . . . (Pause. Looks around. Can't think of what to say.) Okay . . . (All the students start to look with interest at her.) Okay . . . what did we do yesterday?

Gabe: (Looks around at students next to him. Smiles.) Nothin'.

Tia: (Concerned, trying to be helpful.) We were working on verbs.

Anne: . . . And . . . what were we working on . . . ?

Tia: (Worriedly, slowly.) We were working on verbs.

Anne: I know that! What were we working on *about* verbs?! (Tia is startled. No one answers. Anne looks around. Pause.) . . . I'm sorry, Tia. Please excuse me. I'm . . . I'm not feeling well. (Leans back against her desk; puts her hands over her face. Hesitantly, head down.) I'm . . . having a . . . kind of . . . crisis here. (After a moment, looks up at them.) . . . Maybe you can help me out. (Several students sit up straighter. Everyone looks at her intently.) Is anything happening here? (Students are nonplussed.) I mean, are you learning anything? Is anything worthwhile going on here?

Tia: (After a moment, speaking for everyone.) . . . What do you mean?

What will the students tell her if they tell the truth about their experience in her class? What will Gabe say?

Curtain

Faculty Development Activity

You and your colleagues might write your own scenarios about your own and/or your students' experiences—or about any education-relation experience or situation that you imagine. Then you can read, perhaps act out, and discuss what you learn from the scenarios.

Act 1, Scene 3. Believing in Students: The Way

Ruth, an older, experienced teacher at Anne's school

Ken, another teacher

Anne

In the teachers' lounge of Anne's school. At a small table sit three teachers, Ruth, Ken, and Anne. Anne is worried about many of her students being unmotivated, unprepared, and apparently not able to think at a high level.

Anne: How do you keep doing it? Don't you get discouraged? I've been teaching only a year and I'm already very discouraged.

Ken: Oh, you look for the bright students. They make it all worthwhile.

Ruth: That's true. Except every student is bright.

Ken: You say that because you always get all the bright students.

Ruth: That's right. I do.

Anne: How do you do that?

Ruth: (Looks at her for a moment.) Because I'm a mind reader. (Ken looks up with interest.)

Anne: What does that mean?

Ruth: It means I can look into their heads and see their beautiful bright minds. (Ken laughs.) Ask Ken why he thinks I always get all the bright students.

Anne: (To Ken.) Why *do* you?

Ken: Because I'm always telling her how much I like getting her students in my classes because they're all so smart.

Anne: Is that true?

Ken: (Laughs.) Yes. I do and they are.

Anne: (To Ruth.) Okay, so how *do* you get all the smart ones?

Ruth: They're all smart. *All* our students are smart. I just help them see that they're naturally smart and give them the chance to show it.

Ken: (Leaning forward, serious.) How do you do that?

Ruth: I thought you'd never ask. (She smiles at him.)

Curtain

> This is how Ruth helps her students see that they are natural and smart learners.

Act 1, Scene 4. Helping Students Find the Way

Present are some of the same students as in Anne's class, notably Gabe. After greeting the students, Ruth says she has a question for them.

Ruth: Can you all think of something you learned to be good at outside of school? It could be a sport or a hobby or an art or something you did when you were a little kid but don't do anymore. If you drive a car, it could be driving. (Looks around at the students.) If you can't think of anything, raise your hand and I'll come over and help you find something, because everyone is good at something. (Waits a moment, making eye contact with the students. No one raises a hand.) Okay, raise your hand if you *can* think of something. (Everyone raises a hand except Gabe.)

Ruth: (Nods to Gabe.) I'll come over in minute, Gabe, and help you think of something. (Then she speaks to the rest of the class.) Take out a piece of paper. Now think back to before you knew how to do your thing. How did you get from not knowing how to do it to being good at it? Not the world's greatest expert but pretty good at it. Just write some notes on how you got from not knowing how to do it to being good at it. These notes are only to get your memory going, not to hand in. (Paul, Jose, and Gabe have no paper or pens. Ruth gives them some. Paul and Jose start to write. Gabe lets his lie on his desk. Ruth goes over to him and speaks softly.) Gabe? Do you need some help to think of something?

Gabe: (Shakes his head, looks down.)

Ruth: So can you write down how you started to learn it?

Gabe: (Shakes head and smirks.)

Ruth: (Looks at him, assessing the situation.) . . . What's the problem? (Maria and Fran, sitting in front of him, turn to look.)

Gabe: (Yawns and stretches, looks out the window.) This is stupid.

Ruth: Why is it stupid? (Some of the students look at Ruth. Paul and Jose are amused. Vic is worried; Maria is scared.)

Gabe: (Looking bored.) Everybody knows how you learn. (All the students stop writing and pay attention to this interchange.)

Ruth: (Notices everyone is watching and listening. Goes to the front of the room, turns to face the class, and addresses Gabe respectfully.) How *do* people learn?

Gabe: (Shrugs, laughs, keeps looking away.)

Ruth: (Noncombatively.) How *do* you think people learn? (The students are waiting for an explosion.)

Gabe: Oh, man. This is so lame.

Ruth: (Gently.) What is it that you're good at?

Gabe: (Looks at her, amused and belligerent.) Oh, lotsa stuff. Drinkin', gettin' girls. (Paul and Jose laugh.)

Ruth: (Respectfully throughout.) Well, that would work. You could pick one of those skills and tell how you learned to be good at it.

Gabe: (Laughs.)

Ruth: Really, how did you learn to be good at drinking?

Gabe: (Shakes his head, laughs.)

Paul: (Laughing.) Hey, man, tell how you did it and I'll tell you how I did it.

Jose: Yeah, man. How'd you learn to be good at drinkin'?

Ruth: How *did* you start?

Gabe: (Looks away and laughs.)

Ruth: What was the first thing that started you learning how to drink?

Jose and Paul: (Encouraging, laughing.) C'mon, man.

Gabe: (Smiling.) I just tried it.

Ruth: (To the others.) Did anyone else start learning your skill by just trying it?

Paul: Yeah, I did. (Other students join in, agreeing that they, too, had started learning that way. Ruth goes to the board and writes, "I just tried it." Gabe stares at his words written on the board exactly as he had said them.)

Ruth: Can you remember what happened next? Can you write some notes, Gabe, about what you did next to help you learn how to drink? (Gabe shrugs, slowly takes up the pen, and slowly starts to write. The other students also resume writing. After the students have spent a few minutes writing, Ruth stops them.)

Ruth: Okay, now get together with two or three others and tell each other what you're good at and how you got good at it. Then see whether there's anything similar in how you learned your things. (Students, full of curiosity, eagerly start talking. Ruth walks around to observe the groups and make sure everyone is getting a chance to share and that the groups are identifying whether there was anything similar in how they learned. After checking with most groups, she addresses the class.) Okay, it looks like most of you are finished. (Goes to the chalkboard.) So tell me what happened at the very beginning.

Fran: I watched my mother do it. (Ruth writes these words verbatim underneath Gabe's words.)

> Why verbatim? If the teacher edits what students say, it implies, "I'm smart and you're not." This implicit message undermines students' confidence and self-esteem, which are essential for successful learning. Also, if what students say is incorrect, the teacher can now clearly see what they don't understand and so can create a new activity to help them figure it out.

(Others contribute other experiences; she writes whatever they say on the board, verbatim. Then, after a number of contributions, they stop.)

Ruth: Is that it? (Looks around but no one adds anything.) Okay, let's call that Stage 1. (Writes "1" on the board and draws a line next to that list.) So what happened next? (This process is repeated with their contributing a number of items and then stopping. They eventually came up with six stages.) Is that it? (Students nod; no one adds anything else.) Now I'm going to read what you said, and you see whether you want to add or change anything and also be thinking about whether you learned your thing more or less this way, not every word in exactly this order, but in a similar way. (Reads aloud what she's written on the board.) Anything you want to add or change?

Jose: Yeah. I kept making mistakes all along. (Ruth writes "I kept making mistakes all along" and draws arrows to show it relating to all the stages. No one else answers.)

Ruth: So how many of you learned your thing pretty much this way? (Everyone except Maria raises a hand.) And how did you learn your thing, Maria?

Maria: I just kind of knew how to do it from the beginning, when I first did it.

Ruth: What was your thing?

Maria: Playing the piano. I just knew how to do it.

Ruth: Well, that means you have an aptitude. (Writes this word on the board.) You have an inborn talent, a gift. (Ruth smiles at Maria.) You're lucky to have this advantage. (Then Ruth speaks to the others.) So everyone else learned pretty much by this same process? (Everyone but Maria nods or says "yes." Ruth looks around at the students, making eye contact, especially deeply with Gabe.) That means you are all natural-born learners. You have a brain that knows how to learn. (They are silent and sit motionless, looking intently at Ruth, as it sinks in that their teacher believes in them, respects them, is telling them that they are a group of winners and experts.) And what are your things? (She asks the students one by one; and they say such things as cooking, gardening, using the computer, playing football, playing music, dancing, making jokes, painting pictures, fixing cars. They look around and feel respect for their classmates and feel respected by them; they feel they are in a community of natural, successful learners, of respect-worthy experts.)

Curtain

The potential of every student in the class to be a motivated, natural, successful learner is "writ large" on the board for all to see. Ruth sees it. They all see it. Now they are ready—ready and eager and able—to learn, even Gabe, who lives with an alcoholic mother, whose father is in jail, who has a record of truancy, and who, until now, has never done well in school, and who has no self-confidence as a student. But on this day, Gabe sees his life might have a new way to go.

On Their Way

Now Ruth will give her students the opportunity to learn in class by the natural learning process that they have just described, which they have all successfully experienced, even Gabe. As she does that, they will be the same motivated, natural, successful learners in her class that they have been outside school.

RESEARCH ON THE NATURAL HUMAN LEARNING PROCESS (NHLP)

The Missing Link Between Brain Research and Classroom Application

Using the process described above, I have done this research activity with more than 7,000 people from different countries, cultures, and socio-economic status (SES) groups, from second graders to high school students to college students to graduate students to educators. To my continual amazement, every group, without exception, responds in the exact same way as Ruth's students, stopping after making some contributions, and then going on, finally reporting a learning process of four, five, or six group-determined stages that are similar for all groups despite any and all individual differences. (See page 36 for more about individual differences.) Whether a group reports only four stages or six, with four stages more concise and six stages more detailed, the sequence of stages is always the same. See *We're Born to Learn: Using the Brain's Natural Learning Process to Create Today's Curriculum*[2] for more examples of this research, for example, with second, fourth, and sixth graders.[3]

Figures 2.1 and 2.2 are verbatim reports of six very diverse groups (low- and high-SES high school students, reentry and GED students, and

Figure 2.1 Low- and High-SES Student Groups Reporting Their Learning

10th Grade ➢ ***Mid- to high-SES community*** ➢ ***Parents fully involved with school*** ➢ ***Education valued*** ➢ ***College is the goal for every student***	10th Grade ➢ ***Low-SES community*** ➢ ***Parents not involved with school*** ➢ ***Education not valued*** ➢ ***Few students go to college***	11th and 12th Graders in 9th Grade English Class (because of previous failures) ➢ ***Low-SES community*** ➢ ***Parents not involved with school*** ➢ ***Education not valued*** ➢ ***Few students go to college***
Stage 1		
Watching other people Got lucky Curiosity Not having the skills to do something else Looked like something you might want to do after watching someone	Asked my dad about it Watching it Practicing it Having fun Listening Parents introducing you to it Studying it	I did not do very well Needed lots of encouragement Needed better eye-hand coordination I sucked I practiced a lot I was not very confident
Stage 2		
I sucked and this motivated me—that's how it works Researched it Just like messing around with it Playing with it	Committed to it Bought it Practiced it Played it for a while	Practiced for 100s and 1,000s of hours Many years of being grounded* Practiced days on end Learned to lie well from trial and error
Stage 3		
After watching, I was inspired After I questioned, I got answers from coaches or other players Add something new to make it interesting to yourself Try different tactics Competition as a motivator Practice Doing lots of reps of something Start to get the basic skills	You know it Mastered it Perfected it	I was a master I became a Level 23 Black Mage I learned to be a great landscaper* Did it and learned to do it right I learned to let my feelings out in a different way by speaking my mind and heart I got hurt but continued

(Continued)

Figure 2.1 (Continued)

Stage 4		
Refined my skills Made changes to what I'd started to do Trial and error Do harder and harder things Challenge Set a goal or standard Didn't want to get in trouble with the coach so I worked harder	Enjoyed it I loved it Used it Stayed committed to it	Got better I got more confident I could do it without help Awesome eye-hand coordination I learned new words I learned to do it without being grounded and liked it* Started helping others
Stage 5		
Perfection Having fun Teaching others Winning	Worked harder at it Stuck with it Joined a team Could possibly make it a career	Honing the skills More daring More adventuresome
Stage 6		
Reaching thorough understanding		

*I asked this student what she meant about being grounded. She said her parents had made her stay at home, confined to the house and yard, when she misbehaved, which she did a lot.

educators) and their incontrovertibly similar descriptions of—and similar ways of expressing themselves about—how they learned outside school.

First, let's look at the research and, later, how to apply, in any and every classroom, what the research tells us about how human beings naturally learn. Then we can make every classroom a place where students, using their own natural learning process, can and will learn with motivation and success.

Figure 2.3 summarizes and gives a taxonomy for the stages that have been reported by my own and others' research. It is a six-stage taxonomy because that is the most stages learners have ever reported (except one group of adults whose seventh stage was "Then you die"). We can also see that when only four or five stages are reported, the sequence is the same, with the last stages including elements in the typical sixth stage, for example, mastery, teaching others, continuing to learn.

Figure 2.2 High School Dropout Students and Middle School Teachers Reporting Their Learning Process

High School Dropouts Working on Their GED	Inner City Dropouts in a High School Reentry Program	Middle School Teachers
Stage 1		
Did it for the love of the game Rough start Natural Didn't know how to do it In my blood Just did it	Couldn't do it	Frustration Failure Playing Fun Interest
Stage 2		
Practice, practice, practice Practicing Practice makes perfect Watch and learn Studied up	Started learning Practice Someone shows you Start doing Need my glasses	Practice, practice, practice Observation Still frustration
Stage 3		
More practice Too good Perfection after practice Making money off it	Learned how to do it Practice Saw other people Watched Observation Experiment	Started to see good results More positive experiences I needed more instruction Still continue to practice Some success
Stage 4		
Supreme—the best Help someone else Did it all the time Just natural at it Just came naturally	Do it again Watched Mastered the art	Feel good about yourself Start to want to share with others Learn what passion is Gain confidence The will to learn more Started laughing at my mistakes instead of being frustrated with them
Stage 5		
Experience Still doing it	Comes naturally Genetics	
Stage 6		
Stick to the script		

Figure 2.3 Summary of the Natural Human Learning Process (NHLP)

TAXONOMY

STAGE 1: MOTIVATION/Responding to a stimulus: watched, observed, had to, interest, desire, curiosity

STAGE 2: BEGINNING PRACTICE/Doing it: practice, practice, practice, trial and error, ask questions, consult others, basics, make mistakes, lessons, some success

STAGE 3: ADVANCED PRACTICE/Increase of skill and confidence: practice, practice, practice, trial and error, some control, reading, encouragement, experiment, tried new ways, positive attitude, enjoyment, lessons, feedback, confidence, having some success, start sharing

STAGE 4: SKILLFULNESS/Making it your own: practice, doing it your own way, feeling good about yourself, positive reinforcement, sharing knowledge, success, confidence

STAGE 5: REFINEMENT/Further improvement: learning new methods, becoming second nature, continuing to develop, different from anyone else, creativity, independence, validation by others, ownership, habit, teaching

STAGE 6: MASTERY/Broader application: greater challenges, teaching it, continuing improvement or dropping it, feeds into other interests, getting good and better and better, going to higher levels

SOURCE: From Smilkstein (2003), p. 49.

Moreover, amazingly, these natural learning stages parallel the six sub-stages Piaget found in the cognitive development of infants from birth to 18–24 months (Figure 2.4).[4]

> Both Piaget's six stages and the stages parallel to them found in this natural learning research converge with the sequential and constructive process by which the human brain learns (Chapter 3).

It would seem, then, that this natural learning research is showing us the process by which human beings actually learn, in infancy and throughout life. If so, this research is the link that has been missing between neuroscientific research about how the brain learns and how, in and out of the classroom, human beings actually and naturally learn. If so, it gives us

Figure 2.4 Convergence of NHLP's Stages and Piaget's Substages

	PIAGET'S SENSORIMOTOR SUBSTAGES	NATURAL HUMAN LEARNING PROCESS STAGES
	Learning From Birth to Two Years	**Learning Any New Skill or Concept at Any Age**
	Motivation	
1	Reflexive response to external events	Response to stimulus, practice starts basic
	Beginning Practice	
2	Habits formed by repeated cycles of activity	Practice, practice, practice
	Advanced Practice	
3	Beginning of coordination, means-end function clearer	More practice, increase of skill and confidence
	Skillfulness	
4	Purposeful use of means to achieve ends more effectively, combining old means in new ways to get new ends	Doing it one's own way, success
	Refinement	
5	Exploration and discovery of new means by groping to achieve ends more effectively	Further improvements, learning new methods, creativity, independence
	Mastery	
6	Comprehension, finding new means by using the mind (not physical groping)	Full understanding, going to higher levels

SOURCE: From Smilkstein (2003), p. 83.

research-based, specific guidance for how to sequence lessons, courses, and curricula so that all students can learn with motivation and success by their natural human learning process (NHLP).

USING THE MISSING LINK IN MATH EDUCATION

An example of a K–12 curricular need is in the teaching of math. The National Council of Teachers of Mathematics (NCTM) has released their *Principles and Standards for School Mathematics,* which

> underscore the need for a shared, national understanding of the math content that should be emphasized, prekindergarten through 12th grade. . . .
>
> Articulation across the grades is a big concern in mathematics education today, [Mark] Saul[, award-winning teacher,] affirms. The NCTM standards . . . outline the broad areas of mathematical knowledge that students should build over time and grade levels.[5]

These principles and standards describe a concept of teaching math sequentially by which teachers do not unrealistically expect students to make "giant leaps" but, instead, help them, across grades, "make the move [from arithmetic to algebra] seamless."[6] Moreover,

> [r]esearch shows kids learn best when they begin with a thorough grounding in mathematics fundamentals and progress in an orderly sequence. . . .
>
> The secret, [says William] Schmidt[, a math expert at Michigan State University,] is coherence. Instruction should progress in a sequence of topics over the grades that is consistent with the inherent structure and logic of mathematics. . . . Otherwise, kids get confused and don't see the connections between topics. Clutter—teaching kids topics before they are ready for them—and holes in the logical sequence are traps kids may never dig their way out of. . . .
>
> The idea is to build [construct] ideas on each other in an increasingly complex way.[7]

The NCTM is creating a sequential (constructivist) curriculum so that all students can learn with motivation and success by their NHLP. Chapter 3 discusses constructivism, and Part II provides examples of constructivist curricula. Also see Smilkstein[8] for strategies for developing curricula.

IF ALL STUDENTS LEARN THE SAME WAY, WHY ARE STUDENTS' FATES DIFFERENT?

According to the natural learning research, students, whether from a high- or low-SES community, successfully learn outside of school the same sorts of skills by the same process (reports from such schools are in Figures 2.1 and 2.2). Thus, if all these different students have the potential to be successful learners and are motivated to learn, why are their fates so different? Typically, students at a high-SES high school graduate and go on to college and then into professional careers, whereas in some low-SES communities students drop out of school at a rate of 37% or more and typically do not go to college but, instead, become blue-collar workers.

Are their fates different because schools, teachers, administrators, and communities explicitly or implicitly expect, perpetuating a self-fulfilling prophecy, that the capabilities and, therefore, the fates of people are determined by their race, ethnicity, SES, and gender?[9] Are their fates different because the students themselves have different explicit and implicit beliefs and predictions about themselves as students? John Tagg,[10] referencing Carol Dweck's research,[11] points out that students who do not believe they can change their level of success (they have an "entity theory" about themselves) in a specific domain think it would be useless to try to improve and, therefore, do not make an effort to improve. Other students, instead, might believe they can increase their level of success (they have an "incremental theory" about their abilities) in a given domain and so work at trying to improve. However, as Tagg points out, these self-beliefs are not global; a student who has an entity theory about himself in academic subjects can have an incremental theory about himself in sports.

How can we help all students become incremental theorists and believe in their potential to be successful learners in any and all domains? We can do this by showing them, as in Ruth's class, that they are natural-born learners with a brain that knows how to learn, as explained in Chapter 3, "How the Brain Learns: Student Empowerment and Potential." Their having this metacognitive knowledge empowers students.

A PERSON'S FATE: NATURE OR NURTURE?

Is it nature or nurture that determines a person's fate, whether they become entity or incrementalist theorists, whether they believe in themselves or not, and whether they develop their potential to be all they can be? As soon as a baby is born, the environment (nurture) interacts with the baby's nature and has a role in creating who she or he will be. Nature or nurture? This is one of the great unresolved questions.

Here is a conundrum. My father was an identical twin; and even when he and his brother were adults, strangers found it difficult to tell one from the other. When he and his brother were young, his brother became desperately ill with a kidney infection. For almost a year, the effects of his illness kept him bedridden. Their parents, the four other brothers, and especially my father all focused loving attention on the sick child for that year. Guess which twin grew up to be self-centered and which one grew up to be caring? Yes, my father was the one who was always thinking of others. One of my maternal cousins told me several years ago that after his father died my father was the only uncle who called to see how he was doing and offered to help in any way he could. Was it nature or nurture that was responsible for these twins, identical in their genes, to be so different in their personalities? Would they have been similar in personality if one twin had not been nurtured to be the center of attention in the family?

Some twin studies have reported that identical twins parted early in life become adults with uncannily similar personalities and lives. But so far no one has proved that human development is all nature and no nurture.

Here's another situation. Two babies are born in different neighborhoods in the same city in the same year. One is the child of immigrants, nonwhite, both parents working at low-paying jobs. The family lives in a low-SES community in which very few students go to college and many students never graduate from high school. The other is the child of a successful lawyer and a stay-at-home mother. They are white and live in a high-SES community in which almost every child goes to college and very few drop out of high school.

This, of course, does not mean that the low-SES minority child will necessarily grow up to be a high school dropout or that the high-SES child will become a successful professional. Perhaps a teacher takes an interest in the low-SES child and is so supportive and encouraging that the child is inspired to do well in school, to complete high school, and to go on to college to study law to be able to help the needy. James Anderson, in fact, has shown that if even one adult is truly caring about a child, it can change that child's life for the better.[12]

> Bernie Noe, the principal of Lakeside School, a private high school in Seattle, Washington, said, "I've met with our student body each year in groups of 15 in breakfast meetings and a standard question to ask them is, 'What do you want in your teachers, what is it you first and foremost want?' And invariably, from the 5th grade to the 12th grade, they want . . . someone who deeply cares about them as people."

On the other hand, the high-SES privileged child might have been told what to be and what to do and how to do it so often and so absolutely that the child, feeling oppressed, rebels, refuses to do school assignments, doesn't want to go to college, leaves home, drops out of school, and ends up living in a shelter for street people. But there is someone working at the shelter who deeply cares about this young person, who, as a result, then earns a GED and goes to college to study law to help the needy.

Unfortunately, however, there are some students with whom this might not work, students whose negative self-identity is so strongly ingrained or whose sense of self is so oppositional that they cannot allow themselves to participate or cooperate or succeed. These students might even reject a person who clearly cares for them. They need professional therapy, which, unfortunately, they might resist even if it were available to them.

> "What we're learning is that culture and experience actually imprint themselves on the brain, on biology," says science historian Londa Schiebinger of Stanford University in Palo Alto, Calif. In

other words, nature and nurture work together in a much more sophisticated way than many scientists had previously thought.[13]

Gender Differences

There is ongoing research about gender differences. We don't have all the answers yet. Do boys and girls learn so differently that they would do best in same-gender classes? What if teachers—and students—have assumptions and expectations about the innately different natures of males and females? If they do have different assumptions, these assumptions can help create differences that otherwise might not exist. *Are* the genders innately different? Is it nature or nurture? Is it about individual differences affected by nurture? We'll have to keep watching as the research goes on.

However, in a brain-based, natural learning classroom, every student with metacognitive knowledge—and with a teacher who also has this knowledge—is better able to fulfill his or her own potential, whatever that might be.

Nature or nurture? Nature and nurture?

HELPING STUDENTS SEE THEIR POTENTIAL: STUDENTS' SELF-UNDERSTANDING

> Let's go back to Ruth's classroom and see how she helps her students gain further metacognitive knowledge (self-knowledge) about how they learn. (Also see "Metacognition" in Chapter 3.)

Act 1, Scene 4 Continued

After the research activity in Ruth's class is finished, she helps them learn more about their natural learning process.

Ruth: (Writes numbers 1 through 6 vertically on the board, 1 on the bottom to 6 at the top.) What are a few words for how you got from 1, not knowing how to do your thing, to 6, when you were good at it? I'm using 6 because you reported that you learned your things in six stages. (Calls on students who raise their hands.)

Fran: Practice. (Ruth writes this word on the board under the number 1.)

Jose: Perseverance. (Ruth writes this word under "Practice.")

Gabe: I wanted to learn it. (Ruth writes this verbatim under "Perseverance.")

Ruth: Okay, those are enough.

Whatever students say is fine because it's true for them, and this is research. Two to three words are enough. The words *practice* and *time*, used in Figures 2.5 and 2.6, are two of the most frequently volunteered words.

Ruth: Now, this is how it works. (Ruth draws on the board, one at a time, the diagrams in Figure 2.5, replacing "practice and time" with her students' words, "practice," "perseverance," "I wanted to learn it.")

Ruth: (Draws the first diagram in Figure 2.6 and explains to the students what it is about.) If you have an aptitude, like Maria has, you can go higher faster in that area than others can. (Then she draws the second diagram.) But anyone can learn anything to a higher level by putting in enough practice, perseverance, and wanting to learn it. (She uses the students' words and draws the third diagram.) And nobody has an aptitude or gift for everything. Even Einstein, who was at the highest level in math and science, was at lower levels in other areas of life. Can you see who has to make your learning happen? Can you figure this out? (Students sit silently for a few moments, studying the figures on the board.)

Gabe: (Thoughtfully.) We have to do it ourselves.

Ruth: And my job is to give you the opportunities to do it so you can learn in class the way you learn outside of school. (She and the students look at each other warmly. It is clear to the students that their teacher cares about them.)

Curtain

THE BENEFITS OF THE NHLP RESEARCH AND METACOGNITIVE KNOWLEDGE

Principal among the benefits of the NHLP research activity and metacognitive knowledge are the following:

- Students gain invaluable, empowering understanding of their own natural learning process.

- Students' confidence, self-efficacy, self-responsibility, and motivation, as well as respect for themselves and their classmates, increase because this research activity proves to them that they are successful natural learners. They also know that their teacher respects, cares about, and believes in them. All this makes the classroom a safe place to learn, and safety in the classroom is critical for student success.[14]

Figure 2.5 Ceiling Level: People Learn to Higher Levels With More Time and Practice

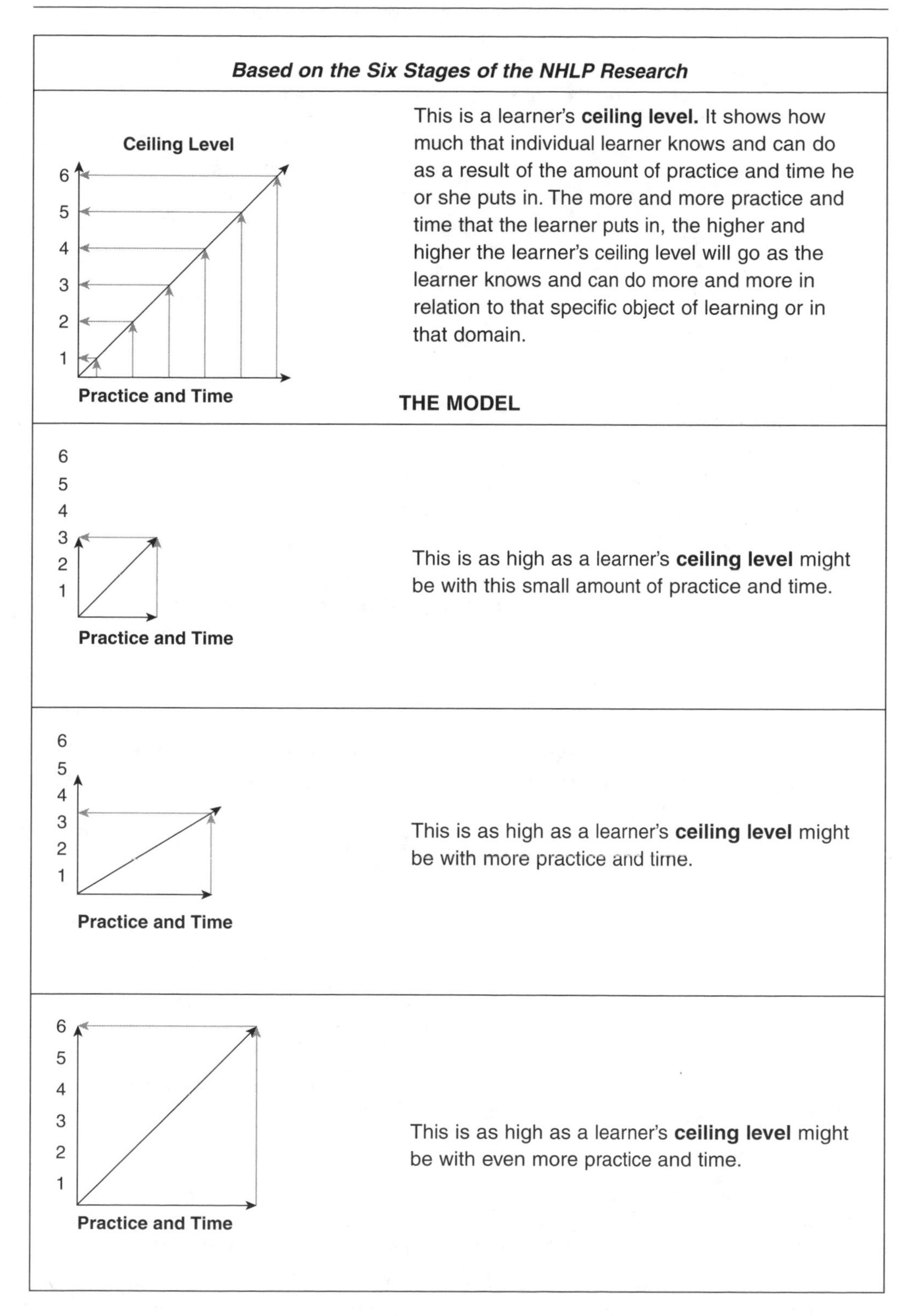

Figure 2.6 Ceiling Level for Individual Differences in Gaining Knowledge and Skill About a Specific Object of Learning or in a Specific Domain

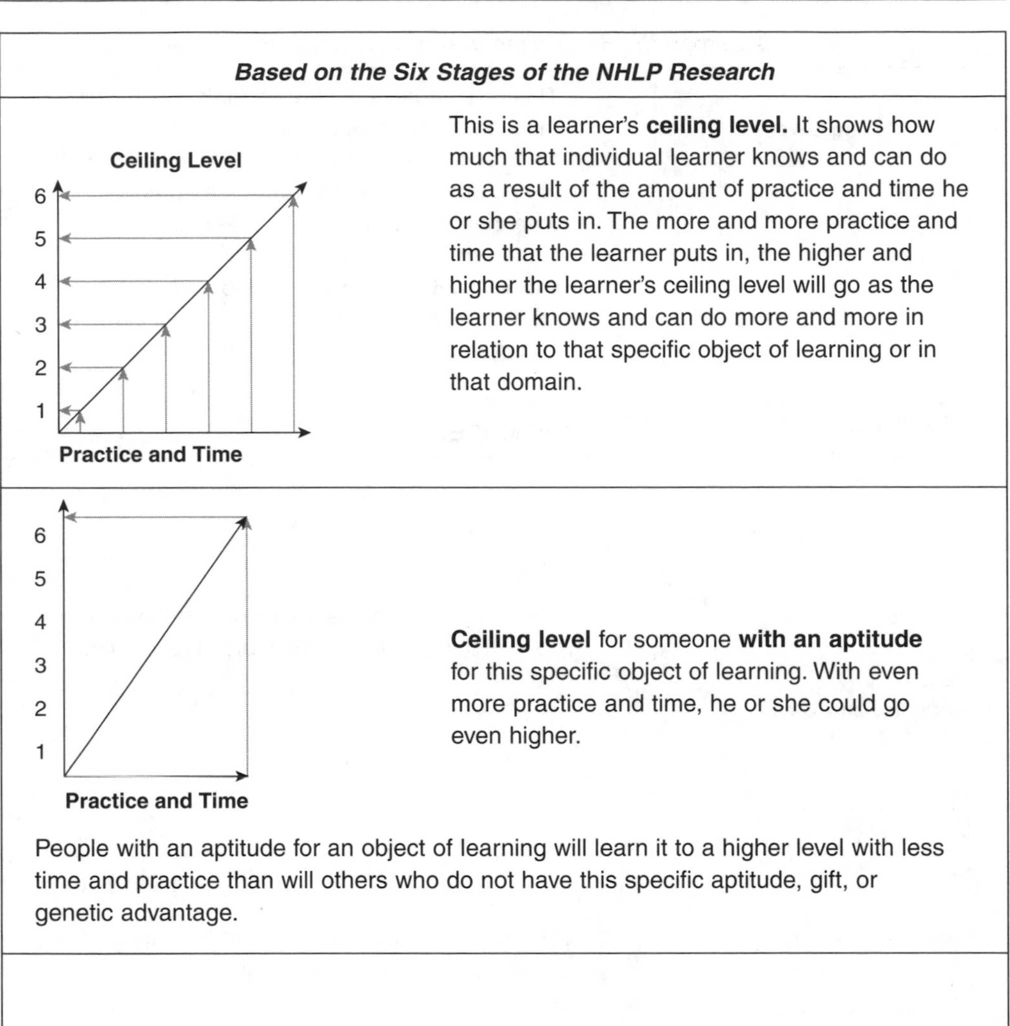

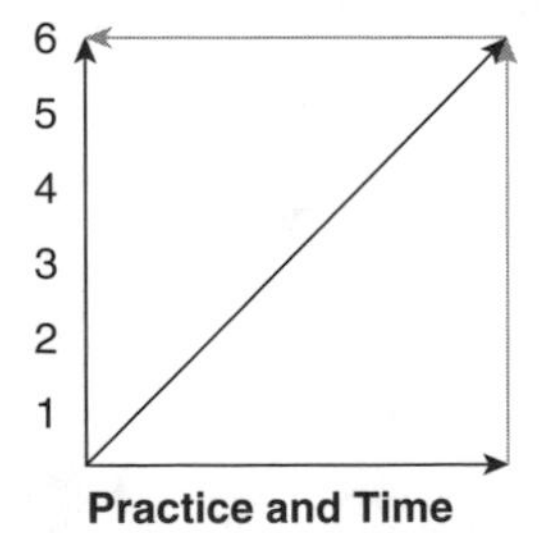

Ceiling level for someone **without an aptitude** for a specific object of learning or domain but who has put in a great deal of practice and time. With even more practice and time, she or he could go even higher.

People without an aptitude, gift, or genetic advantage for a specific object of learning will need to take more time and do more practicing to raise their ceiling level for it. **Different people will reach different levels with different amounts of practice and time.**

• Teachers see that there is an NHLP, that their students are natural learners, that their students learn when they are actively progressing through the stages of the NHLP, and that if they teach in light of this natural learning process, their students will have the opportunity to be the motivated, successful, natural learners they have the potential to be—and are—outside school.

• Students feel safe because their teacher knows they need to practice to learn. Both they and their teacher expect all learners to make mistakes, to learn from their mistakes, and to try again, as many times as they need in order to gain skill and deep understanding.

• Teachers and students now have a common set of concepts and terms for understanding, discussing, and promoting the students' natural learning process.

ALL STUDENTS HAVE AN INNATE POTENTIAL AND MOTIVATION TO LEARN

It is commonly believed that when a person has an interest in a subject, a domain, an object of learning, that person, fueled by an innate motivation, will gladly work long and hard to gain skill, knowledge, and deep understanding about that chosen theme or focus. Notice the 12th-grade student's report in Figure 2.1 that he "practiced for 100s and 1000s of hours."

However, as the NHLP research shows, people who learn to be good at something do not always start with a positive motivation to learn it (see Stage 1 in Figures 2.1 and 2.2). Once they start, though, whether they have personally chosen to learn this particular object of learning or not, the more they are actively engaged in learning by their natural learning process—doing inquiry-based, problem-solving, pattern-seeking, student-centered, thought-provoking activities, which they are born to do and derive pleasure from doing—the more motivated they are to continue learning about that particular object of learning, that unexpectedly pleasing theme or focus. For this reason, any students in any course, if actively engaged in learning the way they are born to learn, will enjoy learning in that course. Students who enjoy a particular course might not choose to take other courses in the same subject; but while they are in that course, they are engaged learners.

The Same Motivation to Learn

When we do as Ruth does, look inside our students and see their innate potential to be engaged, successful learners, we want to give them the opportunity to do in school what they are born to do, to learn by their natural learning process and be all they can be. When we interact with students this way, they know we accept them; they know we care deeply about them. Chapter 3 explains that emotions have a powerful effect on learning, and feeling accepted and cared about are two of the most powerful emotions for igniting students' potential for learning.

As the NHLP research seems to show, every student, of whatever age or level, culture, learning style, or learning preference, learns by the same, apparently invariable, sequence of stages of the NHLP. Learners, whether they are young, old, novices, experienced, used to failure or used to success in school, all seem to learn by the same process outside school, as shown in Figures 2.1 and 2.2, summarized in Figure 2.3, and also found in other research reports.[15] If, indeed, this research shows us the NHLP, if this is how people naturally learn with motivation outside school, then we now know how to teach so that all students can fulfill their potential to be motivated, natural, successful learners.

Part II presents several classroom-proven examples across grade levels of natural learning curricula and lesson plans that do this, that make it possible to ignite the potential of every student.

Do We Need Totally Differentiated Classrooms?

This NHLP research, with its invariable results, indicates that we do not need to create a different lesson or instructional approach or plan for each student. The only differentiation needed is to provide the class with both auditory and visual aids—because some people are auditory learners and some are visual learners, having differently sensitive sensory input channels. Everyone, though, is a kinesthetic learner in that we have to use it, do it, and practice it ourselves in order to learn it.

THE NHLP PEDAGOGY

We also need to use a pedagogy that helps students expand and enrich—rather than be frozen in—their repertoire of learning preferences. It must be a pedagogy that, in combination with natural learning curricula and lessons, makes it possible for every student to be the best that he or she can be. The pedagogical strategy (Individual/Small Group/Whole Group sequence [I/SG/WG]) Ruth used in her classroom does this. First, students work individually because each student has to construct his or her own new knowledge, each one figuring out the task or doing the assignment by him- or herself and consulting his or her own mind-store of knowledge and experience. Then students get together in groups of three—no more than four—or it will take too long for everyone to share; also, in a small group, even a shy student will find it easier to participate. This small-group work is for sharing, discussing, and giving and receiving feedback; and invaluable peer tutoring goes on during small-group work. Also, it gives students the opportunity for social learning and interactive learning, which are reported in the literature as essential for deep learning.[16]

Occasionally I have a student who indicates that she or he doesn't like small-group work. So I tell the student, "Just sit next to the group and listen. You don't have to say anything." It never takes long before that student is actively participating in the group.

After the small-group work, students reconvene as a whole class for a full discussion of all points of view. The teacher asks, "What did you come up with?" and writes every contribution verbatim, without comment, whether right or wrong, on the board. As a result, all students feel safe and respected. Their very own words, their voices, when contributing their own ideas or other ideas they heard in their group, are on the board for all to see—and no contribution is criticized or rejected. If something is wrong, it won't hurt anything to be on the board for a little while. Later, as they progress, the students will be able to correct any mistakes themselves because the teacher, now knowing what the students know and what they don't know, can figure out what the next task might be to help them correct and deepen their understanding and skill.

If necessary, after several more sequential, student-centered I/SG/WG tasks, the teacher might lecture and/or give a reading assignment. Now, more prepared and engaged than if the teacher had started cold with a lecture or reading assignment, the students will be ready—and eager—for this. They say, "I know what you mean!" "I see what you're talking about." "That is something I was wondering about." "That really helps me understand it better." "Is that really true?" "I don't agree." Their excitement can get intense. In fact, the first time I used this method and got to this point, I had to take a few steps backward, blown away by their energy. This was a powerful contrast to the all-too-frequent scene I'd been used to: the students sitting quietly, taking notes on my brilliant lecture; sometimes with a few students, probably those who already had a base of knowledge on which they could construct my lecture, glancing up for a moment with a sparkling eye, but some of them thinking, as was clear from their essay exams, "I don't understand this; but I'll just take notes, memorize them, and I'll pass the test okay."

Also, as students progress through the stages of the NHLP, the conversations in the small groups and whole group—in this community of engaged and critically thinking learners—become ever richer and deeper. This I/SG/WG pedagogy is powerfully effective with any task, topic, subject, and group of students. The examples of successful NHLP lessons for different subjects and grade levels in Part II ignite students' potential.

Chapter 3 explains why this curricular and pedagogical process works. It's because this process is how the brain learns.

NOTES

1. Gabriel, J. G. (2005). *How to thrive as a teacher leader*. Alexandria, VA: ASCD, p. 124.

2. Smilkstein, R. (2003). *We're born to learn: Using the brain's natural learning process to create today's curriculum*. Thousand Oaks, CA: Corwin Press, pp. 40–48.

3. Smilkstein, R. (2003).

4. Piaget, J., & Inhelder, B. (1966/1969). *The psychology of the child*. New York: Basic Books (Original work published 1966).

5. Checkley, K. (2006, April). "Radical" math becomes the standard: Emphasis on algebraic thinking, problem solving, communication. *Education Update*, *48*(4), 2–3, 8.

6. Checkley, K. (2006), p. 8.

7. Mapes, L. V. (2006, April 16). Math: Set of problems. *The Seattle Times*, p. A6.

8. Smilkstein, R. (2003).

9. Delpit, L. (1988). The silenced dialogue: Power and pedagogy in educating other people's children. *Harvard Educational Review*, *58*, 280–297.

Ladson-Billing, G. (1995). Toward a theory of culturally relevant pedagogy. *American Educational Research Journal*, *32*, 465–491.

McPhail, I. P., & McPhail, C. J. (1999). Transforming classroom practice for African American learners: Implications for the learning paradigm. *Removing Vestiges: Research-Based Strategies to Promote Inclusion*, *2*, 49–60.

10. Tagg, J. (2003). *The learning paradigm college*. Bolton, MA: Anker.

11. Dweck, C. (2000). *Self-theories: Their role in motivation, personality, and development*. Philadelphia: Psychology Press.

12. Anderson, J. (1988). Cognitive styles and multicultural populations. *Journal of Teacher Education*, *39*, 2–9.

13. Whalen, J., & Begley, S. (2005, March 30). In England, girls are closing gap with boys in math. *Wall Street Journal*, p. A1.

14. Rose, M. (1995). *Possible lives: The promise of public education in America*. New York: Houghton Mifflin.

15. Smilkstein, R. (2003).

16. Entwistle, N. (2000). Approaches to studying and levels of understanding: The influences of teaching and assessment. In J. C. Smart (Ed.), *Higher education: Handbook of theory and research* (Vol. 15, pp. 156–218). New York: Agathon Press.

Hounsell, D. J. (1997). Understanding teaching and teaching for understanding. In R. Marton, D. J. Hounsell, & N. J. Entwistle (Eds.), *The experience of learning* (2nd ed., pp. 39–58). Edinburgh, Scotland: Scottish Academic Press.

Langer, E. (1997). *The power of mindful learning*. New York: Addison-Wesley.

Tagg, J. (2004, March/April). Why learn? What we may *really* be teaching students. *About Campus*, *8*(6), 2–10.

REFERENCES

Anderson, J. (1988). Cognitive styles and multicultural populations. *Journal of Teacher Education, 39,* 2–9.

Checkley, K. (2006, April). "Radical" math becomes the standard: Emphasis on algebraic thinking, problem solving, communication. *Education Update, 48*(4), 2–3, 8.

Delpit, L. (1988). The silenced dialogue: Power and pedagogy in educating other people's children. *Harvard Educational Review, 58,* 280–297.

Dweck, C. (2000). *Self-theories: Their role in motivation, personality, and development.* Philadelphia: Psychology Press.

Entwistle, N. (2000). Approaches to studying and levels of understanding: The influences of teaching and assessment. In J. C. Smart (Ed.), *Higher education: Handbook of theory and research* (Vol. 15, pp. 156–218). New York: Agathon Press.

Hounsell, D. J. (1997). Understanding teaching and teaching for understanding. In R. Marton, D. J. Hounsell, & N. J. Entwistle (Eds.), *The experience of learning* (2nd ed., pp. 39–58). Edinburgh, Scotland: Scottish Academic Press.

Ladson-Billing, G. (1995). Toward a theory of culturally relevant pedagogy. *American Educational Research Journal, 32,* 465–491.

Langer, E. (1997). *The power of mindful learning.* New York: Addison-Wesley.

Mapes, L. V. (2006, April 16). Math: Set of problems. *The Seattle Times,* p. A6.

McPhail, I. P., & McPhail, C. J. (1999). Transforming classroom practice for African American learners: Implications for the learning paradigm. *Removing Vestiges: Research-Based Strategies to Promote Inclusion, 2,* 49–60.

Piaget, J., & Inhelder, B. (1969). *The psychology of the child.* New York: Basic Books. (Original work published 1966)

Rose, M. (1995). *Possible lives: The promise of public education in America.* New York: Houghton Mifflin.

Smilkstein, R. (2003). *We're born to learn: Using the brain's natural learning process to create today's curriculum.* Thousand Oaks, CA: Corwin Press.

Tagg, J. (2004, March/April). Why learn? What we may *really* be teaching students. *About Campus, 8*(6), 2–10.

Tagg, J. (2003). *The learning paradigm college.* Bolton, MA: Anker.

Whalen, J., & Begley, S. (2005, April 1). In England, girls are closing gap with boys in math. *Wall Street Journal,* p. A1.

3

How the Brain Learns

Student Empowerment and Potential

Because the brain is our learning, thinking, and remembering organ, everyone, especially educators and students, can benefit from knowing how the brain learns. Just as a cardiologist wouldn't treat a patient's heart without knowing how the heart works, so an educator can't really "treat" a student's brain without knowing how the brain learns. As noted in Chapter 2, students gain invaluable, empowering understanding of their own natural learning process. They also need a user's guide to how the brain learns.

Neuroscientists say that the brain is the most complex physical entity in the known universe. Information about the brain and how it functions is voluminous, possibly arcane, and ever increasing. However, we will focus here only on those aspects that will help us ignite our students' potential to be the motivated, engaged learners they were born to be. The information in this chapter is presented in a way that is suitable for—and has been successful in—sharing with students at all levels.

This chapter, especially this section, is not for a science course. It is for any course and every student. Consider this information as a life-skills lesson for students rather than a scientific or scholarly discussion of the brain. However, for readers interested in a more in-depth account of the brain, at the end of the chapter is a list of references to the scientific and scholarly brain research that informs this chapter.

THE SEVEN MAGIC WORDS

> "Humans are motivated to develop competence and to solve problems; they have, as White (1959) put it, 'competence motivation.'"[1]

Human beings are naturally, from infancy, innately motivated to be active, problem-solving learners. How to walk? How to speak? How to feed myself? How to, how to, how to? And why, why, why? Whenever you see a baby crying, but not from pain, hold up in front of her something she has never seen before and ask, "What's this?" She will stop crying and reach out for it so she can figure it out. Figuring things out is something the brain is innately motivated, is impelled, to do. If this is what human beings naturally want to do, are impelled to do, why not teach in a way that engages students in figuring things out for themselves?

See If You Can Figure This Out

The seven words "See if you can figure this out" are, metaphorically, the mating call of the brain. They are the brain's "mating call" because whenever a brain hears those words, either explicitly or implicitly, it enthusiastically responds, "Yes, I will try to figure it out!" This is what the brain is born to do—is, in fact, impelled to do—because it is our survival organ. The brain is always asking, trying to figure out, "What's this? How does it work? How can I make it work for me?" This is how we survive and thrive. A major goal of the brain is to be empowered. Thus, some of its major tasks are to figure things out, to solve problems, to make things work.

Students Figuring It Out for Themselves

The lesson in this section has been successful at the college level and is suitable for high school and middle school history classes as well. Part II provides other examples of successful, classroom-proven lessons that engage students in several elementary, middle school, and high school subjects.

At North Seattle Community College, my colleague Jim Harnish and I were teaching together a course titled "The Russians as People," focusing on both Russian literature and history. Our team-taught program combined two 5-credit courses so that he and I met together for 10 hours a week with one cohort of students. This was a learning community. (See Chapter 8 for a discussion of learning communities.)

Jim, the historian, had taught stand-alone courses on modern European history and was concerned that our students, like his students in previous classes, might not understand how the Russians allowed themselves to be subjugated by Stalin's dictatorship. Jim had previously used a scenario that helped his students connect emotionally to that reality. We decided to use it in our class, too; so we rehearsed this "play," which we performed on the day he was going to introduce Stalinism.

Act 1, Scene 1. The Bad News

Jim: History teacher

Rita: English teacher

A class of 48 students of diverse ages and ethnicities. It's three weeks before the final exam. The students are highly motivated by the course's learning-community style of inquiry-based, problem-based, student-centered, interactive learning. Students work together in small groups, have seminars in which they take turns leading the discussion, do research in teams, and then report together on what they have discovered. There are no exams, only research papers and student projects and presentations. Their work has gained in quality and depth over the term; they are confident, motivated, hardworking, successful learners. In fact, it is just their sense of self-efficacy and self-empowerment that Jim fears will prevent them from fully understanding what happened in Russia under Stalin. How could we help them make a personal connection with—and begin to deeply understand—a society that had accepted living under a totalitarian dictatorship?

Jim and Rita enter class looking downhearted.

Jim: Well, we have some bad news. The state legislature has told us that they aren't going to accept the grades we give in this course because it's so different from other courses. They've hired a test-writing company to write a final exam, which you have to pass in order to get official credit for the course. Because the exam is coming up in just a few weeks and we don't want you to lose the 10 credits for this course, we're going to start focusing on preparing you for the exam. Starting tomorrow, we'll be doing exam preparation in class instead of following the syllabus.

Various Students: (Speaking out.) Did you talk with them and tell them how much we're learning? Do they know how great this class is? Is there any way to get them to change their decision?

Rita: (Waving her hand gently and looking fatigued.) We knew about this two weeks ago and have been trying to reverse the state's decision. We've talked with the president of the college, some of our state legislators, and the state board that governs the community college system, but nobody has been able to change the legislature's decision. So, as Jim said, starting tomorrow we'll be preparing you by having study sessions in class; and we'll also set up study groups so you can study outside class, too.

Various Students: (Calming down and accepting the situation.) Do you think we'll have time to get ready? Do you know what kinds of questions will be on the test?

Kalil: (An international student.) This is wrong. (He gets up, takes his books, and leaves the room. Rita nods to Jim and goes after Kalil.)

Act 1, Scene 2. In the Hallway Outside the Classroom

Rita: Kalil! Wait a minute! (He stops and turns around. She catches up to him.)

Kalil: This is terrible. I'm not going to do this. It is not right.

Rita: It's okay. Listen. What we said isn't true. Jim and I made it up so the class would experience what's it's like living in a dictatorship. Come back and see what happens.

Kalil: (Calming down.) Is this the truth? (Rita nods and Kalil starts to smile.) Okay.

Rita: But when you come back, don't tell anybody that it isn't true. (He agrees. They go back to the classroom.)

Act 1, Scene 3. In the Classroom

Kalil takes his seat. Rita goes up to Jim and stands sadly beside him.

Jim: Okay, since this is our last day before we start the study sessions, we'll go ahead and introduce the topic we'd planned for today. (He turns on the overhead projector and lays down a transparency.) We're not going to have time to do this in our usual interactive way, so I'm just going to give a lecture about it. (He begins to unveil characteristics of totalitarianism: total control over individuals, impersonal authority governs all, fear/terror, the only hope is in conformity. All these our students had experienced and accepted in the previous few minutes.)

Various Students: (Speaking up around the room, making discouraged comments.) This sounds like what's going on here. We might as well be living in Russia. (As Jim continues, students begin to wake up and start making lively comments.) Hey, wait a minute. Was this just a joke? We've been had!

Jim and Rita: (Smiling.) Right. And what do you think about living in a dictatorship? Can you figure out why people might do it?

Various Students: We just gave in. We were scared. They could hurt us. We were ready to submit and obey.

Jim: (Proceeds in the usual way with a student-centered assignment.)

Curtain

Students are now excited, motivated, eager to learn more about this topic. They can now understand Stalinism from having undergone a totalitarian experience and having figured out how and why it had happened to them. Now they can begin to figure out why and how it had happened to the Russian people. Now they are eager to study Russian history. It also helps them figure out the meaning and understand the context in the prerevolutionary Russian literature they are reading.

> "Emerging from all the data is a clear message. . . . [Learning] comes from within, using outside stimuli as material for growth. . . . Explaining things to [learners] won't do the job; they must have a chance to experience, wonder, experiment, and act it out for themselves."[2]

When Students Aren't Invited to Figure It Out in School

If we see students who are not motivated to learn in school, we are seeing people who have been abused in some way out of their natural impulsion to learn—in school. Outside school, however, they are spending hour after hour fascinated by such empowering activities as surfing the Web to see what's in the world; communicating globally via the Internet; trying to figure out, with concentration and by problem solving, how to win at complex video games; and becoming skilled at sports and arts. In Figures 2.1 and 2.2, people report multistage processes of learning, including "practice, practice, practice." Significantly, many groups say these same three words at Stages 2 or 3.

If teachers challenged students with the seven magic words, either implicitly or explicitly, in every lesson, students would be just as engaged in class as they are before their computer or video game screen, on the athletic field, or with their band. The classroom strategy that will ignite student potential is to present students with curricula and lessons that implicitly or explicitly invite them to "see if you can figure this out."

> "Reading problems are the fault of old ideas about reading that do not accurately reflect what the brain requires to read with excellence [which is for the reader to figure it out himself]."[3]

METACOGNITION: BASIC FACTS ABOUT HOW THE BRAIN LEARNS THAT EVERYONE SHOULD KNOW

When both teachers and students have metacognitive knowledge—know how the brain learns and how they themselves learn—every classroom can be a place of vibrant, successful learning.

Our Human Brain

Like the heart and every other body organ, the brain operates by the same processes and performs the same functions in every member of our species. Of course, as with the other body organs, there are variations in performance; but, essentially, the basic functions and nature are the same. For example, if this weren't true, people from all over the world would not be going to China, as is presently the case, for organ transplants; and the organs being transplanted into people from countries and cultures worldwide are all from Chinese cadavers.

When students have knowledge of the natural human learning process and of how the brain learns, they have their user's guide to the brain and their own learning process. This metacognitive knowledge empowers students as learners.

Because this material is essential for students to understand, some of the concepts are presented as metaphors, for example, calling dendrites (these brain structures are discussed below) "branches and twigs." This is a particularly apt metaphor because *dendrite* means "tree-like" and accurately describes the tree-like (branch- and twig-like) form of dendrite brain structures. Students are empowered with this conceptualization because now they can visualize and, thus, understand the concepts better than if they heard only technical terms. Tell them to observe trees in the winter without their leaves and they'll see what dendrites look like.

Students who see learning as growing twigs and branches in their brain—in fact, learning does involve the growing of dendrites in their brain (See Figure 3.3)—will say, as they have actually said in class, with full appreciation of what is happening and how they themselves made it happen, "I feel my dendrites growing!" This is their new and self-empowered way of saying, "I'm getting it—I'm beginning to understand! And I made it happen by growing my own dendrites from thinking about it and practicing a lot!"

When the information in this chapter is shared with students, it empowers them to know why and how they learn—or don't learn. Alex Koerger, a former student of mine, sent me this report about one of his high-school students:

> I just thought I would share this with you. A student was asking me about a specific method of graphing (a method that we had gone over a while ago). I said, "Charlie, you know how to do that. Think about it some." He did, suggesting several wrong methods to me before finally giving me the right answer. I said, "See, I knew you knew how to do that." He responded, "I guess my dendrites were out of practice."
>
> I love that the kids know and use this stuff and that they understand how their brains working on the inside translates to how their bodies behave on the outside. That's pretty darn cool. (Personal communication, February 2, 2006)

Brain Cells (Neurons)

1. Although estimates vary, some researchers report that the brain has more than 100 billion nerve cells (neurons). But all agree that each neuron has one body, thousands of branches and twigs (dendrites), and one narrow tube (axon) (Figure 3.2).

2. Dendrites grow on neurons when we are exploring, practicing, figuring out, and creatively and critically thinking about an object of learning as and because we are going through the activities of our natural learning process (Chapter 2). This *is* learning (Figure 3.3).

3. At the end of the axon are many branches (Figure 3.2). Each branch ends in a bulb filled with chemicals (neurotransmitters) for chemically communicating with other neurons.

Brain Cell (Neuron) Networks

4. There is a tiny gap (synapse) between an axon terminal bulb and another neuron's dendrite or body. When a person is learning, dendrites grow and, also, synapses are created between neurons. Chemicals from an axon bulb go across the synapse to the receiving neuron's dendrite or body (Figure 3.4). Simplifying a very complex process, this chemical

Figure 3.1 The Brain in the Skull

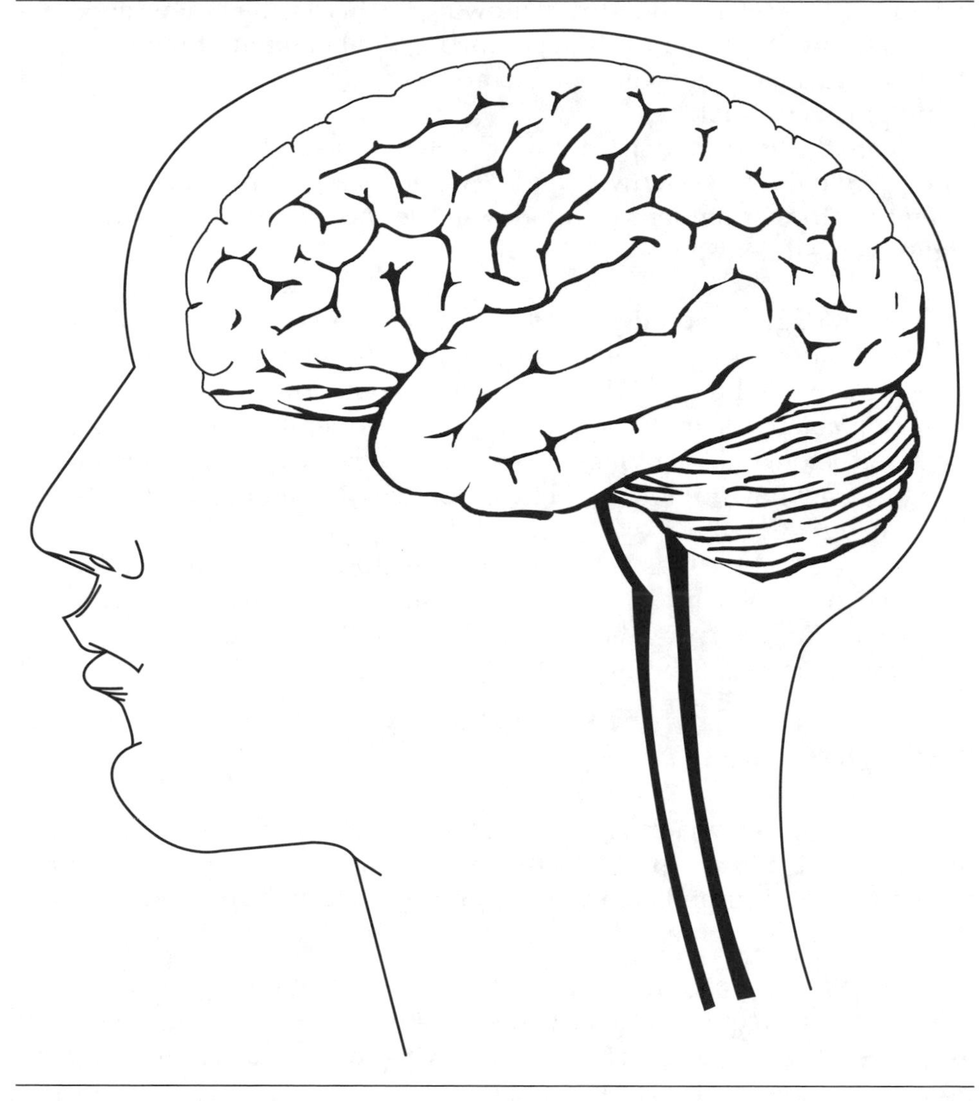

SOURCE: From Smilkstein (2003).

communication between neurons is how the brain learns, thinks, and remembers.

5. When neurons communicate with each other this way, sending and receiving chemical messages at synapses, they form networks for learning, thinking, and remembering (Figure 3.5). There could be as many as 1,000 to 10,000 neurons connected in one network. The more we actively experience, explore, practice, and think about an object of learning and, thus, the higher we go in the stages of our natural learning process, the more dendrites and synapses, specific to that object of learning, are being created. Consequently, more neurons related to that object of learning are connecting at the synapses; and our neural networks for that object of

Figure 3.2 A Neuron

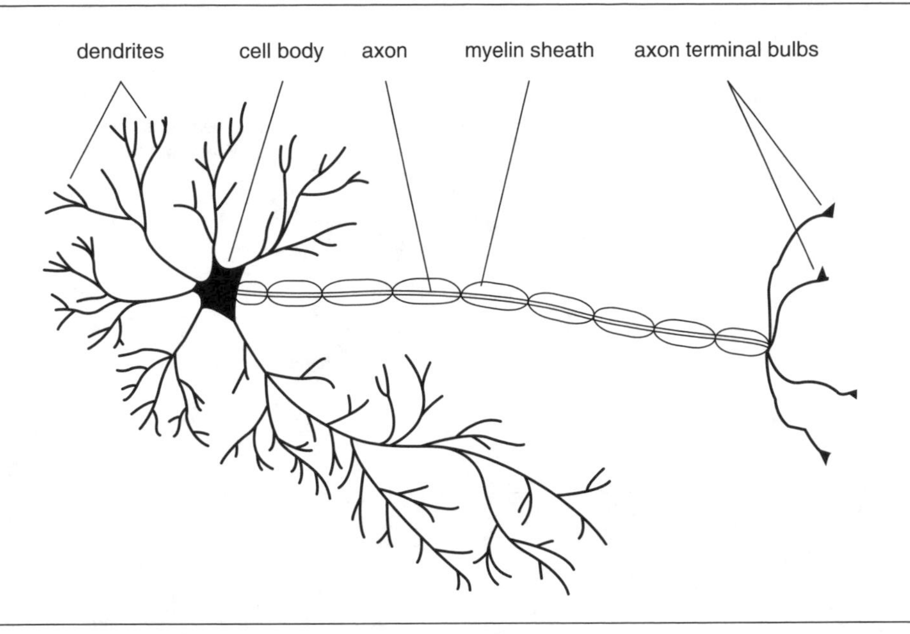

SOURCE: From Smilkstein (2003).

Figure 3.3 Growing Dendrites

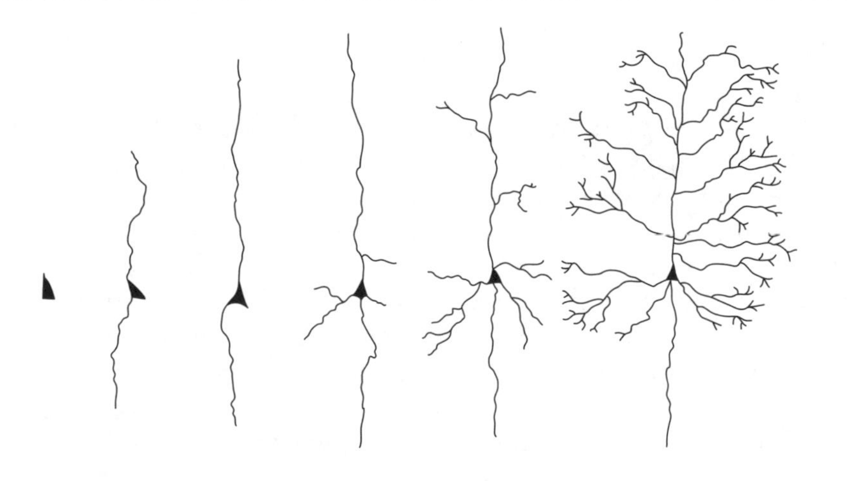

SOURCE: From Smilkstein (2003).

learning are becoming larger, thicker, and more complex. As a specific network grows from our experiences, the more we know about, understand, and can do with that specific object of learning—and the more in-depth, complex, refined, and sophisticated our knowledge and understanding become for that object of learning.

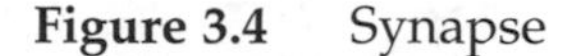

Figure 3.4 Synapse

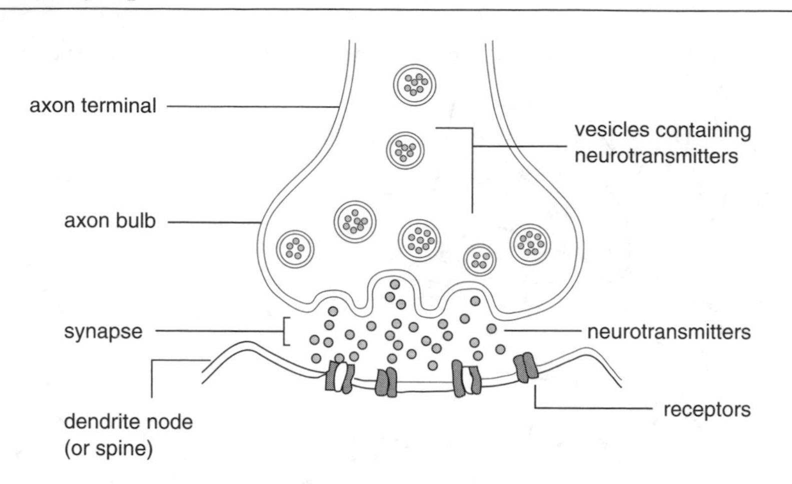

SOURCE: From Smilkstein (2003).

> *The more we process, the more we grow, the more we know.*
>
> "Learning changes the structure of the brain. . . . These structural changes alter the functional organization of the brain."[4]

Rote Learning

We do rote learning also by our activities. However, for rote learning, the activity is usually just copying and/or memorizing. A neural network for rote-learned material is small; and our understanding is superficial, our knowledge and skill limited. Some rote learning is useful, such as the multiplication tables and verb forms. Learners can recite rote material back in its memorized form, such as names and dates in a history course, but typically do not understand the concepts implicit in the material and cannot transfer or apply that knowledge in a thoughtful or creative way. To make rote-learned knowledge useful, students need opportunities to practice it in creative- and critical-thinking ways in meaningful contexts.

The Most Complex Thing in the Known Universe

Why is the brain considered the most complex object in the known universe? Multiply 100,000,000,000 (the number of neurons) by 10,000 (or even only 1,000), which is the number of synapses that a neuron might be using to send and receive chemical messages through the networks. Moreover, these messages can be communicated at 220 miles per hour, in less than a millisecond.

Figure 3.5 A Neural Network

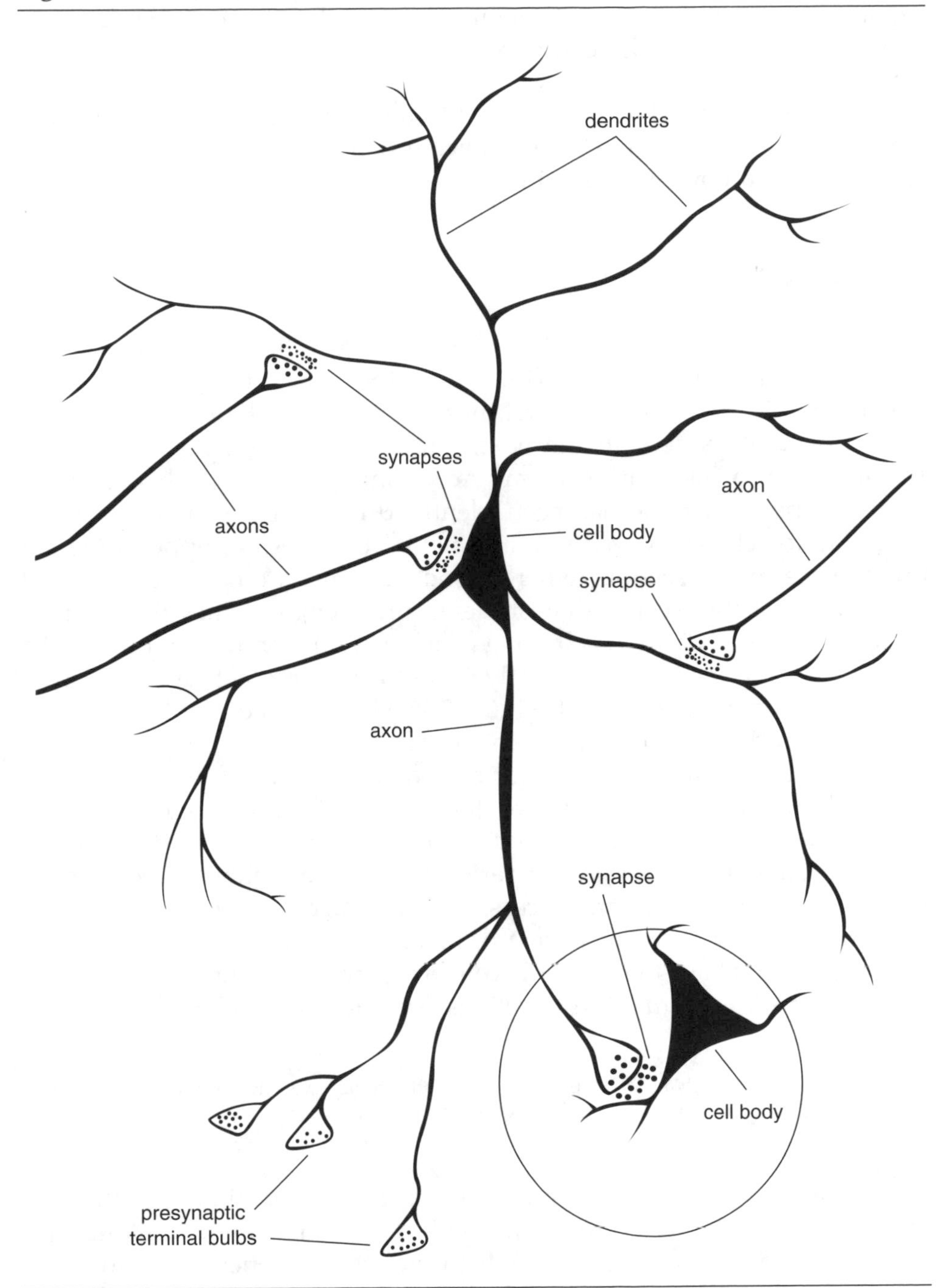

SOURCE: From Smilkstein (2003).

This is why the human brain, the soft, three-pound, grapefruit-size organ in our skull, which is the source of everything human beings have ever created, is the most complex—and amazing—object in the known universe.

When students have this accessible understanding, they know that learning isn't a vague, mysterious, uncontrollable process; and it engages them in self-empowering learning.

MOTIVATION

James Paul McGee, in his article "High Score Education: Games, Not School, Are Teaching Kids to Think,"[5] writes that video games "tend to encourage players to achieve total mastery at one level, only to challenge and undo that mastery in the next, forcing kids to adapt and evolve." Forcing them or motivating them? According to McGee, "This carefully choreographed dialectic has been identified by learning theorists as the best way to achieve expertise in any field. This doesn't happen much in our routine-driven schools, where 'good' students are often just good at 'doing school.'" It seems that students must enjoy achieving mastery, being challenged further, adapting, and evolving or they wouldn't be spending hours and hours intently focused on these activities and outcomes. Remember the student (Figure 2.1) who reported that he practiced for "100s and 1000s of hours" and became a video game master and another student who practiced "for days on end."

And in school? According to John Tagg, "Nearly all high school students are essentially disengaged from their mandatory academic work at an emotional level . . . and experience negative feelings [about their] potency, skill, involvement, success, and self-esteem." He points out that "[e]xtracurricular activities pose a dramatic contrast with the classroom" in that students have highly positive feelings when engaged in these voluntary activities and that these feelings "sustain involvement."[6]

> Rarely is a student unwilling to learn—if a student hears, explicitly or implicitly, those seven magic words, "See if you can figure this out."

Are students more motivated and engaged in classes in which they are given the opportunity—and challenged—to do their own thinking and problem-solving or in classes in which, quietly and obediently, they are expected only to listen and watch? McGee believes that schools today are in the "cognitive-science dark ages."

Motivated to Survive Outside School

Unfortunately, not all students are engaged in positive ways outside school. Although the learning they are doing isn't always fascinating or enjoyable, the motivation for some students, out of necessity, is to figure out how to become as empowered as possible to cope with and survive in their environment. But they are all using their brains to learn how to become as empowered as possible, how to survive and thrive.

CREATIVITY

George Land reported that in 1968 he gave a NASA creativity test to 1,600 five-year-olds and 98% passed it. Then he retested them when they were ten and only 30% passed. When he tested them again in five more years, only 12% passed. He also gave this same test to 28,000 adults and not more than 2% passed. "What we have concluded," he wrote, "is that non-creative behavior is learned."[7] How is it learned? Linda Naiman, in reviewing Land's results, asks, "Why aren't adults as creative as children?" Her answer is that "creativity has been buried by rules and regulations. Our educational system was designed during the Industrial Revolution over 200 years ago, to train us to be good workers and follow instructions."[8]

In fact, our educational system was once called "the factory model," which describes those classrooms, some of which still exist, in which students follow the rules, are obedient, and focus on trying to remember what the teacher is telling them and on coming up with the teacher-determined or curriculum-determined right answers.

If this is what students have been experiencing, this is what they have been learning: school is boring. But outside school, the brain seeks creativity in challenges, problems to solve, things to figure out—because this is what it is innately impelled to do. It is also internally rewarded for being creative because the brain produces feel-good chemicals, endorphins, when it is solving problems, meeting challenges, and figuring things out. In other words, the brain rewards itself when it is engaged in this kind of learning.

EMOTIONS AND THE BRAIN: FIGHT OR FLIGHT

Organs in the body, including the brain itself, produce different chemicals in response to the brain's perception of whether something is a danger or whether it is an intriguing challenge, whether she must flee (the flight response) or whether she can confidently take up the challenge (the fight response). If the perception is that it is a danger that the person cannot handle, chemicals immediately flood the synapses and shut some of them down, saying, in effect, "There is no time to think! Just flee!" The brain is our survival organ, and its job is to keep us safe from any situation it perceives as dangerous. For some students, taking a test is in this category.

On the other hand, because the brain is also the organ that helps us thrive, if the perception is of a challenge that the person can handle, different chemicals flood the synapses and facilitate the flow of neurotransmitters through them, which causes thinking and remembering: "I can figure this out! I'm going for it!"

For example, a student who fears tests has studied hard for the upcoming test; but then, when he is handed the test, his perception, because of his fear, is that he can't handle it. As a result, survival-related flight chemicals ("You're in danger! No time to think! Just flee!") enter his synapses. His memory goes blank because his brain has decided it's too dangerous to waste time thinking and that he should just run away from the perceived danger. Because he can't jump up and run out of the room, he sits there—but his brain is in escape mode.

He sits in the classroom, test in hand, with no memory of what he has studied. "I have a bad memory," he will think. However, with metacognitive knowledge of how the brain learns, thinks, and remembers, he will be able to say instead, "No, my memory is fine. I studied. I grew my dendrites, connected my synapses, and constructed some networks for this subject. They're actual, physical brain structures and can't disappear all of a sudden. So it's just that my emotions are sabotaging me."

With this empowering metacognitive knowledge, students can "brainwash" themselves. By relaxing, deep breathing, and visualizing the flight chemicals going away and the fight chemicals flowing in ("I can handle this!"), they are able to get their synapses working again, their brain thinking and remembering again. Students need to know they have the ability to do this. With this metacognitive knowledge, students are empowered to be self-responsible, confident learners.

> Stress causes the body to produce cortisol, which prepares the body to respond to danger. However, too much cortisol too often from the highly stressful emotions of powerlessness, fear, and anxiety can kill neurons. Thus, it is critical that students have metacognitive knowledge to help them understand how their emotions affect their brain and to empower them to understand what they are feeling and why—and how to deal with these feelings.

CONSTRUCTIVISM

> In the most general sense, the contemporary view of learning is that people construct new knowledge and understanding based on what they already know and believe. . . . [P]eople construct new knowledge based on their current knowledge. [E]xisting knowledge is used to build new knowledge.[9]

Sternberg and Williams describe constructivism from a pedagogical and teaching perspective:

> Researchers have shifted from viewing the *teacher* as belonging at the center of the learning process, to viewing the *student* as having a more central and active role. . . . Consistent with the **student-centered approach** is a view sometimes called **constructivism**, because it sees students as constructing their own understanding.[10] [Emphasis in original]

In addition, Piaget and others have described and explained constructivism in various complex neurophysiological and theoretical ways.[11] For example, in 1993, Jacobs, Schall, and Scheibel discovered that human dendrite growth reflects the learner's educational and avocational experiences. They also found that the highest-grown dendrites, those furthest from the neuron's body, are the most mature, the most capable of responding to complex stimuli in the environment. They found that our neural network, our "tree of knowledge," for a specific object of learning, which *is* our learning, grows by physiologically constructing each higher level of knowledge on a lower level until it reaches a mature level of knowledge, skill, and understanding[12] (Figures 3.2, 3.3, and 3.5). In other words, their research found a neurophysiological constructivist process of learning.

The Converging Research

When different areas of research converge, it suggests that something significant has been discovered. The natural learning research findings (Chapter 2, Figures 2.1 and 2.2) converge with Jacobs, Schall, and Scheibel's research and with other research on the brain's constructive learning process. These findings also correspond with the constructive process Piaget found in his research as the one by which infants from birth to two years learn new skills and concepts.

This converging research is also in accordance with the pedagogical approach described by Bransford et al. and also by Sternberg and Williams. These various views all explain that learning starts with what the learner already knows, that new knowledge must be connected to it and then constructed through experiencing and processing, stage upon stage, neural structure upon neural structure, to higher and more complex levels of knowledge, skill, and understanding (Figure 3.6).

McGee's "choreographed dialectic [that] has been identified by learning theorists as the best way to achieve expertise in any field" (page 58) also seems to be a constructivist approach, converging with the views above.

Transfer

"Transfer means carrying over knowledge from one problem or situation to a new problem [or situation]."[13] Transfer is one of the most

Figure 3.6 Ceiling Level and Neural Networks: Convergence of the Natural Human Learning Process Research and Brain Research

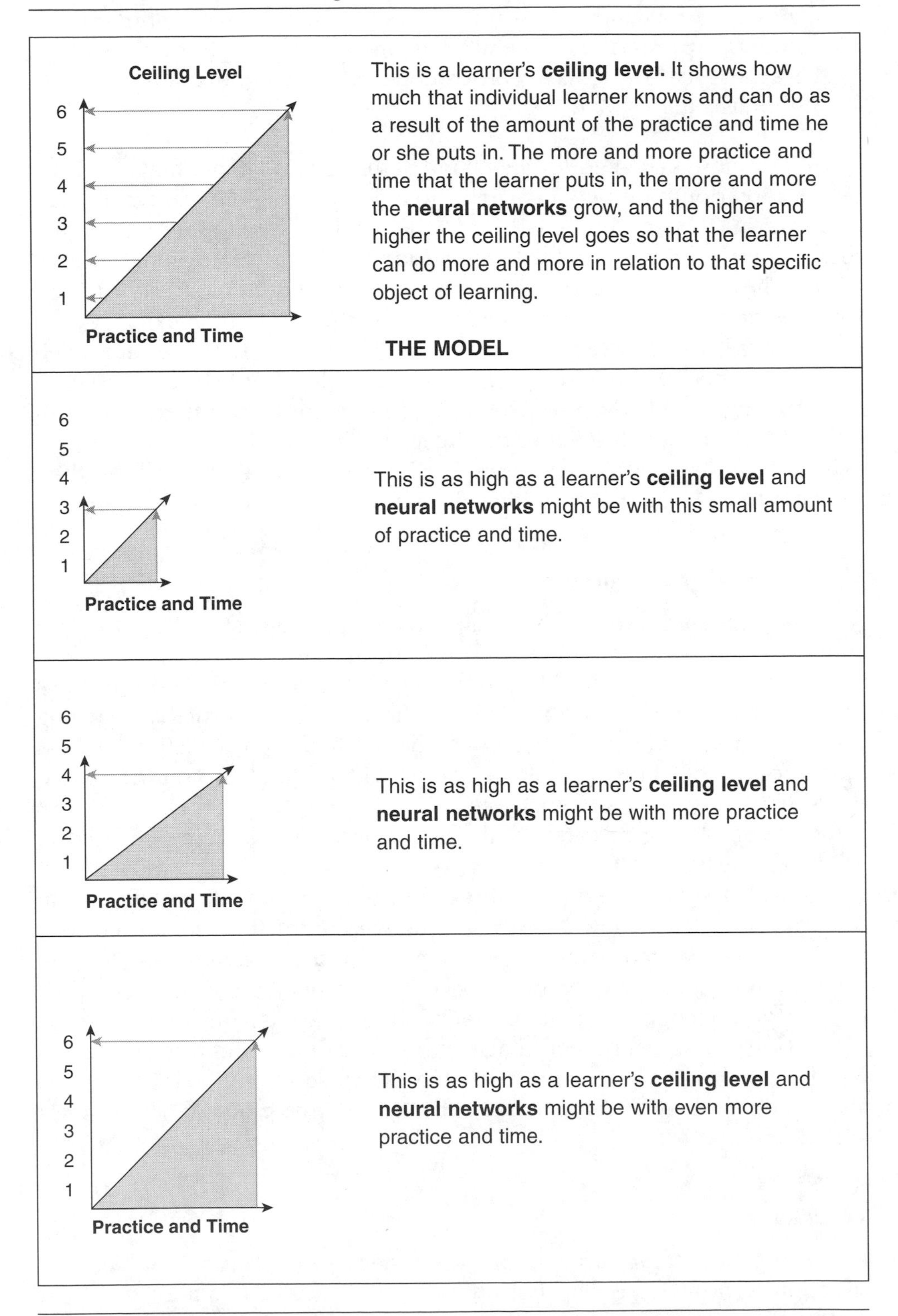

SOURCE: From Smilkstein (2003).

problematic and complex issues in educational psychology. However, the main point students and teachers need to know about transfer is that a person starts learning a new topic by making a connection between what the person knows (the neural networks the person already has) and the new topic. See "They Can't Connect" (pages 68–69) for examples.

REASONS STUDENTS ARE NOT MOTIVATED IN SCHOOL

If we see students who look like they don't want to learn or can't learn, we are seeing an anomaly, because the brain is born to learn; it is born to figure things out; it wants to learn and it enjoys learning. Are students unmotivated if they aren't given the opportunity in school to figure things out for themselves? Is the teacher starting out above and beyond where they are so that they cannot make a connection? Are they suffering from an undiagnosed or untreated learning disability? Have they been abused (criticized, ridiculed) by others (e.g., teachers, parents, peers) for figuring things out themselves, for coming up with their own ideas, for doing their own critical and creative thinking?

One or more of the following reasons might be why students are not motivated in school:

1. Their brain has not been invited, not given an opportunity, to learn by its natural learning process.
2. They have a diagnosed learning disability.
3. They have an undiagnosed learning disability.
4. They fear success.
5. The teacher doesn't start where they are, so they can't connect.

The Brain Hasn't Been Invited

The Adolescent Brain

Why do so many adolescents do risky, dangerous things? Recently, there have been reports that the reason adolescents do not have good judgment and do not make good decisions is that the adolescent brain, specifically the prefrontal cortex, is not yet fully developed. This is not the problem. The brain is 95% developed by the age of five. What is lacking in the adolescent brain are the dendrites and synapses for the knowledge and understanding required for having good judgment and for making good decisions, which is the province of the prefrontal cortex. What is needed in order for adolescents to grow these brain structures? They need the opportunity to practice thinking about and making important decisions, and using and reflecting on their own judgment.

The brain grows its dendrites, synapses, and neural networks for higher-level thinking and responsible decision making, as for anything else, from what it experiences. If adolescents haven't had the opportunity to experience and practice serious and responsible decision making in or out of school, they haven't learned how to do it. They haven't had the opportunity to grow the neural structures for doing that.

The human brain, which grows specific neural/knowledge structures from specific experiences, "is a dynamic organ, shaped to a great extent by experience—by what a living being does, and has done."[14]

> At Harvard Medical School, Sara Lazar took magnetic resonance imaging (MRI) scans of 20 subjects who were students of "insight meditation," which focuses on breath awareness and bodily sensations, and compared them with brain scans from 15 people with no meditation or yoga experience. Her team found that specific cortical regions of the brain were significantly thicker in people who meditated than in those who did not . . . [and that c]ortical thickening was correlated with experience: the longer a subject had been practicing meditation, the thicker the cortex was.[15]

Studying the human brain, John Ratey wrote, "Extra use means extra cortex. The lesson, again, is that ongoing perception reshapes the ongoing brain. Practice makes new brain."[16] Thus, since the brain grows from what it experiences and practices, if an adolescent hasn't had the opportunity to practice responsible decision making, that person hasn't had the opportunity to grow the specific structures that would increase or develop the prefrontal cortex. So, of course, this adolescent's brain will be less developed than an adult's brain.

Teenagers have brains that are ready to figure out, work on, and try to solve big problems and meet great challenges; but too often they are not invited to do that in school or, in some cases, in their family or community. As a result, some will be impelled by their frustrated brains to do something, anything, that is challenging and exciting, even risky. Or they will medicate themselves. And these students won't be interested in school when it doesn't challenge them to the height of their creative and critical thinking abilities.

Let us, however, also look at the teenagers who are responsible citizens, who volunteer with civic organizations, who care for their younger siblings when their parents are ill or unable to do so, who have afterschool jobs to make money to save for college, who take an interest in the social and political realities of the community, the nation, and the world. Their brains are probably more like adults' brains than their disengaged peers' brains.

What's the solution to the problem of disengaged teens? Treat all students, especially teenagers, with respect for their brains' innate need and desire to think independently, creatively, and even deeply. And provide curricula that invite them to do that.

But we also need to be sure the students know about all this. It is invaluable knowledge that will convince them that they can be successful learners in school—but, of course, only if school is a brain-based, natural learning, constructivist place. If it is, they will be motivated learners in school, as they are outside school with their computers and video games and other extracurricular activities. Chapter 6 also discusses adolescents, their memories, their emotions, and the importance of a caring teacher in their lives.

Diagnosed With a Learning Disability

Students with a learning disability also want to learn, are able to learn, enjoy learning, and seek empowerment and affirmation. These students, like any others, learn by the same brain-based, natural learning, constructivist processes. They might go slower and not reach as high a level of understanding and skill (not construct as big and thick a neural network), but they can certainly progress and learn by constructing new and larger networks (Figure 3.7). When treated with the acceptance and assurance of safety that all students need, and, if necessary, with appropriate accommodations, they, too, will do their best and experience success.[17]

Undiagnosed Learning Disability

What if a student has not been diagnosed with an existing learning disability? Will the teacher know enough about learning disabilities to suspect there is one? If so, will there be appropriate resources at the school to test and then support the student? Unfortunately, in some states a diagnosis is made merely by checking off items on a list of behaviors. Then drugs might be prescribed. These methods, though, can miss the real problem. For example, a student with a reading problem—caused either by a true disability or by being underprepared and therefore not able to connect with the class work—might choose to be disruptive and gain a reputation for being bad rather than let the teacher and other students find out that she cannot read.

They Fear Success

Some networks might not be desirable ones. For example, a child's dysfunctional, perhaps alcoholic, mother has told him all his life that he is stupid, useless, no good, a loser and doesn't give him respect or show him love or keep him safe. As a result, the child is growing a big, strongly constructed network of a negative self-image: "I'm stupid, no good, can't do anything right, no one can love me." This can be a conscious or, if it is too

Figure 3.7 Individual Differences: Learners With Different Levels of Ability

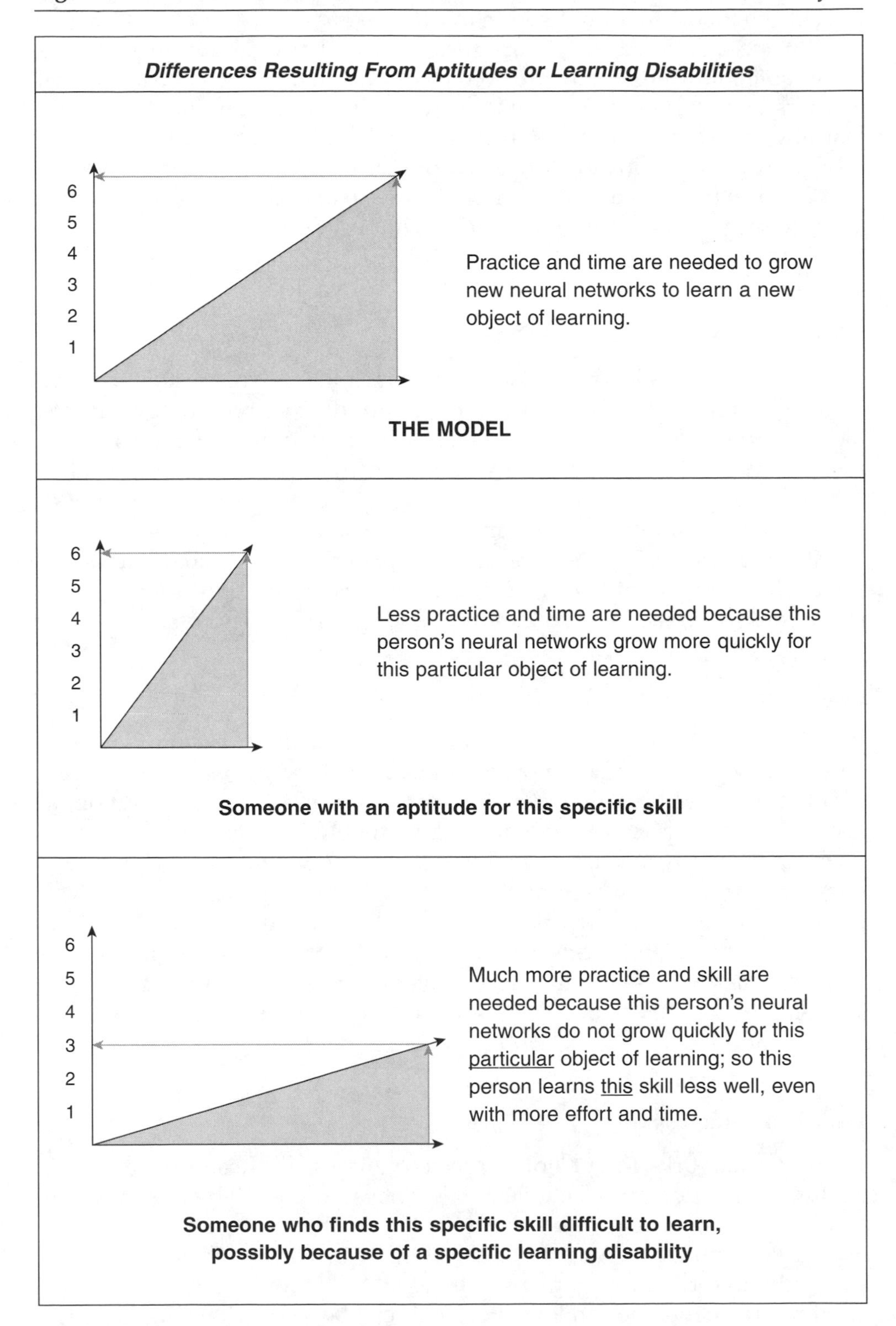

SOURCE: From Smilkstein (2003).

painful to hear, a subconscious self-image. But the effect, in either case, is the same: fear of success. Why fear success? To succeed would contradict that strong network of negative sense of self; it would leave the person without any sense of self, lost, or experiencing a subconscious fear of contradicting the introjected, violent mother. Many of us have known a student like this. Just as he is about to succeed—which might have been a struggle uphill to get to that point—instead of going all the way, he sabotages himself: he doesn't come to class, doesn't do his work, misbehaves. He breaks a teacher's heart.

At the other end of the spectrum, students who fear *failure* don't present the same kind of problem. These students want to succeed and would be happy to do so. With metacognitive knowledge and brain-compatible, natural learning curriculum and pedagogy, they can experience success and, consequently, will become confident about their ability to learn.

The student who fears success has no inner resources to help him overcome his negative self-image. But then one day at the beginning of a new term, he is in class and his teacher does something different.

Getting Rid of Bad Networks

Act 1

His teacher is Ruth and he is Gabe. After they do the natural learning research activities described in Chapter 2, Ruth explains how the brain learns. It grows dendrites and networks for what the person experiences, practices, and thinks about; the more the person does this, the more the dendrites and networks grow, which means the more the person's knowledge and skill grow for what he or she has been experiencing, practicing, and thinking about.

Then Ruth makes the connection for her students who fear success.

Ruth: If you have the idea that you are stupid or bad, it's just the dendrites and networks that someone else made your brain grow by telling you this a lot or treating you this way. So whenever you hear that voice in your head or have the feeling that you're stupid or bad or shouldn't try to succeed, say, "You're just a bunch of dumb dendrites! If I don't use you, if I don't listen to you, I'll lose you. And I'll also be growing new, good dendrites by reminding myself I'm a natural-born learner with a brain that knows how to learn, which is the truth!" It won't be quick or easy to lose the old bad dendrites and grow the new good ones; but it will happen with this metacognitive knowledge, which tells you how your brain learns. And you have a wonderful brain that knows how to learn. Didn't you just prove it by saying how you learned to be good at something?

(Students nod and smile. Gabe is motionless. He is beginning to get the feeling that something good is happening. He doesn't know it yet, but he now has a resource that can possibly save him from a life of failure and misery.)

His new resources are this metacognitive knowledge and this teacher, who shows her students that she accepts, respects, and cares for them and that her classroom is a safe place. The metacognitive knowledge motivates and empowers her students to be the successful learners they are born to be and deeply want to be.

Curtain

They Can't Connect

However, if the teacher doesn't find out where the students are, what they already know, and just starts where the teacher thinks they are or ought to be, some or many or all of the students cannot connect. For students who aren't where the teacher thinks they should be, trying to learn from what the teacher is saying or demonstrating would be like a tree trying to grow new twigs and branches in the air above its existing structures. Would we blame the tree or think it incapable of growing new twigs and branches if it couldn't grow them out of thin air?

"A logical extension of the view that new knowledge must be constructed from existing knowledge is that teachers need to pay attention to the incomplete understandings, the false beliefs, and the naïve renditions of concepts that learners bring with them to a given subject. Teachers then need to build on these ideas in ways that help each student achieve a more mature understanding."[18]

When a teacher presents a new concept or skill in class, students from a culture or educational background different from the teacher's might not have the requisite, preliminary, foundation knowledge upon which to construct the new knowledge. They might want to say in frustration, and perhaps even misery, to a teacher who doesn't take this difference and its implications for learning into account, "I don't understand what you are saying or what you want. I don't see what you mean."

A common exchange between these students and this teacher might, in essence, be as follows, even if not verbalized:

"You're missing the point," says the teacher, thinking they are less able students.

"But I don't see what you mean," think the students.

"Let me show you again. This is how it works. This is what it means."

"But I don't see it. Please help me understand and see. I don't think I'm stupid. I just don't know what you're talking about. But maybe I am stupid."

As current research shows, if a teacher's implicit attitude is that a student is less able, the student is aware of that attitude and is negatively impacted, losing confidence and motivation.[19]

For example, in a math class students have constructed specific, dedicated math-in-workbook networks and have become adept at doing workbook math. The next topic, however, is learning how to solve novel math word problems using critical and creative thinking. This is another, and very different, specific object of learning that they need to process so their brains can construct the new, different, specific networks that will *be* their specific new knowledge and skill. Just because these students have highly developed knowledge—well-grown specific networks—for doing workbook math operations, it does not mean they have highly developed, or any, understanding, knowledge, skill—any networks—for solving novel math word problems. Unfortunately, without the relevant networks, they will keep trying to use the math networks (knowledge) they already have in their brains. However, those networks alone cannot solve these word problems.

The major task now is that they will have to begin constructing their new specific network for the new object of learning, their new understanding and skill. Part of this will be their processing and practicing how to use their previous knowledge in a new way for a new purpose. This will create the "seamless" transition through subject and grade levels that the National Council of Teachers of Mathematics is advocating (pages 33–34, Chapter 2) and that is discussed and illustrated in Chapter 4. This means that they will need to grow new dendrites from already existing ones to construct a new, more complex network. As a result, the students will have more complex understanding, knowledge, and skill because the new network, for these combined objects of learning, will be thicker, larger, more complex.

How can a teacher start a new unit or topic so that every student, even in a diverse classroom, can connect with something she or he already knows? There are several sample lessons later in this chapter (pages 72–74) as well as examples in Part II for different subjects and grade levels. Other examples are in Smilkstein 2003, along with examples of curricula for whole units and programs.[20]

PLASTICITY (NEUROPLASTICITY)

Ruth gave Gabe and his classmates a lesson about the brain's plasticity, which is that our ideas and beliefs can change. With new and different experiences, our brain can grow new and different neural networks, new and different "trees of knowledge." And, as in Gabe's case, it can also get rid of negative or destructive ideas (networks). The brain can change its structures in two ways. The first way is by pruning.

Use It or Lose It: Pruning

If a network isn't being used anymore because a person has stopped thinking about or practicing that specific object of learning, as when Gabe will now refuse to focus on or listen to his negative self-image network anymore, the brain, the great ecologist, will prune away those unused structures, which will then just dissolve back into brain tissue.

However, if a network is very large and long-standing, as when a person has played the piano for many years, from when she was 12 until she was 22, and then doesn't play for 10 years, she will most likely be able to remember and resume her piano playing without too much trouble. This is especially true if she had many experiences related to her playing: playing duets with friends, playing in recitals and school shows, practicing every day. All these related experiences will have constructed such thick, rich networks that they won't easily disappear. But a person who played the piano for only a few months when she was 12 would probably have to start all over again after a 10-year hiatus.

Gabe will have to struggle hard against his long-standing negative self-image network to make it stop influencing his thoughts, feelings, and actions. At the same time, he can begin constructing an alternate and positive self-image network:

> You're just a bunch of dumb dendrites, and I'm not going to listen to you. Shut up! Get out of my brain! Instead, I'm going to spend my time thinking about how smart and good and worthwhile I am because I'm good at some things, like driving a car and playing my guitar. And I'm worth something because my teacher believes in me and cares about me and wants to help me.

With effort and determination, and with the help and support of his teacher—or any other person who believes in him—his brain will eventually prune away the network he's not using anymore while it constructs the new one he's focusing on.

Use it or lose it. This also explains why students might not remember in September everything they knew in June if they give it no thought and don't use it in July and August.

Improve Networks

Another way a network can change is by a person's learning something more and/or different about something he already knows (a network already in use), as Ruth is trying to help Gabe do.

Suppose someone has been using incorrect grammar and consistently makes errors in subject-verb agreement, saying, "Everyone succeeds at their work" instead of "Everyone succeeds at his or her work." The teacher might correct this person many times. However, unless the person makes an effort to stop using (and, thus, losing) the incorrect usage (incorrect network), that old network will remain; the student will continue to make those same mistakes. This student needs metacognitive knowledge about how a person learns: "I have to practice a lot to grow my new dendrites."[21]

This same is true, of course, for all life-related networks, like those that are our personal beliefs, assumptions, and prejudices. If we don't question our views, if we aren't open to other, different views and don't make an effort to construct possibly better ones, we will keep those same beliefs, assumptions, and prejudices. Students with metacognitive knowledge are more likely to examine their own views, and they will also be better equipped to change them if they choose to do so.

NO-FAIL FIRST-STAGE LEARNING TASKS

If a teacher wants to help every student in the class make the critical first personal connection with a new topic, the teacher needs to assign a no-fail task that all students, no matter how different from each other, can initially relate to and do. Once they all have made that first connection, they will all be engaged and ready to continue figuring it out.

Differentiation and the Same Activities for Everyone in Class?

Don't all students have different areas and levels of knowledge and experience? Aren't they all different in what they can do? Aren't they all motivated by different tasks? So how can one task or the same activities, lessons, and pedagogy fit all students when all students are unique and have their own unique personalities, preferences, abilities, types of intelligences, experiences, thoughts, feelings, talents, beliefs, histories, cultures, likes, dislikes, learning preferences, learning styles, and knowledge?

Carol Tomlinson, a major authority on differentiation, believes the heart and soul of teaching is creating a real relationship between teacher and student and seeing, affirming, and caring for each student as a unique individual. She advocates teaching that is responsive to the individual student and not a one-size-fits-all activity—and that this is the same for 5-year-olds and 50-year-olds.[22]

Yes, all of us are different—but as members of the same species, we're all similar in our neurobiological functions and processes. For this reason, one task can, as in the examples below, engage every student because every student has a brain that learns by the same neurophysiological process unless there is a severe impairment or dysfunction. Moreover, all students come to class with knowledge they have already learned, with experiences they have already lived through. It is with these preexisting resources that a constructive no-fail first task begins.

EXAMPLES OF NO-FAIL FIRST-STAGE LEARNING TASKS

Following are examples of no-fail first activities to which every student can make a personal connection and, thus, start to construct the new neural structures that *are* the new knowledge. The only exceptions might be students with a severe learning disability or a fear of success but who have no resources to help them overcome these conditions.

If a teacher begins every new unit or topic with a no-fail task to which every student can make an initial personal connection or which every student can figure out, all the students will be together on the same playing field. Even in a heterogeneous class in which some students have more relevant experience, knowledge, and/or skill than other students, the first task, nevertheless, needs to—and can—engage everyone. And what engages every student? When the brain hears, either explicitly or implicitly, its "mating call," those seven magic words, about anything, it wants to figure it out. Then, the Individual/Small Group/Whole Group (I/SG/WG) pedagogy, described in Chapter 2, provides a variety of opportunities for students to experience different modes and styles of learning. With this pedagogy, students enrich and broaden their intelligences, learning styles, and learning preferences while remaining engaged in learning.

Three Tasks

1. With middle school or younger students, the teacher assigns this activity: "Think of something you don't like about school. Write a short letter to tell what you don't like about school to your teacher, or write a short letter about what you don't like about school to your friend, or just write it down privately for yourself. You're not going to hand these in to be graded. It's just so you can say whatever you want to say about this." After they have done their writing, the teacher asks them to get together with two other students and tell each other whom they wrote to and why. Finally, the teacher calls them back together and has a general class discussion about their reasons for choosing the person to whom they wrote their letter. This is the first task in an English unit to introduce students to the concept of "audience."

After this, to strengthen the new concept (new neural network), the teacher might have the students write three short letters, one to each of these audiences, about another topic and then process their work, as above, through the I/SG/WG active, interactive process. By the end of this activity, all the students will have a clearer, deeper understanding of the concept of "audience."

2. For high school or college students, the teacher gives them this problem to solve (to figure out): "You are a student who finds out that your new stepfather, the head of the mafia in your city, has killed your father and then married your mother. But you have no physical proof of this murder. What do you feel? What can you do?" Students are instructed to think about it and write down their ideas just as notes for discussion. Every student, no matter how different in temperament, background, educational level, and GPA, will be able to figure out a personal answer to this question, this no-fail first task. Then, after a few minutes, they are instructed to get together with two or three others and share and discuss their ideas. They are always excited about doing this. Finally, they get together as a whole class and have a general discussion about what they would feel and do, including why they would or would not follow some of the other students' suggested plans. All answers, questions, comments are equally accepted and respected. In short, every student is a contributing member of this interactive, social learning, cooperative community.

Guess what class this is and what their next assignment is. This is an English literature class and their assignment will be to read *Hamlet*. Now when they read the play, they will read it with lively curiosity and personal interest. What *does* he feel? What *does* he do? Is it anything like what they themselves would feel and do? Why or why not? They are motivated to read, think, discuss, and figure it out. Now they are all on the same playing field—to say nothing of the positive emotional effect in the classroom of everyone's being able to understand and participate. We also need to remember that these positive emotions will facilitate communication through the synapses so that the brain can think and remember more completely and confidently (the fight response).

3. In a class for high school or college students, the teacher gives the students this problem to figure out: "It is the year 2020 and you and millions of other people are unable to find work. The government is doing nothing to help you. It is interested only in its own power and has no concern for the suffering of the citizens. Some people want to revolt against the government and overthrow it. Would you join the revolution? Why or why not?" Again, they figure it out individually, then share in interactive small groups, finally reconvening for an all-class, community discussion.

What class is this and what is the next assignment? It's a European history class and the assignment is to read about the French Revolution of 1789. Now when they read about it, they will have a personal orientation. They will be curious, motivated to find out what those other people did and what happened.

Faculty Development Activity

You and your colleagues might each create a no-fail first task for one of your own courses. You can test them out on each other and provide feedback. After this, you might use your tasks with your students and then report back to your group for debriefing, discussion, and more feedback; and then, following the same process, create another no-fail task.

THINGS THAT CAN MAKE THE BRAIN GO WRONG

Drugs and Alcohol

The brain is impelled to figure things out, learn, and seek empowerment—unless something goes wrong. Drugs, alcohol, some illnesses, and stress (page 60) can make it go wrong. Drugs like marijuana and cocaine at first make the synapses communicate more quickly, but then the drugs begin to burn them out. After much usage of these drugs, the synapses can become so damaged that they cannot perform their function—and the brain becomes less and less able to learn, think, and remember.

Too much alcohol kills neurons. Too much alcohol over many years kills so many neurons that the person's brain becomes severely impaired. However, if people stop using these substances before too much damage is done, the brain might be able to recover. Students need this metacognitive information.

Alzheimer's Disease

For older students, the major illness that makes the brain unable to do its work of learning, thinking, and remembering is Alzheimer's disease. No one yet knows what causes it or how to cure it. But we do know that when susceptible people keep learning and doing intellectually challenging activities, having an active social life, doing everyday activities differently, exercising, and learning new things, they develop the disease later than others; and, when it does appear, its progress is slower.[23] As a result, many care facilities for the elderly are now providing brain-challenging activities and exercise opportunities for their residents to help them keep

Alzheimer's at bay. Apparently, the younger a person starts this regimen, the better.

FEEDING THE BRAIN

The brain, which is only 3% of the body's weight, uses up to 20% of the body's energy. It uses this much energy because it is the hardest-working organ, active at all times, monitoring and controlling all the organs and systems in the body, including all our conscious and unconscious learning, thinking, and remembering. Consequently, the brain must be nourished so that it can successfully perform all its tasks. We know that children who come to school ill nourished will be at a disadvantage.[24]

> Moreover, when it is working especially hard, as when solving a problem or doing a complex critical- or creative-thinking activity, it uses even more energy and fuel.
>
> It is essential, then, that we ingest enough glucose [except refined sugar] and water [the basic brain nutrients] to provide the energy the brain needs to work well. Exercising is another way to increase our intake of oxygen. We also need certain vitamins and chemicals, for example, calcium, sodium, and potassium.[25]

"Our brain craves nutrients based on its evolutionary history, such as fruits, vegetables, nuts, legumes, lean meat, eggs, fish, and shellfish."[26] Every student needs to know this and what to eat to nourish his or her brain so that the brain can do its job of figuring things out, thinking, learning, and remembering.[27]

OPPORTUNITIES TO FULFILL THEIR POTENTIAL

Since it is in every student's nature to be a motivated, engaged learner, how can we be sure all students have access to an environment that will make it possible for them to fulfill their potential? If every parent, teacher, administrator, legislator, politician, and citizen believes every student has this potential, would the educational system be different? Would there be major national and local efforts to make sure every student has the opportunity to fulfill his or her potential to be a creative and critical thinker? If not, why not?

Other examples of classroom-proven, successful lessons and activities based on the converging natural learning research, brain research, and

Figure 3.8 A Tree of Knowledge Is Like This Real Tree

Photo by Ronald P. Phipps, 2005. Used with permission.

constructivist research are in Part II. If this approach ignites students' potential to be all they can be, why not teach this way?

Learning Is an Organic Process

Learning, which is the growing of dendrites, synapses, and neural networks to higher and higher levels, is an organic process—like the growing of branches and twigs on trees, each one constructed on another (Figure 3.8).

NOTES

1. Bransford, J. D., Brown, A. L., & Cocking, R. R. (Eds.). (1999). *How people learn: Brain, mind, experience, and school.* Washington, DC: National Academy Press, p. 48.

2. Healy, J. M. (1994). *Your child's growing mind: A practical guide to brain development and learning from birth to adolescence.* New York: Doubleday, p. 39.

3. Tadlock, D. (2005). *Read right! Coaching your child to excellence in reading.* New York: McGraw-Hill, pp. 192–193, 144–145.

4. Bransford, J. D., Brown, A. L., & Cocking, R. R. (Eds.). (1999), p. 103.

5. McGee, J. P. (2003, May). High score education: Games, not school, are teaching kids to think. *Wired*, 11.05. Retrieved August 3, 2006, from http://www.wired.com/wired/archive/11.05/view.html

6. Tagg, J. (2003). *The learning paradigm college*. Bolton, MA: Anker, p. 45.

7. Land, G., & Jarman, B. (1992). *Breakpoint and beyond: Mastering the future today*. New York: HarperCollins.

8. Naiman, L. (2000, February). Numbers tell the story. *Creativity at Work Newsletter*. Retrieved August 3, 2006, from http://www.creativityatwork.com/articlesContent/currency.html

9. Bransford, J. D., Brown, A. L., & Cocking, R. R. (Eds.). (1999), pp. 10–11.

10. Sternberg, R. J., & Williams, W. M. (2002). *Educational psychology*. Boston: Allyn & Bacon, p. 444.

Adapted from Smilkstein, R. (2006). Constructivism. In S. Feinstein (Ed.), *The Praeger handbook on learning and the brain*. Westport, CT: Greenwood Press.

11. Piaget, J. (1971). *Biology and knowledge*. Chicago: University of Chicago Press.

12. Jacobs, B., Schall, M., & Scheibel, A. B. (1993). A quantitative dendritic analysis of Wernicke's area in humans: II. Gender, hemispheric, and environmental factors. *Journal of Comparative Neurology, 327*, 97–111.

13. Sternberg, R. J., & Williams, W. M. (2002), p. 329.

14. Bransford, J. D., Brown, A. L., & Cocking, R. R. (Eds.). (1999), p. 114.

15. Patione, B. (2006, January/February). Meditation may change the brain. *BrainWork, 16*(1), 10.

Goldberg, E. (2005). *The wisdom of paradox*. New York: Gotham Books, pp. 249–261.

16. Ratey, J. J. (2001). *A user's guide to the brain: Perception, attention, and the four theaters of the brain*. New York: Pantheon, p. 60.

17. Levine, M. (2002). *A mind at a time*. New York: Simon & Schuster.

Sousa, D. (2001). *How the special needs brain learns*. Thousand Oaks, CA: Corwin Press.

18. Bransford, J. D., Brown, A. L., & Cocking, R. R. (Eds.). (1999), p. 10.

19. Delpit, L. (1988). The silenced dialogue: Power and pedagogy in educating other people's children. *Harvard Educational Review, 58*, 280–297.

Heath, S. B. (1982). *Ways with words: Language, life, and work in communities and classrooms*. New York: Cambridge University Press.

Ladson-Billing, G. (1995). Toward a theory of culturally relevant pedagogy. *American Educational Research Journal, 32*, 465–491.

McPhail, I. P., & McPhail, C. J. (1999). Transforming classroom practice for African American learners: Implications for the learning paradigm. *Removing Vestiges: Research-Based Strategies to Promote Inclusion, 2*, 49–60.

20. Smilkstein, R. (2003). *We're born to learn: Using the brain's natural learning process to create today's curriculum*. Thousand Oaks, CA: Corwin Press, pp. 160–161, 184–185, 196–199, 208–211.

21. Smilkstein, R. (2003), pp. 111–113.

22. Tomlinson, C. (2006, February). Keynote speech, National Association for Developmental Education (NADE) National Conference, Philadelphia.

23. Ratey, J. J. (2001), p. 364.

Snowdon, D. (2001). *Aging with grace: What the Nun Study teaches us about leading longer, healthier, and more meaningful lives*. New York: Bantam Books.

24. Carper, J. (2000). *Your miracle brain*. New York: HarperCollins.
25. Smilkstein, R. (2003), p. 69–70.
26. Carper, J. (2000), p. 42.
27. Brownlee, C. (2006, March 4). Eat smart: Foods may affect the brain as well as the body. *Science News, 169*(9), 136–137.

Harder, B. (April 22, 2006). Dementia off the menu: Mediterranean diet tied to low Alzheimer's risk. *Science News, 169*(16), 245.

REFERENCES

Berninger, V. W., & Richards, T. L. (2002). *Brain literacy for educators and psychologists*. San Diego, CA: Academic Press.

Bjorklund, D. E. (2000). *Children's thinking: Developmental function and individual differences* (3rd ed.). Belmont, CA: Wadsworth/Thompson Learning.

Boylan, H. R. (2002). *What works: Research-based best practices in developmental education*. Boone, NC: Continuous Quality Improvement Network and National Center for Developmental Education, Appalachian State University.

The Brain in the News. To subscribe: 1001 G Street, NW, Suite 1025, Washington, DC 20001.

Bransford, J. D., Brown, A. L., & Cocking, R. R. (Eds.). (1999). *How people learn: Brain, mind, experience, and school*. Washington, DC: National Academy Press.

Brownlee, C. (2006, March 4). Eat smart: Foods may affect the brain as well as the body. *Science News, 169*(9), 136–137.

Caine, G., & Caine, R. N. (1991). *Making connections: Teaching and the human brain*. Alexandria, VA: Association for Supervision and Curriculum Development.

Campione, J. C., Brown, A. L., & Ferrara, R. A. (1982). Mental retardation and intelligence. In R. J. Sternberg (Ed.), *Handbook of human intelligence* (p. 461). New York: Cambridge University Press.

Damasio, A. (2003). *Looking for Spinoza: Joy, sorrow, and the feeling brain*. Orlando, FL: A Harvest Book/Harcourt.

Delpit, L. (1988). The silenced dialogue: Power and pedagogy in educating other people's children. *Harvard Educational Review, 58*, 280–297.

Diamond, M. (1967). Extensive cortical depth measurements and neuron size increases in the cortex of environmentally enriched rats. *Journal of Comparative Neurology, 131*, 357–364.

Diamond, M. (1988). *Enriching heredity*. New York: Free Press.

Gopnik, A., Meltzoff, A. N., & Kuhl, P. K. (1999). *The scientist in the crib: Minds, brains, and how children learn*. New York: William Morrow.

Greenough, W. T., Black, J. E., & Wallace, C. S. (1987). Experience and brain development. *Child Development, 58*, 547.

Harder, B. (2006, April 22). Dementia off the menu: Mediterranean diet tied to low Alzheimer's risk. *Science News, 169*(16), 245.

Hart, L. (1999). *Human brain and human learning* (5th ed.). Kent, WA: Books for Educators.

Healy, J. M. (1994). *Your child's growing mind: A practical guide to brain development and learning from birth to adolescence*. New York: Doubleday.

Heath, S. B. (1982). *Ways with words: Language, life, and work in communities and classrooms*. New York: Cambridge University Press.

Jacobs, B., Schall, M., & Scheibel, A. B. (1993). A quantitative dendritic analysis of Wernicke's area in humans: II. Gender, hemispheric, and environmental factors. *Journal of Comparative Neurology, 327*, 97–111.

Jensen, E. (1998). *Teaching with the brain in mind*. Alexandria, VA: Association for Supervision and Curriculum Development.

Ladson-Billing, G. (1995). Toward a theory of culturally relevant pedagogy. *American Educational Research Journal, 32*, 465–491.

Land, G., & Jarman, B. (1992). *Breakpoint and beyond: Mastering the future today*. New York: HarperCollins.

Levine, M. (2002). *A mind at a time*. New York: Simon & Schuster.

Marzano, R. J., Pickering, D., & Pollock, J. E. (2004). *Classroom instruction that works: Research-based strategies for increasing student achievement*. Alexandria, VA: Association for Supervision and Curriculum Development.

McGee, J. P. (2003, May). High score education: Games, not school, are teaching kids to think. *Wired*, 11.05. Retrieved August 3, 2006, from http://www.wired.com/wired/archive/11.05/view.html

McPhail, I. P., & McPhail, C. J. (1999). Transforming classroom practice for African American learners: Implications for the learning paradigm. *Removing Vestiges: Research-Based Strategies to Promote Inclusion, 2*, 49–60.

Naiman, L. (2000, February). Numbers tell the story. *Creativity at Work Newsletter*. Retrieved August 3, 2006, from http://www.creativityatwork.com/articlesContent/currency.html

Perkins, D. N. (1992). *Smart schools: Better thinking and learning for every child*. New York: Simon & Schuster.

Patione, B. (2006, January/February). Meditation may change the brain. *BrainWork, 16*(1), 10.

Petit, T. L., & Markus, E. J. (1987). The cellular basis of learning and memory: The anatomical sequel to neuronal use. In H. W. Milgram, C. M. Macleod, & T. L. Petit (Eds.), *Neuroplasticity, learning, and memory* (pp. 87–124). New York: Alan R. Liss.

Piaget, J. (1971). *Biology and knowledge*. Chicago: University of Chicago Press.

Piaget, J., & Inhelder, B. (1969). *The psychology of the child*. New York: Basic Books.

Plomin, R., & Kosslyn, S. M. (2001). Genes, brain and cognition. *Nature Neuroscience, 4*(12), 1153–1155.

Rapport, R. (2005). *Nerve endings: The discovery of the synapse*. New York: W.W. Norton.

Ratey, J. J. (2001). *A user's guide to the brain: Perception, attention, and the four theaters of the brain*. New York: Pantheon.

Renner, M., & Rosenzweig, M. (1987). *Enriched and impoverished environments: Effects on brain and behavior*. New York: Springer Verlag.

Rose, S. (2005). *The future of the brain: The promise and perils of tomorrow's neuroscience*. New York: Oxford University Press.

Royer, J. M. (1986). Designing instruction to produce understanding: An approach based on cognitive theory. In G. D. Phye & T. Andre (Eds.), *Cognitive classroom learning: Understanding, thinking, and problem solving* (pp. 83–113). Orlando, FL: Academic Press.

Sawyer, C. (2005, Fall). CRLA (College Reading and Learning Association) brain-compatible teaching and SIG (special interest group). *Newsletter, 1*(2), 1–2.

Smilkstein, R. (2003). *We're born to learn: Using the brain's natural learning process to create today's curriculum*. Thousand Oaks, CA: Corwin Press.

Smilkstein, R. (2006). Constructivism. In S. Feinstein (Ed.), *The Praeger handbook on learning and the brain*. Westport, CT: Greenwood Press.
Sousa, D. (2001). *How the special needs brain learns*. Thousand Oaks, CA: Corwin Press.
Sprenger, M. (1999). *Learning and memory: The brain in action*. Alexandria, VA: Association for Supervision and Curriculum Development.
Sternberg, R. J. (Ed.). (1982). *Handbook of human intelligence*. New York: Cambridge University Press.
Sternberg, R. J., & Williams, W. M. (2002). *Educational psychology*. Boston: Allyn & Bacon.
Sylwester, R. (1993, December/1994, January). What the biology of the brain tells us about learning. *Educational Leadership, 51*(4), 46–51.
Sylwester, R. (1995). *Celebration of neurons: An educator's guide to the human brain*. Alexandria, VA: Association for Supervision and Curriculum Development.
Sylwester, R. (2003). *A biological brain in a cultural classroom* (2nd ed.). Thousand Oaks, CA: Corwin Press.
Tagg, J. (2003). *The learning paradigm college*. Bolton, MA: Anker.
Tomlinson, C. (1999). *The differentiated classroom: Responding to the needs of all students*. Alexandria, VA: Association for Supervision and Curriculum Development.
Triesman, U. (1992). Studying students studying calculus: A look at the lives of minority mathematics students in college. *College Mathematics Journal, 23*(5), 362–372.
Vasquez, S. (2000). Calculator use in developmental mathematics. *Research in Developmental Education, 15*(5), 1–4.
Vedantum, S. (2002, May 20). Descartes notwithstanding, some neuroscientists find the answer in chemistry, not philosophy. *The Washington Post*, p. A9.
Walker, S. (1998). *The hyperactivity hoax*. New York: St. Martin's.
Wesson, K. (2000, August). What everyone should know about the latest brain research. Retrieved April 4, 2002, from http://www.sciencemaster.com/Wesson/home.php
Wolfe, P. (2001). *Brain matters: Translating research into classroom practice*. Alexandria, VA: Association for Supervision and Curriculum Development.
Zull, J. E. (2002). *The art of changing the brain: Enriching the practice of teaching by exploring the biology of learning*. Sterling, VA: Stylus.

Web Sites for Related Topics

http://brainrules.com (interactive site for children and adults)
www.aan.com (American Academy of Neurology)
www.chadd.org (Children and Adults With Attention Deficit/Hyperactivity Disorder)
www.interdys.org (International Dyslexia Association)
www.ldantl.org (Learning Disabilities Association of America)
www.ncld.org (National Center for Learning Disabilities)
www.pbs.org/net/brain (five-part special on brain development, three-dimensional anatomical studies)

PART II

Classroom Applications

How Tall Am I? 4

Real-World Math for Early Learners

The knowledge differences among early learners in elementary grades K–3 are linked to the quantity and quality of the knowledge they acquire as they act on and think about their experiences. Their experiences will vary greatly from student to student. From the earliest age, young people learn at different rates depending on the opportunities offered to them and the nature of the learning environment. Given an equal opportunity, every student can achieve maximum potential. More will be said about this later in the chapter. The important thing to note at this point is that learning is a physiological activity, just like breathing; and like breathing, it happens naturally. It takes place as our brain cells, known as neurons, encounter and think about new experiences. As was explained in Chapter 3, tiny fibers called *dendrites*, which are attached to our neurons, grow as a result of these experiences. As they grow and, thus, provide places for neurons to connect in new or larger networks, we learn and retain what has been learned. These new dendrites and new or larger networks are our new or more complex knowledge.

Babies are born with certain innate observation skills, enabling them to distinguish between exceptional and ordinary events. Jean Piaget, the Swiss cognitive psychologist, found that young people as early as the age of two, long before they go to school, are well able to tackle the puzzles and problems that confront them in daily experiences. The success of books like the Harry Potter series among all ages is a good indicator of the ability of young people to visualize new and different worlds and phenomena. Their imaginations are very much alive. It is a common sight to see a six-year-old transform a stick into an airplane or a space rocket. It is equally interesting to note how a child responds to his or her schoolmates.

Social skills, whether positive or negative, seem to be developed before a child goes to school. The tens of thousands of new neurons that appear every minute in the human brain both before birth and in the first few years of life need multiple experiences in order to develop the dendrites. In these early years, there is a threefold expansion in the size of a child's brain. All of this physiological view of learning is only new because recent research findings have given it strong support. The actual practice is as old as the history of education. It was the way John Dewey's students learned almost a hundred years ago.

Long before the time of Dewey, however, other teachers also saw learning as a natural process. They thought that minds grow by themselves, at their own rate, similar to the way plants grow. They knew that teachers cannot make this growth happen. They can only arrange or offer stimulating environments and experiences so that children can do the growing themselves, naturally. If we go back to antiquity, we can find the same approach taken by Confucius in China and Quintilian in Rome. The only teachers from antiquity, though, about whom we have a detailed record of this mode of teaching are Jesus and Socrates. Jesus' favorite method seems to have been to tell a story in which learners were presented with new information that greatly interested them but required serious thought to be understood. Jesus always insisted that they figure out the meanings among themselves rather than have him explain them. His story method of brain-compatible learning is one that many first grade teachers employ today. Socrates presented learners with problems to solve and questions to answer that challenged them to figure out the solutions and answers themselves by using their store of prior knowledge and sense of logic. Socrates thought their prior knowledge was born in them, while we now know learners construct their knowledge from and during their experiences in life.

TRANSITION FROM HOME TO SCHOOL

The kinds of experiences provided at home in the years before kindergarten vary greatly from home to home, from community to community, and from cultural group to cultural group, so learning activities have to take account of this. How is this done? By a sharp focus on each student's problem-solving abilities, not initially on the subject matter of math. As a student is given freedom to investigate something, others in the class join in, not only to help but to understand what is going on. For a five- or six-year-old, speech is closely tied to understanding. Constant chatter is the way to cope with new things. A few years ago, a Chicago kindergarten teacher was puzzled by this behavior among her students. She taped their conversations for an hour each day, and then at home she analyzed them. She discovered that their words had nothing to do with sharing information but only with comprehension about their experiences. A silent kindergarten room is not a good learning environment. A home without conversation is not a good learning environment.

Young learners who come from homes with computers have access to programs where literacy aids are available. These children arrive at school as readers. Many of them also had exposure to a variety of community learning centers such as museums, science centers, and libraries. Many of them are acquainted with calculators. It is quite a different story in homes where resources are limited and where children are left in day care centers while both parents work. These disparities, far from being handicaps, encourage teachers to focus on games, puzzles, and problems that give maximum responsibility to the learner. Personal collections fit well. They might be sticks, leaves, or buttons and they are the child's security blanket, providing an identity in an unfamiliar place. Differences are not the focus of attention. Children can move toward their maximum capacity for learning as they are free to explore and talk. Confidence is gained, relationships are nurtured, and a healthy, brain-friendly environment is created.

A MATH-FRIENDLY ENVIRONMENT

The classroom environment within which learning takes place is a vital component of the learning process. It profoundly affects what is taught and known and it plays a large part in a person's attitude all through life to the things experienced there. People remember minute details of earlier experiences all through life. If these experiences carry happy memories, all is well. If not, we tend to be negative toward what was learned in that setting. Brain-friendly experiences for the youngest students carry a power of suggestion that is highly motivating and accelerates learning. Benjamin Bloom, in his study of highly successful students, discovered that the early learning environment was the key to later success.

To create a brain-friendly environment for new math learners, we need to understand the nature of math. Its attractiveness lies in its patterns, and these patterns can be found in art, nature, or music. It so happens that the human brain works in patterns. Take, for instance, our way of recognizing someone when we meet. Unlike acquiring an accumulation of discrete bits of information about a person, we recognize him or her as a whole. We do not identify eyes, then face, then arms, and so on. Instead there is an instant awareness of the whole person. All the different parts are seen as forming a single pattern, a pattern that is linked to one already in the observer's brain. It is like this in all aspects of what we might call natural learning, coping with new situations in ways that take account of what the brain already knows.

Figure 4.1 All About Me

There is a temptation to speed up the learning process because there is so much to cover, but the reality is that the best learning often takes place in the process of solving a problem, not in the end product. The brain of a young person is curious about anything and everything. There is a spirit of wonderment because there is so much that is new in the environment. In the kindergarten environment, the classroom, the furniture, the teacher, and the other students are all new. The spirit of wonderment needs to be fostered by encouraging freedom, especially freedom of movement within the classroom, while exposing the learners to a variety of new things. A good starter for the first days of school is a simple personal diary in which students record, or the teacher records for them, basic data about their experiences. This is updated later in the year.

At the university of British Columbia in Canada, there was a Child Study Center staffed by two teachers for every 12 youngsters of ages three or four. The purpose of the center was both to provide a brain-friendly learning environment and, at the same time, demonstrate for teachers in training good ways of teaching preschoolers. One third of the learners came from the children of faculty, one third from the children of graduate students, and the rest from the surrounding community. In this way, a mix of backgrounds was found in every class. Children were often introduced to the Center in a personal way. For one four-year-old who was about to join the Center, one of the teachers came to his home, sat down on the floor, introduced himself, and talked with the new learner for a time about his toys and activities. Thus, when this youngster went to the Center next day, the teacher was someone he knew.

The various activities of the Center were quite structured and sufficiently varied so that every young person or any group of them could gravitate toward things that were interesting and within their abilities to do. Teachers in training could observe what was going on through one-way observation mirrors. The Center was intended to show what a brain-friendly environment should look like, and the evidence became clear in subsequent interviews. When asked what the teacher had told them to do or what the teacher had taught them, every three- and four-year-old looked puzzled. Although both teachers were present, helping here and there and sorting out minor conflicts over possessions, none of the young people was aware of them as part of their learning. The response that always came back was, "We did so and so."

Creating and maintaining an environment of wonderment is an essential foundation for lifelong learning. Attitudes are developed in such a setting that will influence future learning. Constant exposure to new and unexpected things and experiences is the curriculum for wonderment development! I knew a parent who was so influenced by Marian Diamond's book, *Magic Trees of the Mind*, that she decided to give her week-old child a different experience every day. Unlike many parents, she had the freedom to do this. One day might be examining a worm that they found in the garden and another observing an ambulance passing with its sirens sounding. The parent sustained this practice for three years. She did not realize that researchers had written about the self-motivating effects of her efforts if continued for a period of three years, but she did observe what began to occur. Her three-year-old took initiatives, asking questions about things that no one had ever drawn to his attention. He had become a self-motivated learner.

Young learners frequently express their understandings in mythical stories that they have created. If they are given enough freedom to explore on their own, they will readily share a story about anything and everything. It may be their explanation of how the moon got into the sky or why some birds can fly and some cannot. Their stories are extremely important. They need to be heard and appreciated because they are the expressions of wonderment. All too often, teachers' enthusiasm to see children learn reality makes them indifferent to imaginative stories. That is not good. It weakens the natural instinct of wonderment. One writer suggested that this sense of wonder is so important that, like a muscle, it has to be exercised continually. Young students need opportunities to explore, to make choices, to have thoughtful conversations, and to be left alone at times to ponder new experiences.

There is one more good reason for creating a brain-friendly math environment. Unlike some other subjects, math deals with abstract concepts, and the necessary transitions from real-world experiences can create emotional barriers. The classroom environment needs to be supportive by first letting students start where they are so they can construct their new knowledge dendrite by dendrite, and second by letting them figure things out individually and with classmates. Evidence from teaching mathematics at junior and high school levels reveals how these early barriers persist and how difficult it is to dislodge them. A common response is this: I cannot do math. I have never been good at it. Could it be that these long-standing emotional barriers are the reason for the weak performance of U.S. math students internationally? In 2001, for example, in a math competition, U.S. eighth-grade students came in 18th among students of the same age in 37 developed countries.

MATH CONTENT FOR EARLY GRADES

The repeated emphasis above on letting young students learn at their own pace and in ways that are brain-friendly does not imply indifference to math content. There is a body of math knowledge that first- and second-grade students must acquire. The emphasis in this book is on methods that ensure both comprehension and retention of this important content. Curriculum guides for Grades 1 and 2 all across North America spell out math content under three general categories: numbers, measurement, and geometry.

Numbers

Numbers includes counting and estimating. They can be studied in a variety of ways that help to make the transfer complete from real objects to the abstract world of symbols, or *numerals*, as they are often called. One effective way of involving students in exercises that require adding and subtracting is the competitive "climb the ladder" game. Here two dice are used, and at each throw, the two values are added, and the student moves up by that amount. The ladder can be as simple as a drawing on the blackboard. Some scores can be preselected in this game to move players back down the ladder when they are required to subtract two numerals.

Personal experience is probably the best resource to use in developing fractional values of numerals such as halves or thirds. Real-world recipes and the frequency of one half, one third, or three quarters in them is a means of introducing fractions. In a sequence of watching a recipe for cookies being made, then cooked, and cut up into smaller pieces, there is no difficulty in getting the attention of the beneficiaries as arrangements are made to share the end product in halves or quarters depending on the number of children. The waiting time for the cookies to bake is an occasion to do clock reading, either with a face of 12 numbers and two hands or the digital variety in which two numbers are separated by a colon. In the past, many societies used different ways of indicating numbers. Students can be asked to draw clocks using one or more of these alternative systems.

A discussion of teeth is always a popular one. Students can be asked if they remember when they lost a baby tooth. They can be asked if the new one has grown in, and then asked to count how many teeth they have.

Figure 4.2 Numbers in the Past

Egypt	I	II	III	IIII	III II	III III	IIII III	IIII IIII	III III III	∩
Babylon	▽	▽▽	▽▽▽	▽▽▽ ▽	▽▽▽ ▽▽	▽▽▽ ▽▽▽	▽▽▽▽ ▽▽▽	▽▽▽▽ ▽▽▽▽	▽▽▽▽▽ ▽▽▽▽	▷
Rome	I	II	III	IV	V	VI	VII	VIII	IX	X

Help from other students, a valuable component of all learning activities, is needed for this. Shopping, by introducing money, is another valuable experience in the learning of numbering. The regular multiplier as one goes from penny to nickel to dime and so on enables a teacher to introduce more complex fractions. Playing at shopping is a game that can reinforce these larger numbers. It can also be used for handling the more complex fractional exchanges that occur as change is given. Here also it is possible to have counting backward introduced. Many store clerks do this as they count back from the money you give them to the change they give you.

Estimating too can be introduced in relation to shopping. How long does it take for you to walk to the store? Guess! Then check next time you go, and see how close you came to it. Numerous class activities that involve estimating are well worth doing. They are interesting with young people because estimates are entirely in their own hands. They are also competitive in a healthy way as they observe the differing abilities of other students. Give the class a length of string and ask how many times it will go round a particular book.

Measurement

The second category is measurement. Ask students to estimate the number of lengths of a ruler needed to reach from one side of the classroom to the other. Another activity involves volumes of a liquid. Estimate the number of times needed to fill a small glass and pour it into a bigger one before the bigger one is full. Measurement can be linked to the content of Figure 4.1, not necessarily adding the results to the personal diary. There is a huge advantage in using the measurements of parts of a student's own body. These are the most readily understood real-world data. Students can decide the units they will use for finding out their height. They might suggest using the length of an arm or foot, or the distance from mid-finger to mid-finger when they stretch out their arms on either side. If, for example, they decide to use hand width, they might be interested to know that the height of horses is still measured in that way. It is a small step from measuring the heights of students to putting the results on a set of bar graphs. These graphs can then be updated in the course of the year to see how much each boy or girl has grown.

Geometry

Introducing ideas about geometry, the third main area of content, leads to patterns of all kinds, and, as indicated above, patterns are the brain's normal way of understanding content. Perhaps that is why geometry is often a more popular branch of mathematics than either numbers or measurement. A good starter involves a sheet of graph paper on which students are asked to color all the squares. Only two colors are used, and students must not allow two squares of the same color to touch each other except at a corner. Another pattern activity is a competitive game of joining dots. A set of vertical and horizontal dots are laid out on a sheet of paper, and students are asked to join any group of three dots vertically, horizontally, or obliquely. They cannot use a dot more than once. The game is over when it becomes impossible to find another set of three dots. Differences among patterns are illustrated in Figure 4.3 where a student is asked to identify an irregular element in a set of regular ones. Others of the same kind can be laid out on a classroom wall for independent work before and after formal classroom activities. There can be lively discussions of them and of ways of figuring them out.

As always, if an activity in geometry can be framed within a story, success is guaranteed. The series of books published by Charlesbridge, each with a variation of the general title *Sir Cumference*, exemplify this approach very well by creating problems related to shapes in the court of King Arthur in order to teach geometrical concepts. Stories about castles, knights, and moats are popular with a wide range of ages. Suppose, for example, the king of one castle was trying to arrange a peace conference with another king. They had been fighting each other for years, and now one king was determined to make peace. He appointed 10 of his knights to meet with 10 from the other king but, in order not to offend the other side, he had to arrange seating around a table so that each one of the 20 knights had exactly the same kind of position around the table. No one could be seen as sitting at the head of the table, because that position was always reserved for the most important person. At the same time, no one person could be farther than 12 feet from another so that all of the conversation would be heard by every knight. Ask the class to figure out what sort of table and what size would be needed for the peace conference. A simple story embellishing the past life of these two kings and their knights could introduce the problem.

Figure 4.3 Which One Is Different?

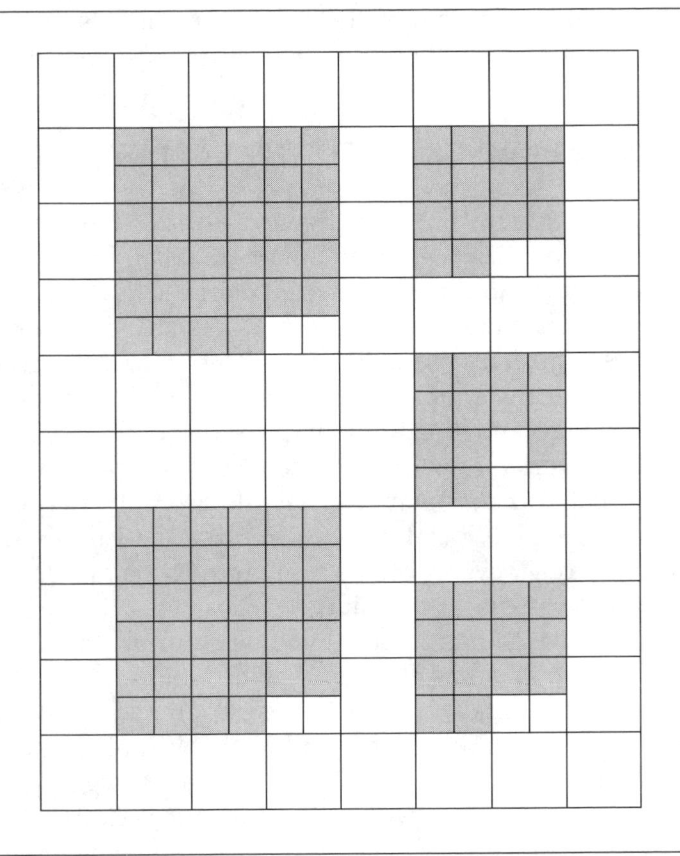

Games

It would be difficult to overestimate the value of games in the development of mathematical skills. Again and again, educational researchers and teachers at all age levels insist that experience with games greatly improves a student's performance in mathematics. One expert claimed that students from homes where board games such as Scrabble, chess, or checkers were frequently in use were consistently one year ahead of those students who lacked that kind of home background. It does not seem to matter what kind of game is used. The value lies in the creative thinking demanded by the game. Because such thinking is entirely an initiative on the part of each student, without any help from either peers or the teacher, it fits perfectly with all that has already been said about brain-friendly activity, both by the individual student and in the social environment within which the game is played. Perhaps the title of this section of the chapter is not the best to use for this aspect of natural learning, but it is the one that is often employed because of its popularity. The purpose here is the discovery and development of young learners' talents, and in that context, things not usually described as games need to be included.

MULTIPLE INTELLIGENCES AND STUDENT POTENTIAL

The idea of different kinds of intelligence is now familiar, and it fits perfectly here. Traditionally, verbal and mathematical skills were given top priority in assessing the abilities of young people. This approach left out a large number of other mental resources, and it is only in recent times that the value of these alternative intelligences came to be fully recognized. It is likely that both the ancient Greek emphasis on mathematics as the main key to all knowledge and the Roman stress of verbal skills lingered in the minds of educators all through the centuries as measures of superior intelligence. Verbal and mathematical talents are only two of the many latent abilities of people. Social, musical, spatial, and interpersonal relational skills are among several others that are now being recognized. It is vital that all of these be discovered at the earliest ages. Spatial intelligence, the ability to visualize things as occupying specific areas of space, can be recognized in preschoolers as they play with blocks, building towers or castles, or assembling jigsaw puzzles. These are the kinds of people who often go on in later years to become architects or engineers. It would be tragic if their abilities were not identified at an early stage.

In earlier times, when verbal and mathematical skills were the only recognized measures of intelligence, young people were often pressured into careers that required these skills, thereby preventing them entering more appropriate careers. We are all familiar with one of the more extreme examples, fortunately no longer practiced, of this kind of misguided counseling: forcing left-handed children to write with their right hand. Musical talent can now be spotted at a very early age, both in terms of the presence of perfect pitch and physical evidence in the brain in an area known as the planum temporale, an area that grows if musical studies are begun before the age of seven. The free activities associated with games continue in other areas of latent ability. These and other self-directed initiatives are the best ways of discovering and nurturing latent abilities at the earliest possible stage of life. Play, of one kind or another, is always the activity of choice whenever six-year-olds have free time.

Mention has already been made of the value of standard games such as chess or checkers. However, it is evident from any consideration of multiple intelligences that other endeavors give better expression to the abilities of some. Dressing to represent famous people or some personal interest, making and using puppets in plays with the aid of a puppet stage and audience, and music of various kinds all serve the basic purpose of uncovering the hidden abilities of young people. Storytelling serves the

Figure 4.4 A Maze

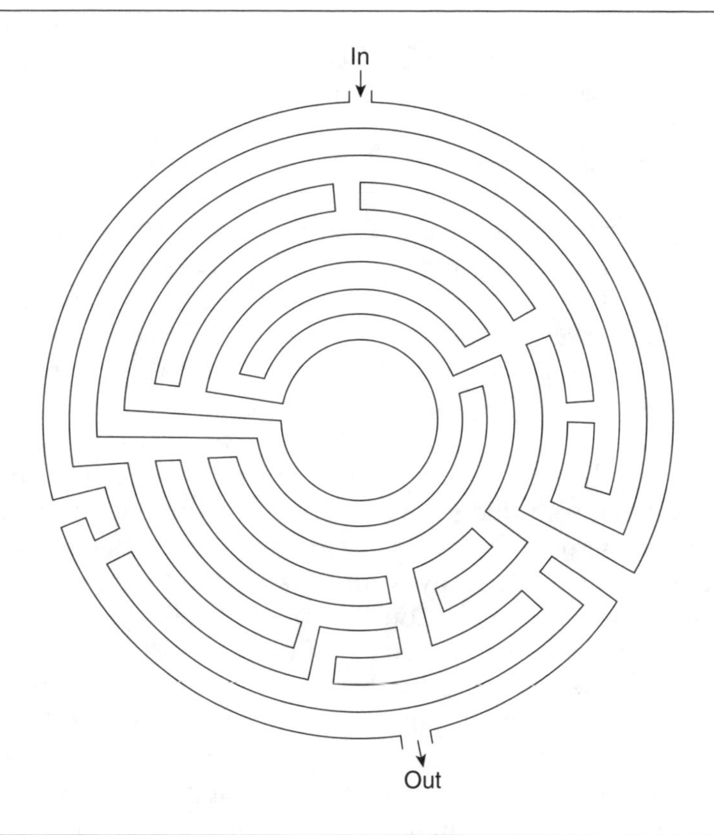

same purpose as games in inviting participation. The questions and comments of students in response to stories, sometimes from young people who do not seem to have any special aptitudes, raises their levels of thinking to new heights. Aesop's fables, thousands of years old, still live on in many schools and homes. Stories that are puzzles, or ones in which the outcome has to be figured out, are also valuable ways of identifying talent. So is the simple example shown above of a maze.

EXPLORING OUTSIDE THE CLASSROOM

A very large part of a first-grade student's day is spent out of doors, including traveling to and from school. Schools often organize visits to nearby sites and events. These trips, along with the regular exposures to the outdoors, are ideal settings for matching abstract aspects of math with the real world. The reason for such an assertion is that the world around us is familiar in detail and anything in it is quickly recognized. Think back to what was said above about the environment in which learning takes place. Our brains instinctively observe the environment in which we are at any given moment. The game "I Spy" can be used to identify and describe things that are tall or long or round, and in every instance the answer can be the introduction to a short discussion. What do you notice about the tallest tree? Why does it have more leaves than the others?

Imagine a school visit to an airport. Once there, the students see the types of planes on the ground and observe others as they take off or land, and inside the terminal they note the various places where passengers go through the boarding process. Now let the children talk about the things they saw and ask a few questions to focus their thinking. The journey to and from the airport must not be wasted. Use it to sharpen observation skills. Say, for example, "As we come close to the airport, I want you to look out for different kinds of very tall posts. What do you see on them? What might they be for?" There is no need for answers to be provided immediately. Ask the students how can they find out what they are for. On return to the classroom, the most valuable part of the whole exercise occurs as they are asked to draw what they saw and then to show and tell their class what they had seen. Concepts of space, distance, length, height, and depth all will soon be featured as different reports are presented.

The visit provides an opportunity to talk about the rules that apply in air travel. Students who had flying experience will have ready answers to questions about these rules. What does a passenger do if the air pressure drops while the plane is in the air? Some students may even be able to explain why such an event might occur. What must every passenger do at the time of takeoff and also when the plane is about to land? There is an added value in this discussion. Air travel is the type of event that brings the whole world into the classroom. The class can be shown on a globe how air routes are very different from other ways of traveling around the world. In the process, every student has a vicarious experience of being an important player in something that goes on all the time all over the world.

This was the kind of activity that characterized John Dewey's famous pragmatist philosophy. It was enormously successful all over the world, especially in the United States, where it remained dominant for most of the twentieth century. Why was it so successful? Because it matched the brain's natural way of learning. The subject matter was always local and therefore relevant and interesting to young people. Responsibility for choosing content within that framework and for seeking out information about it rested on the students. The teacher's role was that of a guide rather than a source of knowledge, asking questions on occasion when needed. When, in the late 1950s, Dewey's philosophy of learning was rejected by many educational authorities, it was because they wanted to impose specific learning skills on learners in order to improve national standards in various subjects. The development of the individual learners in order to raise them to their maximum potential was rejected, and the old-fashioned, imposed learning took its place. Some educational leaders still fail to understand the difference between these two very different approaches to learning.

EVALUATION

The essence of brain-compatible teaching can be captured through short evaluations that put the onus on students' interests and reactions to the content of the chapter. For example, a series of games and puzzles can be placed around the classroom and student interest observed by their behavior before and after class. Simple instruments of evaluation like this are particularly appropriate for any age, as will be evident from Chapter 10. We are so accustomed to think of evaluation as exams that measure achievement that we forget the main purpose of evaluation, to identify areas of competence and its opposite in order to improve subsequent teaching. Students can be involved in their own evaluations by explaining to one another why they like some activities. However conducted, evaluation must be a continuous process, even in small ways, sometimes after individual lessons, at other times at the end of the day.

REFERENCES

Coates, G. D., & Stenmark, J. K. (1997). *Family math for young children*. Berkeley, CA: Lawrence Hall of Science.

Diamond, M., & Hopson, J. (1999). *Magic trees of the mind*. New York: Penguin.

Ledoux, J. (2003). *Our synaptic self: How our brains become who we are*. New York: Prentice Hall.

Neuschwander, C., & Geehan, W. (1997). *Sir Cumference and the First Round Table*. Watertown, MA: Charlesbridge.

5

Can You Build an Igloo?

Understanding the Past With Elementary Learners

At the upper elementary level, natural learning flourishes because these 10- and 11-year-olds experience a fairly quiet time of physical development. They are free from the distractions of the dramatic and rapid changes of the earlier years, and they have not yet encountered the challenges of puberty and adolescence. Theirs is a time of freedom to explore. Their interests run in all directions: collecting, cycling, reading comics, playing an instrument, or competing at video games, even learning table manners. Dendrite networks explode and unused circuits get trimmed back. It's always inspiring to be with a class of 10- and 11-year-olds. They are lively, active, able to absorb and think about an enormous amount of information. They do not need external motivation. Rather, they need what Carl Rogers called "freedom to learn." Like A. S. Neill of Summerhill fame, and others from the present time, Rogers had discovered that achievement levels go sky high when students have the opportunity to do their own thinking, that is to say, their own exploring, reflecting, problem solving, and experimenting. At times there are tensions when elements of bullying appear. One parent who experienced this problem at her son's school decided to invite the offending boy to join a soccer game in which her son played every week. As a result, the two boys became good friends and stayed like that for the rest of the school year.

DISCOVERING THE PAST

Preadolescents' lived experiences of home and community, along with their innate ability to do logical thinking and problem solving, equip them to examine other places and times and to construct their new learning on what they already know. Hence, the focus of this chapter will be on learning about the past through adventures into the past, in both time and place. The contrasts between the students' own lifestyles and those of people at a distance provide the kind of dissonances that can lead to an in-depth learning experience because they will naturally trigger lots of questions. Even five-year-olds get interested in contrasting lifestyles. Recently, one young person of that age, having heard a bit about genes and looking at pictures of people in another country, asked, "Mommy, if these people have the same genes as we have, why don't they look like us?" This is a question with many thought-provoking answers, and it does not require a teacher to ask it.

Natural learning, as explained in Chapters 2 and 3, always depends of students' curiosity and their past experiences. These are the learners' assets; the brain learns with eagerness, and the memory successfully retains what is being learned, when these assets are invested in the learning process, as they are in this unit's constructivist curriculum and pedagogy. The construction of a house is another metaphor for the construction of knowledge. Floors are added one above the other using materials that fit. The materials for any higher floor must be of the right weight and type so that they can firmly interconnect with, and be constructed on, the floor below. In the same way, each higher, more complex level of content in this constructivist natural learning unit must interconnect with what has already been learned. This is the brain's natural and, therefore, most effective way of learning. It ignites students' potential to learn.

If we pursue this comparison of learning being like constructing a house, the teacher's role can be seen as manifold. First, like the requirement for constructing a firm foundation for a building, the teacher needs to assign a task that can help every student connect to his or her own background as the foundation for the student's new learning. Then, at each higher level, the teacher needs to assign a learning task that can interconnect with the previous level of knowledge and understanding. For example, if any research work is to be done, partly inspired by probing questions from the teacher, partly the result of students' curiosity, it can be a task or activity assigned after students have made a connection to the topic through one or more foundation-constructing activities. The students' research can then be presented orally or in displays, accompanied by analysis of and reflections about the subject of the unit.

As discussed in Chapter 3, the pedagogy most appropriate for the brain's constructive process of learning is one that first invites each learner to construct his or her own personal foundation; thus, each task is begun individually. Then, because cognitive construction is best done with several doing the thinking, small groups of three or four explore what they bring to it, each trying to find the group's best strengths and any concerns or questions that individual members might have. Finally, to ensure that all the groups' best strengths are brought to bear on the task, all the "builders" convene and, with their combined efforts, ensure that the new "floor" is correctly interconnected with the previous one and is thus a firm basis for the next "floor," that is to say, the next concept or skill that will be constructed. It is tempting to think of learning as a sequential collection of information, one bit at a time. This approach might seem to make sense, and the results can easily be tested. The human brain, however, does not work like that. It connects new information naturally to acquired knowledge and understanding in interconnected clusters, not in separate individual bits.

The makers of computers know all about this aspect of the brain because they want computers to do as much as possible of the brain's work. Take, for example, the kinds of problems faced by an aircraft company in the design of a new airplane. A certain amount of information is available from past experience, but the company wants to introduce changes to make the final product more attractive and more efficient. It knows that any change to any one part of the plane might affect the performance of all the other parts, so it sets up a cluster of measuring instruments on a working model of the plane under consideration, each instrument designed to measure the performance of one area and also to adjust the activity in that area to accommodate any new stresses caused by changes elsewhere. Thus, immediately as a new feature is introduced in one part of the plane, every other part of the model moves or changes as it adjusts to the new stresses occurring in its location. That's how our brains work. Billions of cells in different networked clusters respond to inputs that might affect the whole person and accept, modify, or reject them in accordance with what sustains or improves the person's self-understood best interests and equilibrium.

BEGINNING THE UNIT

As the teacher begins a series of learning activities about life in the past, the constructivist sequence begins. The class is told they are going to find out what it was like to live a long time ago when many of the things we have today were not available. "A long time ago" means when their parents' grandparents lived, and maybe their parents know something about those times. To begin this adventure, students are assigned to find out all they can about the differences between past and present by asking their parents, or any older people living in the community, how people lived a long time ago. Thus, this task connects to each student's personal foundation of his or her own family and community. The small groups then share, compare, contrast, and discuss their individual findings and come to conclusions about how people lived a long time ago. After this, the groups reconvene as a whole class and share their conclusions for a full-class discussion. All of this will then provide a foundation that they can use when they later examine a new place that is located at a distance from them in both time and space.

The next task in this constructivist curriculum will take them to the "next higher floor" of understanding. The teacher asks them if what they had been told is accurate and how they could find out more accurately what it was like a long time ago. To fully engage them in this task, to fully develop their critical and creative thinking, the teacher can have them answer these questions using the natural learning constructivist pedagogy: first by using their own personal foundation of knowledge and experience, then sharing in a small group, and finally debriefing and discussing as a whole group. With their curiosity further aroused by this constructivist combination of discovery, inquiry, and cooperative learning, the students have a foundation upon which to construct the next level of their growing "house" of knowledge and understanding. As they conduct their research, the school library and computers can be employed to expand on whatever was individually gleaned from family and community sources and on what was inspired by their own and their teacher's questions about what life was really like back then. Groups could tackle different topics: schools, homes, travel arrangements, and so on. Their findings would then be presented to and discussed with the whole class. The entire process, as before, follows the constructivist pedagogical sequence of Individual/Small Group/Whole Group activities.

Questions posed by their teacher and themselves might include the following: How did they travel? How did they get their news about events in other countries? What about music? Did they play the same games as today? Did they wear the same kinds of things to school? Was school the same as today? Were there movies? How did they get along without items that were not available at that time: radio, television, cell phones, only a few people having cars? Questions might follow about how the absence of these things affected living conditions. Were people happier, do you think? What sorts of things might scare them? Were there doctors and hospitals like today? They would soon make a number of discoveries, for example, that many of the resources for entertainment, sports, and home life had to be created by people's own efforts, and that life in general depended much more than it does today on what they could do for themselves.

The great variety of topics and questions that surface in investigations of this kind give opportunities to capture the curiosity and interests even of students who, for various reasons such as home problems, might not be fitting into school life very well. Natural learning constructivist curriculum and pedagogy are effective ways to meet the needs and ignite the potential of all students, including those at risk. To conclude the research project, let them see a list of 10 facts about 1900 as listed below and let them discuss, question, and comment on the list in the light of their own discoveries.

Ten facts about America in 1900, when the total population of the country was about 80 million:

1. The average length of life was 47 years.
2. One home in every 7 had a bathtub.
3. One home in every 12 had a telephone.
4. There was one car for every 10,000 people.
5. The speed limit in most cities was 10 miles/hour.
6. No building in the nation was as high as 1,000 feet.
7. The average wage was 22 cents/hour.
8. Sugar was 4 cents/pound; eggs were 14 cents/dozen.
9. Babies were born at home, not in hospitals.
10. One in 16 graduated from high school.

EXAMINING A DISTANT PLACE

The class discussion that completes the learning sequence above is the introduction to and becomes the foundation for the next higher level and a more ambitious project, living in another, more distant place, about a hundred years ago. In this unit's curriculum, in an upper elementary classroom in British Columbia, the place is Cambridge Bay in northern Canada, where the people known as the Inuit live. The students are to imagine traveling to that part of North America to Cambridge Bay on Victoria Island in the month of January. They would go to Cambridge Bay and then travel by snowmobile to a place nearby on the coast where Inuit used to live a hundred years ago. Life for the Inuit is quite different today, but they had lived in the old ways for thousands of years with very little contact between them and other parts of the world. "How did they live then, about the same time as your great-grandparents lived?" That is what has to be discovered; that is the research question. Finding out what the class already knows about this part of the world is the first task of the teacher: the temperatures, the weather, the terrain, what it's like in winter time, and so on. These are things that are not very different today from the way they were a hundred years ago. Students might also know some other things about that part of the world, and there might well be someone in class who happens to know quite a lot about Cambridge Bay. As they share what they know, it soon becomes clear to the teacher what has yet to be learned.

The class is asked to think about all that they need to know about Cambridge Bay to answer the research question, and as various things are suggested, groups are organized to do the necessary research. There is no shortage of resources for their investigations. All kinds of library books and encyclopedias can be starters. On the Internet, it will be a surprise to most students to find many files dealing with the community of Cambridge Bay on the Google site. They can even get all the climatic data they need to construct climographs, not too difficult for upper elementary students and an interesting way to show the difference between summer and winter. Two simple climographs, one for Cambridge Bay and one for where they live, can be constructed by the students with the teacher's help, and alongside them, a chart can be constructed to show the number of hours of daylight in both places in January. Some measurements here are in Canadian units, and they can be changed into American ones for making comparisons.

Cambridge Bay, Nunavut, Canada
Latitude: 69.06 N Longitude: 105.07 W Altitude: 23 m

	J	F	M	A	M	J	J	A	S	O	N	D
Temperature (degrees C)	–32	–33	–30	–21	–9	2	8	6	0	–11	–23	–29
Snow Cover (cm)	19	23	25	27	17	0	0	0	2	11	14	17
Sunshine (h)	0	59	176	262	253	287	322	178	76	60	12	0

Information can also be collected from the Atlas of Canada site (http://atlas.gc.ca), which is free to all and can provide a map and other details about Cambridge Bay. Students can be walked through these cyber-research directions: "This is the Internet site we'll be using. Start by clicking on 'English.' On the left side of the next frame that comes up, under 'Explore our Maps,' click on 'provincial and territorial'; and when the list appears, click on Nunavut (NU), which is the territory of Canada that includes Cambridge Bay. To see the map click on 'jpeg.'"

At the end of the research period, after the students have shared and discussed their research findings in the whole class, they are asked, "What do you need to take with you for the trip?" As before, this can also be done individually, in small groups, and then as a whole class so that all students have the opportunity to participate fully. Some background, if not discovered by the students, might be appropriate for the teacher to add here as a further resource for students. At this point, with their curiosity now fully engaged, students are eager to hear what life was really like for the Inuit a hundred years ago.

Figure 5.1 Catching a Seal

The Inuit, in the time we are examining, lived a nomadic life as they searched for food. In summer, they moved south on land to catch caribou or collect berries. In the fall, they found fish near the mouths of rivers. They clothed themselves with the furs of the animals they caught, and their hunting instruments were made from the bones of these same animals. Over time, they learned to detect the slightest changes in the weather because their survival depended on understanding it. They had 12 different words for the wind, depending on where it blew from or how strong it was. These words told them how far they were from a shoreline, and the wind-etched marks on the shoreline told them where that particular area of land was. In ways like these, the wind served the purpose that a compass would serve today. As winter descended on them and ice covered everything, their only available source of food was seal meat. There was never enough food in the previous seasons to enable them to save up for winter. Everything they needed to survive in winter had to come from the seals they caught.

To catch seals, they had to move out onto the frozen Arctic Ocean or onto large floating sheets of ice called *ice floes*. Seals are warm-blooded animals; that is to say, they have lungs like us, and though they live beneath the ice, they have to come up to breathing holes near the surface from time to time to get air. It is when they come up to these breathing holes that the Inuit catch them. Every seal has to come up for fresh air once a day. The Inuit hunter tries to catch a seal at these times. First he has to find a breathing hole. Regular winds blow snow over the surface of the ice, and over a period of time, every breathing hole is covered with several inches of snow. The seal can breathe through the snow, but there must be a hole in the ice below in order to reach that level. Seals create these holes using their hot breath to enable them to live under water for long periods of time and feed on the fish they catch there. The hunter has a friend to help him find the breathing holes: a dog that is his constant companion and that, at other times of the year, is part of a dog team to pull a sled. Dogs have very sensitive noses, and they can detect through the snow the slighted indication of a seal's previous visit because seal meat is part of their diet. As soon as the dog detects one of these breathing holes, it digs away the snow and reveals the place the hunter is seeking.

Life on the surface of the ocean ice is difficult. It is windy and very cold, just as the land is. Often the hunter has to stand for hours waiting for the seal to come up to the breathing hole. The strong winds that are common in the high latitudes of Cambridge Bay make the temperature feel much lower than it actually is.

Fortunately, the furs in which the hunter is clothed are taken from animals that are accustomed to living in these low temperatures. The Inuit discovered, just by trying and trying until they succeeded, that they could build snow houses that would protect them from the cold. There are no exact measurements, even today, for building snow houses, or *igloos*, as they are known in the far north of Canada. With plenty of practice, the Inuit learned how to do it. Today, they can erect a snow house in an hour. Often, in the few hours of sunlight available to them in the winter, that is all the time available for doing it. Blocks of snow, 3 feet long, 2 feet wide, and 1.5 feet high, form the walls. A dozen of them are laid on the ground for the first layer, and then fewer and fewer are used for the remaining four layers, which leaves space for one more block at the top, 5 feet above the ground, to seal the walls.

The blocks themselves create a 5-foot-high shelter, but an extra foot is gained on the inside by digging down below ground level inside the igloo. Each block of snow has to slope upward and inward in order to have the walls curve in gradually. When the igloo is finished, a lamp inside, made from animal fat, raises the temperature a bit above zero so that some melting occurs between the snow blocks. This melting binds the individual snow blocks into a solid snow wall, so strong and resistant to outside pressure that not even a polar bear could knock down the igloo. Some light comes through the snow walls, but the cold air is kept out because the snow blocks are good insulators.

The whole class can imagine life in an igloo by creating a space on the classroom floor, a circle of 12 feet in diameter. They can then decide where they would put everything for a family of four. There is little need for teacher input here. Lively discussions quickly emerge as student interests clash with what would be appropriate for living in the way the Inuit lived.

Figure 5.2 An Igloo

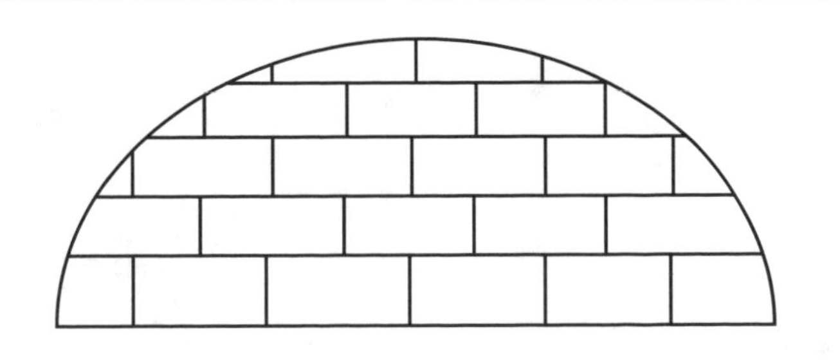

For example, a narrow entrance allowing people to crawl into the igloo allows cold air to come in whenever anyone enters or leaves. If no one asks a question about this, the teacher might pose one because this phenomenon is not common in lower latitudes. "How did the Inuit solve this problem?" After the students try to discover the answer to this question individually, then cooperatively in small groups, and, finally, in a whole-class interactive discussion, perhaps with some probing questions by the teacher, they will discover—or the teacher will tell them—the answer. The answer is that the Inuit built platforms for seating and sleeping above the level of the entrance because the cold air will always stay below since it is heavier than the warmer air above. The temperature, though, stays just below freezing. Another way to imagine life in an igloo is to build one, using standard white home insulation sheets, 16 by 24 by 2 inches, and using inches rather than feet for the sizes of the blocks. With such a scale, they would build an igloo a foot in width and a little less than that in height.

The seal hunting game is yet another valuable way of understanding Inuit life. It is based on actual conditions in northern Canada. In this game, the students pretend that they are seal hunters, and the game takes them through the daily search for seals, the Inuit's main food supply and their source of materials for clothing, boots, and bone tools. Additionally, because the harsh climate prevents the growing of vegetables, the Inuit depend on fresh liver from the seal as a substitute source of essential nutrients. In this seal hunt game, there are three ice floes with five clusters of ice on each floe; each cluster has six breathing holes as shown in Figure 5.3,

Figure 5.3 Seal Hunt Game

	Ice Floe A	Ice Floe B	Ice Floe C
	1 2 3	1 2 3	1 2 3
Range N			
	4 5 6	4 5 6	4 5 6
	1 2 3	1 2 3	1 2 3
Range O			
	4 5 6	4 5 6	4 5 6
	1 2 3	1 2 3	1 2 3
Range R			
	4 5 6	4 5 6	4 5 6
	1 2 3	1 2 3	1 2 3
Range T			
	4 5 6	4 5 6	4 5 6
	1 2 3	1 2 3	1 2 3
Range H			
	4 5 6	4 5 6	4 5 6

and each seal has to come up to one of these breathing holes once a day. The six breathing holes of each cluster represent the area beneath the ice in which a seal roams and finds food. To make it easier to play the game, a chart of six layers is needed, each like the one in Figure 5.3 but separately identified by the letters *N* to *H*. This chart should be given to a student who is selected to referee the game. The game begins by each student picking any one of the breathing holes in any one cluster for a day of hunting. The referee for the class records results and makes sure that no two students select the same breathing hole. Twenty days of hunting are then played, and the results are tabulated. The rules of the game are as follows:

1. Toss a die (mark a sugar cube if no dice are available) to indicate the end of one day's hunting. If the number does not match the number of the location chosen by the hunter, the seal has not come up to breathe at that spot, and the hunter has lost one day's hunting. If the number does match, throw the die again. If the number matches the spot again, a seal has already been caught by another hunter, and no seal will come to that breathing hole that day. If the number is different, the student-hunter has caught one seal.

2. A seal provides food for one hunter for six days. At the beginning of the game, each hunter has a four-day supply of food. He can go for four hungry days (after the first four days with food), and then he is dead. Each hunter is on his own, with no sharing of food or information except that he or she has to tell the referee which hole is being watched before the dice are thrown. At the end of 20 days, the student referee counts the total number of hungry days and the number of hunters dead.

The devastating results of the individual style of hunting will be obvious to the class. The teacher can then ask the students, "How did these people survive for so long with this kind of result?" If the teacher takes enough time to let them figure it out individually, in small groups, and then as a whole class, they will certainly figure out some pattern of shared hunting or shared food. At that stage, they can play the game again with some sort of cooperative hunting in place. The teacher could then help the students construct their next higher level of understanding by assigning a new higher level task: "Discuss the outcomes of the shared hunting and discover how, in our society, we survive using cooperative methods of securing food." In all of the natural learning constructive processes outlined in this chapter, a student's potential is fully employed to make him or her a motivated and successful learner.

There is one other aspect of life in Cambridge Bay that existed in the past and also exists today. It's something that links the past with the present and introduces some of the problems of modern life in Cambridge Bay. A hundred years ago, there were more boys than girls. It is the same today, 155 boys and 135 girls in the age range of 5 to 14. The total population of Cambridge Bay today is 1,300. The teacher can ask the students why they think that is so and whether they think it is good to have such a condition. It might be possible to raise thought-provoking questions: "Do you think that boys get more advantages than girls because they are the hunters and so they are able to live longer?" "Why could girls not be hunters too?" Another unusual thing in Nunavut is the language spoken by most of the people. It is called Inuktitut. Very few speak English. What might be the reason for this?

INUIT SOCIETY TODAY

There are other questions too that arise from modern living. The old ways have greatly changed, and with these changes new problems have come. Some of these changes are good, others not so good. In about the middle of the twentieth century, the introduction of x-rays identified and led to treatment of the biggest health hazard in the old ways, tuberculosis. This is a common disease among people who have to spend long periods of time indoors in crowded accommodations. At about the same time, improved health services reduced the infant death rate. The result of both of these developments was a steady increase in the population. As noted above, Cambridge Bay today has a population of 1,300, far more than ever was the case a hundred years ago. At first glance, these changes seem to be good. However, they were accompanied by other aspects of modern life, such as the availability of rifles for hunting, and that one change quickly depleted the numbers of seals because many more could be caught in a short time.

Students should be presented with some of these changes, both the good and the bad, and asked to discuss them in small groups as a culmination to their study of Inuit life. Once again, as before, their conclusions should be presented to the whole class, who should suggest possible answers to the problems that arise. Here are some of the things that might be discussed. The news that Inuit people could catch many more seals than they needed attracted the attention of fur manufacturers farther south, who were anxious to get seal skins with their fur. They paid a lot of money for these skins, and Inuit people were able to buy many of the things they never were able to get before. Because they did not need all the meat of the seals that they now were able to catch, they took only the skins and left the meat for wolves to eat. As a result, the population of wolves increased rapidly, and they began to kill more and more caribou, the animals on which the Inuit depended for their living in spring and early summer. The Federal Government launched a major campaign against wolves when they saw what was happening. About 5,000 wolves were killed in one five-year period. What should have been done in a situation like this?

In more recent years, everything changed for the Inuit. In 1993, the Territory of Nunavut was created, giving them self-government over an area almost as big as the state of California. Cambridge Bay, as was noted earlier, is within this new territory. It stretches from about 55 degrees north to 80 degrees north, to within 500 miles of the North Pole, and from 60 degrees west to 120 degrees west. The Inuit have to govern this vast amount of land with a total population of less than 30,000, less than one would find in a small Californian town. This new territory has been divided into two parts, one of which is administered by people who want to preserve the old ways of living from the land but with the advantages of modern help. The other part of Nunavut is involved in the global industrial economy. It will develop new industries in the north and trade with different countries around the world. Students should be asked, "If you had to make the choice as a citizen of Nunavut, in which one of these two areas would you choose to live?"

REFERENCES

Freedman, R. (1980). *Immigrant kids*. New York: Puffin Books.

Gunn, A. M. (1974). *Canada's northland*. Toronto, Ontario, Canada: Oxford University Press.

Macdonald, F. (2001). *The world in the time of Albert Einstein*. Philadelphia: Chelsea House.

Purich, D. (1992). *The Inuit and their land: The story of Nunavut*. Toronto, Ontario, Canada: Dormer.

6

Where Would You Locate Your Castle?

Developing Potential in Early Adolescent Learners

If we want to draw out talent and potential, early adolescence is a pivotal time. It can be a stage in human development when the promise that has been dormant in many children comes alive. Unfortunately, it is sometimes a defining time when young people who have extraordinary but not necessarily obvious gifts lose their drive and retreat from the potential they might have fulfilled. What happens at this critical stage that enables some students to soar and others to flounder? What part can school and teachers play in launching and nurturing the talent that all young people possess but not all fully express?

This chapter will initially look at the often tumultuous physical, mental, and emotional transformations that are taking place in the early adolescent child. Because brain development is so central to this stage of child development, we will look particularly at what is being learned about the adolescent brain. Subsequently, the chapter will focus on classroom strategies that will give us the greatest opportunity to help these dynamic human beings be successful.

We have long understood that early adolescence was a period of dramatic instability, vulnerability, and change. While each child will have a unique timetable and experience, someplace between 9 and 17, virtually all young people will go through wide-ranging physical changes that prepare their bodies to create and bear children. The transformations that characterize puberty are occurring at an earlier age than we have previously understood. The Carnegie Council on Adolescent Development reported that in the nineteenth century, the average age for an American girl to reach menarche was 16. In a study of 17,000 girls, Herman-Giddens reports that today the average is 12.5 years.[1] Two thirds of 10-year-olds in the study were showing breast development and other evidences of menarche. Where the onset of puberty used to be associated with secondary school, today it is understood to be an elementary school reality. Boys too are going through the physical changes of puberty earlier than in the past, and from 18 months to three years later than adolescent girls.

WHAT ARE THE RELATIVELY NORMAL PHYSICAL CHANGES THAT OCCUR WITH THE BEGINNING OF PUBERTY?

The child will experience rapid physical growth, though maturation rates differ dramatically from individual to individual. Between 12 and 16, they will gain 4 to 12 inches in height and they will add between 15 and 65 pounds. In boys, feet and arms will grow faster than the rest of their bodies. Their shoulders also broaden. Body proportions change in females as their hips widen. Both genders may experience joints that ache due to rapid growth.[2]

Numerous physical changes occur that are associated with the pituitary gland's triggering of testosterone, estrogen, progesterone, and other hormones. Skin becomes more oily. They become susceptible to developing pimples. Sweating increases and they might develop body odor. Hair grows under the arms and on the pubis. In males, it also occurs on their face and chest. In males, genitals mature, their voice deepens, sperm is produced, and erections might occur with or without any sexual thought. Their muscles and strength increase. In females, genitals mature, breasts develop, and ovulation begins.[3]

These physiological changes would be a challenge by themselves, but they are often accompanied by wild mood swings and overwrought emotions. One day they are in love, and the next day they can't stand the same person. One moment they might be very close to their parents, and the next, without any apparent cause, they will be distant or even hostile.

Ronald Dahl, a psychiatrist at the University of Pittsburgh, attributes these mood swings to chemical changes in the limbic system of the brain. Not only do feelings reach a flash point more readily, but adolescents seek out situations where they can allow their emotions to run wild. Dahl says they actively look for experiences to create intense feelings.[4]

Early adolescents frequently critical of themselves and others. They're sure that they are too fat or too skinny, too hairy, or too large breasted. If they are not picking themselves apart, they might be sniping at their locker partner or younger brother. They can be exceedingly sensitive about who likes them and who does not. They spend inordinate amounts of time checking each other out and fretting over having the right people to eat lunch with or simply to be in the company of. Above all else, this is a period of considerable insecurity and difficulty with self-concept. Surveys show that girls experience a marked drop in self-esteem at this time.[5]

These physical and emotional changes that the early adolescent is experiencing are taking place within the context of important adult relationships, whether at home or school. This is often a time when open communication with adults is strained and when the adolescent is more likely to challenge authority and test limits. There are many ways that this testing might be manifested. Teen smoking has actually decreased nationally since the late 1990s, but alcohol consumption and drugs continue to be growing concerns. A survey of the drinking habits of Michigan teens was published in 2003. The study reported that 62 percent of all high school seniors in that state revealed having been drunk at some point during their high school years. In another study reported by the Carnegie Foundation, 92 percent of high school seniors had experimented with alcohol more than once before graduating. Of that percent, more than half indicated that they had begun drinking in the sixth to ninth grades.[6] Fourteen percent of the eighth graders in the Michigan study reported having consumed five or more drinks at one sitting at some point in the past two weeks.[7]

At the very time when adolescents are most wanting to challenge authority and push to be independent, they often experience family situations that are both unstable and unsupportive. The present era of our culture is characterized by the "dissolution of the American family." Divorce is a reality for a majority of young people today. In any class of 30 students that a teacher might have, the odds are that only 16 will live with their two biological parents, 7 will live only with their mother, and 6 will live with at least one stepparent. Only a small fraction will live with only their father or with adoptive parents. This situation will always be in flux for these students because 75 percent of all divorced people will remarry, and the divorce rate for second and subsequent marriages is higher than for first marriages. By some estimates, re-divorce rates are more than 60 percent.[8]

While there are many children from divorced families who are successful in school and beyond, there are also many studies that point to the increased difficulty these students face because of challenging home situations. The ability of the child to navigate the difficulties and adjustments of divorce will in some measure depend on the age of the child at the divorce. A child at age 12 who experienced his parents' divorce at age 6 is different from a child of age 12 who is now going through his parents' divorce. Researchers have found, however, that boys of divorce show significantly higher incidences of school behavior problems, such as aggression and hyperactivity, immediately after a divorce.[9] For girls, a parent's remarriage introduces many new behavioral and emotional issues. Niolon reported several studies of 13- to 18-year-olds of both genders where the subjects showed significantly greater problems with anger, shame, and depression related to their parents' divorce. In some of these studies, the problems could be identified in a boy's behavior as early as four years before the actual divorce. Wallerstein makes an important point that home situations where there are contentious, angry partners who stay together for "the children's sake" or any other reason are no better for young people than is going through divorce.[10]

While there are many examples of young people who succeeded in the face of the difficulties they deal with as children, far more social pathologies can be found among children from single-parent households. Sixty-three percent of all youth suicides are committed by children from single-parent homes. Seventy percent of all teenage pregnancies occur in women from single-parent families. Eighty percent of all prison inmates and 90 percent of all homeless and runaway children are from families with only one parent.[11] There can be no doubt that these home circumstances put significant additional pressures on the early adolescent child, who is already struggling with the challenges of puberty.

HOW THEN WOULD WE TEACH?

Despite all these physical and family challenges and self-absorbed behaviors, early adolescents can be a joy to work with. They have special needs for nurture, security, and a positive environment, but with the right teacher, they are remarkable learners and producers. When aroused, their curiosity propels them into surprisingly deep investigations. When it is tapped, they have an idealism that will lead them to put enormous energy into famine relief or aid to tsunami victims. They, too, have boundless energy that can sometimes be channeled to projects like creating a very professional brochure about their community for visitors or new residents. In one instance, such a brochure showing climate and history and community services was so well done by a group of sixth graders that the Chamber of Commerce of their community bought the brochure for several thousand dollars and distributed it to newcomers for years after.

What follows is a vignette, a true story about a fairly normal adolescent and his teacher who earnestly desired to see him reach his potential.

Justin was just another sullen seventh grader when he showed up for Mr. Colburn's World Geography class. He wouldn't make eye contact when Colburn greeted him at the door. Because there weren't assigned seats, he always sat in the back of the room. He never participated in class unless forced to. He didn't turn in homework. He earned mostly D's on his tests. There wasn't much evidence to suggest that he was a child with ability.

Early each fall, Colburn made phone calls to the parents of each of his students, not a small task when you have 180 or more students in class each day. With each call, he simply introduced himself and commented on how much he was looking forward to working with their son or daughter. He asked if the parent or representative of the family had any questions or concerns. He invited them to come to Back to School Night and gave them his home phone number in case they ever needed to get in touch with him outside of school hours. Colburn felt that the more you interact with a child and his family, the more valuable information you have to work with. His call to Justin's home netted some of that important information. He learned that Justin's mother had passed away while he was in the sixth grade. One day in class, later in the semester, Mr. Colburn had given the class a reading assignment to be done in class. He was circulating around, answering questions and checking to see if his students were on task. When he came up behind Justin, Colburn could see that Justin had a copy of *Playboy* tucked surreptitiously within the pages of his text. Justin was engrossed in graphic anatomy and not geography. Colburn made a snap decision. Instead of confiscating the illicit material and reprimanding Justin, he reached over to a nearby shelf and handed Justin a novel and simply said, "I think you will find this more interesting."

Colburn's approach might not have worked with all students, but it worked with Justin. The simple act of not admonishing him when he clearly expected to be disciplined was the basis of a new bond that would form between the two. Over time, Justin found Colburn as someone he could trust, and someone who really cared for him. Justin would sometimes come by Colburn's classroom before school or during lunch, just to talk. Colburn found that Justin liked to use his imagination and make up stories. He encouraged Justin to write them down and even showed one of them to a colleague in the English Department. It made Justin feel special that he had an advocate, someone who believed in him.

Justin didn't immediately become a star student. His effort and grades improved, but he wasn't suddenly an outstanding student. The payoff in this true story didn't come for 15 years. Colburn was invited to a book-signing party for a young author of children's fiction. The author was celebrating the publication of his eighth children's book and wanted Colburn present. Sure enough, it was Justin Matott, and his book *Drinking Fountain Joe* was dedicated to Mr. Colburn, "a wonderful teacher who once looked upon this 'Joe' with kinder eyes than most."

JUSTIN'S TEACHER

Teachers like Mr. Colburn, who are successful in bringing out the best in the Justins of the world, tend to have a different perspective about their goals for teaching. Like all teachers, the "Colburn-like" teachers work with subject matter and a curriculum. They work with textbooks that are filled with facts and generalizations and skills, just as others do. Colburn has a strong academic background in geography and a genuine enthusiasm about teaching the subject. He certainly wants his students to learn ideas and perspectives about the world that will make them wiser about global issues and more interested in studying and traveling to other parts of the world.

Colburn also has a broader set of goals that are not curriculum specific. These have to do with the skills and attitudes he knows his students will need to possess in order to be effective in the world. These would certainly include skills of communication: the ability to read, write, speak, and listen. He would want his students to learn social skills and how to work effectively as a part of a team. He would be concerned, too, that they would develop good work habits and learn how to discover and evaluate knowledge and make good decisions. All of these skills and dispositions are fundamental to their success as adults.

No one would argue against the importance of curriculum goals like these. The difference between teachers like Ed Colburn and many others is in the way they work with and use the curriculum. These outcomes will often not be realized because they aren't the teacher's first priority. The real priorities for these Colburn-like teachers are certainly complex and much more difficult to accomplish than simply transmitting their knowledge. Their focus is on the development of the child. They want to see all their students grow in their excitement about their learning. They want to see them become more confident that they can be successful, not just in school but in the broader endeavors of life. When these teachers can help their students see what they are capable of, the students are never the same. Ron Berger describes this as "catching a glimpse of who they could be." He believes it is "transformational." It might not even happen in school, but when it does, students can become inspired learners.[12]

BUILDING RELATIONSHIPS: THE KEY TO EARLY ADOLESCENTS

Colburn often encounters students whom he taught 10, 20, or even 30 years earlier. He will talk to these former students about many things, but he usually gets around to asking them, "What do you remember from our World Geography class when you were a seventh grader?" Typically in answering, they don't recall academic things. They might mention a special project they did, but much more often they would comment, "We liked coming to class and we knew that you cared about us." The relationship he developed with his students was the key, and relationship remains the key in working with all adolescents.

How do teachers develop the relationships that open up student potential when they work with 150 to 180 students each day? It certainly isn't easy, and it takes a lot of energy. Here are just a few ideas from Colburn's "bag of tricks."

1. On the first day of class, Colburn has his students fill out a questionnaire whereby he accesses important information about each child. In his "Project Getting to Know You," he asks them what their hobbies and interests are. Where have they traveled? When is their birthday? He also has them do sentence completions to surface cues about what is going on in their lives and how they view teachers, the subject that they will study, and school.

- When I think about what's going on for me right now, I'm nervous about . . .
- For me school is . . .
- Teachers help me learn best when they . . .

He also asks them if there is anything he should know about them as their teacher and to tell him one thing that they feel comfortable to share that is unique about them. All of this information becomes useful in building relationships with students and a climate in his classroom that fosters student success.

2. Another idea in the "bag of tricks" that teachers like Colburn use is to find ways to make each child in the classroom the center of attention for focused times. Even the most shy student wants to be noticed in a positive way as a unique person. There are many ways to do this. Some teachers periodically compile a "people scavenger hunt" in which they list positive characteristics of individuals in the room, such as "someone who has been to New York," "someone with an August birthday," or "someone who can play an electric guitar." The teacher might give the class five minutes at the beginning of class, while he is taking care of attendance and other logistical matters, to interview each other and find as many of the people with those characteristics as they can. The message that comes across is that each person is important in this classroom. It also allows the students to find individuals they might not have known who share common interests.

Another valuable relationship-building idea is to assign "people bag" presentations early in the year. The students must come up with some sort of "bag" or container that characterizes them. It might be a back pack or an athletic bag or just a decorated paper bag. They put in the bag three artifacts that represent things that are important to them. Then they have five minutes to share their people bag. At the end of each presentation, two or three other students are encouraged to indicate ways they relate to the people bag presenter. It will take some class time to do these activities, but the dividends are well worth the time.

3. Relationally oriented teachers know how to turn over strategic aspects of control in the classroom to their students. This can take different forms, but the result in many cases is that the learners are empowered. Here are a few ways that this can take place. At the beginning of an instructional unit, many teachers ask the simple question, "What would

you like to learn about as we study _____?" There are some situations in which a teacher wouldn't ask such a question because there is some sort of problem that is creating a negative atmosphere, but in most circumstances, students give enthusiastic reasons for studying a new topic. One version of this is called *KWL*. In this approach, students work in small groups to identify what they already "know" about a new topic. That's the *K*. Then they list what they "want to know." That's the *W*. If they have written these lists on large sheets of paper, they can post them in the classroom where the lists can readily be seen. When students notice that they have "learned" something they had listed as a "want to know," they go up and put a check mark next to that learning. This is the *L* in KWL.

Ed Colburn has a simple but important tool that he uses to give students more control in the instructional process. He teaches his students phrases like "70 in a 30." The students then can use the phrase to get him to slow down in his explanation of some idea. When they say "70 in a 30," they are telling him, you are going 70 miles an hour, when this "neighborhood" has a 30-mile-an-hour speed limit. If they can be in control of the pace, they can be more successful learners.

Other teachers empower their students through contract grading systems, where they spell out the requirements for an A, B, or C grade in the class. The students learn what projects, minimum test score average, and so forth are required for each grade. They "contract" for the grade they want, understanding that it must be a C or better. The differences between each grade are usually on the basis of quantity of work. When tests or papers are returned, the teacher simply indicates whether they are "satisfactory" or "unsatisfactory" as fulfilling the agreed-upon contract. If the paper is not satisfactory, the student must redo what was not satisfactory and resubmit it. When it works well, students feel a security about their grade because they can see that they control it. With groups in which it doesn't work well, the teacher sees the same paper over and over, and in the end they might have to recontract because the grading period is about to end and some students still have work that has not been determined to be satisfactory.

Each of these ideas will work in some middle-level classrooms but might not in others. Teaching is highly contextual. However, what is universal is the idea that in order to get the best from students, the teacher must develop positive relationships with them. These relationships are the foundation of a nurturing and productive classroom.

ENRICHED ENVIRONMENTS

One of the clear messages of neuroscience research is the importance of the environment in learning. As discussed in Chapter 3, in research on rats that has been ongoing since the 1960s, Marion Diamond and her

Figure 6.1 Dendritic Branching

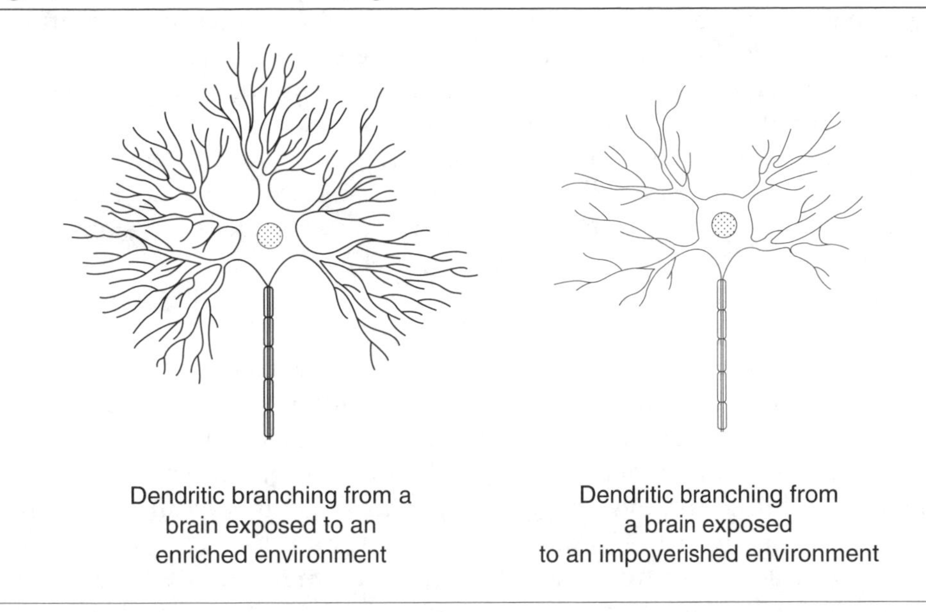

colleagues at the University of California, Berkeley, demonstrated that a stimulating environment causes a change in the structure and chemistry of their brain cells. Using laboratory rats, researchers found that groups of rats with access to "toys" and other stimuli develop a thicker cerebral cortex and larger brain cells than did those without this stimulation. The rats were able to use their more developed brains better, too. After being in this more stimulating environment for even short periods of time, they were able to navigate mazes better than rats that didn't play.[13]

The environment turns out to be particularly important in working with the early adolescent. There appears to be no limit of possibilities for ways to encourage similar brain growth or "neuroplasticity," that is, learning, in our middle-level classrooms. Jenson identifies music, mind games, puzzles, manipulatives, lighting, color, and plants as components of an enriched classroom environment.[14] Diamond says the essence of creating an enriched environment is providing opportunities for the learner to be mentally active and participative. As illustrations, she identifies circumstances where students are using their imaginations, building models, and even teaching other students.[15] Novelty, curiosity, and figuring things out are keys. Arnold Scheibel at the Brain Research Institute at UCLA says that "unfamiliar activities are the brain's best friend."[16] The brain's attraction to the novel might be a survival response, as noted in Chapter 3. Anything new in our environment might represent a potential danger, so our brain has to pay attention to it. Once we have grown accustomed to it, it becomes routine and we tend to ignore it.

Although incorporating novelty—with the opportunity for students to experience and process the novelty and figure it out—is important in any classroom, the early adolescent craves it. We see this in their fascination with video games and ever-changing media stimulation. Middle-level teachers often understand and utilize this fascination and work to create experiences that capture their interest in that which is different and unique. However, especially with novelty, students need to be able to make an initial connection to their own emotions, ideas, or experiences and, on that basis, be challenged to "figure it out."

Here are just a couple of examples:

1. A sixth-grade teacher in Hibbing, Minnesota, helped her students learn the Pythagorean theorem in Math by giving her class an aerial photo of Tiger Stadium in Detroit and asking them if they would help her determine if a home run hit there by Mickey Mantle on September 10, 1960, was the longest home run ever hit. It seems that the ball was hit over a light stand in right center field and out of the stadium. It landed in a lumber yard across the street from the stadium. They knew right where the ball landed because a lumber yard worker saw it hit the ground. Unfortunately, however, there was no way to measure straight to home plate from there because the stadium blocks the path. The students got into it and started asking questions. From the photo, they could see that there was a door in the wall of the stadium along the right-field foul line at the 325-foot marker. Did the teacher happen to know whether the door went all the way through to the street, they asked. "Yes it did," she answered. It was used to bring equipment into the park and it was 47 feet from the right field wall through the stands to the street. Pretty soon, the class had the whole thing figured out, and by incorporating the formula for determining the hypotenuse of a right triangle, they determined that the ball traveled over 640 feet. With some excited Internet research, they determined Mantle's was the longest home run ever hit, at 643 feet.

2. The students of a seventh-grade social studies teacher in Ft. Collins, Colorado, will never forget the day their teacher, Mr. Dornan, conducted a human sacrifice ceremony as it would have taken place a thousand years ago in the ancient Aztec civilization. He wanted them to understand the power of religious belief in that culture, so he dressed as an Aztec priest and simulated the entire ceremony, ending with the tearing out of the heart of a captured prisoner. While this lesson might be too gory, the students were emotionally captivated and intent on learning more about the Aztecs and their civilization.

3. A ninth-grade science teacher in Ontario, Canada, responded to a simple question by a student who had seen the Academy Award–winning movie about the sinking of the *Titanic*. "Mr. Howell, did so many people

have to die when the *Titanic* went down?" Howell turned this question into an opportunity for the students to research what happened and offer creative ideas about what could have been done to save lives. After finding pictures and information about the ship from Web research, they figured out a detailed plan that could have been implemented by the captain in the two hours between the time the ship hit the iceberg that fateful April night and the time the ship actually sank. The lesson didn't end there, however. The students wanted to "try their ideas out," so they found a naval historian in England through the Internet and made a formal presentation to him. This was an experience these students would never forget, for reasons we will understand later in the chapter.

BOREDOM REDUCES THE ADOLESCENT BRAIN

The effect of boredom on the brain turns out to be as dramatic as the effects of providing enrichment. In the research done by Marion Diamond's group, young rats who had been in enriched environments and were known to have developed more complex cortical structures were subsequently put into plain cages and allowed to experience an unstimulating environment. In a matter of only weeks, their cortex grew thinner. Diamond concludes from this research that the message "for teenage and young adult brains is startling: An impoverished, unstimulating environment has as much impact on the adolescent brain as does deliberate enrichment."[17]

"It's boring" is unfortunately one of the most common utterances from the adolescent mouth. While boredom might be a fact of life in the teen's world, Dr. Diamond's research is compelling. Wherever possible, we want to challenge their inclination to be bored. Teamwork with parents might help alleviate boredom in afterschool hours, but fighting boredom in school is one of our biggest challenges.

Some teachers utilize the walls, bulletin boards, and even ceilings of their classroom to battle student boredom. Colorful posters and intriguing quotes not only make the room warmer and more hospitable, they might challenge the student when he is momentarily not on task with the lesson being taught. When students are invited to figure something out, their interest will be engaged. For example, many middle-level teachers utilize ongoing "mystery contests" as a means of promoting curiosity and providing brain-stimulating events in their classroom. They might utilize a bulletin board that is readily visible. They post a clue a day in a three- or four-day sequence, and students compete to figure out the answer for extra credit. The clues are posted in print that is large enough to be seen all over the room. In a seventh-grade World Geography class, the clue sequence might be as follows.

Can you figure out what nation this is?

Day 1: This nation is the second most populous on its continent, but virtually all of its people live on only 3.5 percent of the nation's land. This is because an important physical feature dominates this nation's way of life. (A correct answer is worth 5 points.)

Day 2: The most important crop of this nation is cotton. It is among the world's leading producers of this crop, which was first developed here during the American Civil War to supply the British textile industry when the Union blockaded southern ports. (A correct answer is worth 4 points.)

Day 3: There are records describing the history of this nation that date back more than 5,000 years. Some of the most remarkable engineering feats in all of world history have taken place here. (A correct answer is worth 3 points.)

The answer is: Egypt.

Participation is usually elective, and those participating submit their guesses on 3 × 5 cards with a reference to get credit. By posting this sort of mystery contest each day, whether students participate actively in the contest or not, they have a novel, curiosity-inducing element in their environment. This is, of course, just one type of brain-stimulating activity. Ideally, our classrooms should regularly feature many, often-changing "brain challenges." In doing this, the environment actually "teaches" and, in fact, might change the brain. Of course, the same thing can be done with mysterious animals, substances in science, or authors in literature. The point is that mysteries compel the brain to think and wonder and try to figure out which are good antidotes to boredom, because it is what the brain, our survival organ, wants and needs to do.

A fun variation of the mystery contest idea is to post questions about obscure facts that students won't know but might find intriguing to research answers to. Here are a few examples.

- What unusual thing did Babe Ruth do to keep himself cool while playing baseball? Answer: He put a wet cabbage leaf under his cap.
- What is the longest word that can be made utilizing only one row of a standard keyboard? Answer: typewriter.
- How are Israeli postage stamps different from those of any other nation? Answer: The glue is certified kosher.
- What is the shortest complete sentence in the English language? Answer: Go.
- On average, how much pizza do Americans eat each day? Answer: 18 acres.

A teacher can post one of these a day and offer simple prizes for as many correct answers as are turned in to this "Weird Things That Hardly

Anyone Knows Contest." Typically, students love these and are eager to find answers to them. There is a side benefit in that these become topics for discussion at the dinner table when parents ask the inevitable "What did you do in school today?" question.

THE IMPORTANCE OF PLAY

Teachers might utilize their classroom environment to stimulate brain activity, but they might not realize the power of doing so. In our high-stakes-testing culture, teachers might hesitate to use academic games or creative projects, for example, because they might feel play is frivolous. Psychologist Stuart Margulies studied third and fourth graders in New York City to learn how playing games would affect their learning. One randomly determined group of students received 45 minutes of chess instruction each week, while the other group received 45 minutes of extra schoolwork each school day. On reading tests administered a semester later, the chess players significantly outperformed the extra schoolwork group.[18] Neuroanatomists would say of this study that it is evidence that the mental exercise of playing challenging games builds on the neurons in the thinking regions of our brain. It might turn out that an environment that utilizes academic games and mentally challenging play will result in greater achievement gains than will more conventional instruction, and play works especially well with the early adolescent.

THE OPPOSITE OF PLAY IS STRESS

Teachers need to be aware of other dimensions of the classroom environment besides stimulation. The brain is especially sensitive to the presence of excessive stress and or threats. Because the first priority of the human brain is survival, potential threat, whether social, emotional, or physical, triggers neurochemicals that inhibit learning.

There are countless incidents in schools every day that illustrate this reaction and its effect upon learning. On an elementary playground in Colorado, just before the school day was to begin, a group of sixth graders were attracted to a German shepherd that had wandered into their play area. The dog seemed to be friendly, so they surrounded it and began petting it; suddenly it went berserk and started barking and biting. No one was seriously injured, but as the school day opened, the teachers throughout the building noted that it took hours for the students to calm down and be able to focus and learn.

We now understand that brain chemistry was involved in that event. Chapter 3, in the section on the "flight or fight" response, discusses the role of chemicals, especially cortisol, in our ability to think and remember.

ACTIVE LEARNING AND PROBLEM SOLVING

There is a substantial body of research to support the use of teaching strategies that promote active learning with all levels of students, but particularly with the middle-level child. Active by nature, this child learns better when his or her instruction involves more than listening and when less emphasis is placed on the teacher's merely transmitting information. These students thrive when the emphasis is on developing their thinking and investigating skills. There are many and varied active-learning strategies: inquiry, simulation, problem solving, and others. The common denominator is that when students learn via the process of "figuring something out," the brain learns and retains that material more effectively.

In Chapter 2, Rita Smilkstein argues that the brain, like other human organs, has developed instinctive traits that affect how it operates best. We don't have to teach the lungs to breathe or the heart to beat. Similarly, we don't have to teach the brain to think or figure things out. The human brain, as part of its survival priorities, naturally looks for problems to solve. In our early eras as a species, this trait was probably honed by the need to outwit saber-toothed tigers or simply find enough to eat. It has become an instinctive behavior. Our brain is naturally inquisitive and consistently searches for questions to answer and problems to solve.

We sometimes don't believe this is true of our students in classroom situations because the problems we give them to work on might not intrigue them. Scardamalia and Bereiter put the challenge to teachers this way: "We must find ways for the brain to satisfy its natural curiosity and desire for novelty, discovery and challenge. We need to focus on wonderment questions. Questions which spring from the deep interests of the child."[19] The tendency in many of our classrooms is to give students answers to questions they have never asked. History students might not be interested in what was going on in Europe during the Middle Ages, but they become curious to consider where in their county a castle would be located if they could apply the locational factors that were employed by European princes in that time period. And in the process of figuring this problem out, they have a better probability of retaining knowledge about a broad range of things associated with the feudal system because of the way the brain processes and stores knowledge when higher-order thinking, such as this, is involved.

When the teen brain is engaged with a complex problem that it is interested in figuring out, circuits or networks of neurons from all over the cortex grow in complexity as they exchange information related to the problem. Dr. Marta Denny of the University of Wisconsin described it this way: "Problem solving is to the brain what serious aerobic exercise is to the body. It creates a virtual explosion of activity, causing synapses to form, neurotransmitters to live and blood flow to increase."[20] I have used a seventh-grade World Geography activity that can illustrate how these circuits work in a "figure-it-out" context. In this particular activity, students work in cooperative groups to decide where in the world women receive the best and worst treatment. Each group has tabled data for a region of the world and considers eight variables regarding women's circumstances in the nations of their region. They have such information as women's mortality rate in giving birth, comparative literacy rates by gender, the average numbers of children per adult female, life expectancy rates, female share of their nation's labor force, and so on. After considering these variables in their assigned region, the students decide which nations of the world offer women the best and worst treatment. Then they make recommendations about how women's circumstances could be improved in each of these regions.[21]

Because there is always comparative data for the United States on each region's data sheet, the students can make sense of the information they are working with. Moreover, someplace in their cerebral cortex, they have circuitry regarding "fairness." They will immediately view a statistic that in some parts of the world women occupy less then 5 percent of the labor force or have more than seven children per adult female as not being "fair" or "just." That circuitry or neural network in turn is further developed by associating parts of the world with these facts about women's circumstances.

CONNECTED LEARNING

Middle school teachers have long understood intuitively the necessity of relating content back to the experience base of their students. We sometimes struggle with how to relate topics like equity or justice to the lives of eighth graders, but we know the victorious feeling when we are able to do this. We can see from their expressions that "they get it," which means every student's brain had made a connection with something the student already knows and can now begin constructing a new network or connect to an existing network. An oversimplified example of this might involve the concept of "power," which could be a topic in a junior high Civics curriculum. We can certainly explain it and illustrate it from examples in Washington or even with adults in our own community. Dutiful students will write definitions in their notes and, when called upon, if they have reviewed, might be able to give the definition back on a test. If they have given the correct definition, we say they have learned the concept. The problem is that nothing might have changed in their brain's circuitry.

Another approach to this concept will certainly take longer but might work better because the adolescent brain might comprehend it and store it better. In this approach, the teacher might begin with a task rather than direct instruction. She might then display seven or eight magazine pictures of individuals the students would readily recognize, such as Britney

Spears, Donald Trump, Bill Gates, Mother Theresa, George W. Bush, Jennifer Lopez, Martin Luther King, and Ricky Martin. Without giving any definitions, she would pose the question: "How would you rank these individuals according to who has the most power?" The students would think about it individually for a few minutes, and then they would be paired up and start talking about their task. Obviously, before they can make the rankings, they have to arrive at their own explanation of power. The ranking effort yields a lively discussion and many views of not only who has the most power, but how many different sorts of power there are. This lesson could be followed up with an assignment to keep a journal record of how they use power in their own relationships, how others use power over them, and where they see power exhibited around them.

The learning benefits of this sort of lesson are many. Most importantly, the challenge is intriguing enough and personal enough that adolescent learners are likely to be "engaged mentally." They are figuring out what power is from their own base of knowledge. They are compelled to relate a new idea to their previous understandings, which they are eager to do because the task is relevant to their world of ideas. Physiologically, as Smilkstein explains, "Connected learning is a physiological imperative. Dendrites don't grow from nothing. They grow from lower dendrites that have already been constructed."[22]

SOCIAL LEARNING

There will always be a small percent of middle school/junior high students who would prefer to work on class projects by themselves. Feeling shy or awkward in social situations is a significant part of adolescence for many students. Simply being introverted or wanting to do a project by themselves is also common for this age group. It is also their nature, however, to be social and to be attracted to projects and discussions in which they can interact in a comfortable and productive way with their peers. The wise teacher provides opportunities for both individual work and collaborative activities.

Neuroscientists such as Eisenberg argue that "the human brain is constructed socially."[23] Getting students to dialogue with each other turns out to be essential for their learning. Where there is a rich dialogue and students are sharing from their own experience as they consider a concept, the resultant exchange can be powerful. The act of formulating and expressing a thought as part of an exchange between students and from a student to her teacher is itself a form of learning. The brain is far more apt to be engaged in doing this than it is in merely listening. When students are exchanging insights, they are both hearing from each other and explaining to each other, and the back-and-forth of this can result in greater dendritic development and thus more actual learning.

In large measure, the sort of exchange described above only occurs in the right mix of classroom factors. Simply because a teacher wants students to dialogue won't make it happen. He must first establish an environment that promotes this positive give-and-take. Because this age group normally seeks opportunities to get off task, there must be a significant measure of respect for the teacher that allows him to maintain the class's focus. Balanced with this is a sense of security that the students must feel. They must know that it will be safe to offer their ideas. Little interaction will take place if the students are concerned that they can be embarrassed or attacked by a fellow student or their teacher. This safety only happens where a teacher invests the time to develop and enforce rules that put-downs are never allowed in the classroom. Beyond this, the teacher must also take time to make sure that students get to know each other and have friendships in the classroom. The teacher who would utilize the power of social learning will plan regular relationship-enhancing activities in the classroom.

A powerful activity for creating respect, safety, social interaction, and community building is the natural learning research described in Chapter 2.

THE IMPORTANCE OF EMOTION

Brain researchers are calling educators' attention to the importance of a small, almond-shaped structure in the limbic system in the middle of the brain: the amygdala. The amygdala processes emotional stimuli coming into our senses. When we have an experience with fear, embarrassment, or anger or with positive emotions like joy, these experiences are processed into long-term memory through the functioning of the amygdala.

Years ago, before I understood anything about brain research, I had the privilege to teach both junior and senior high school students. After they had moved on to other grade levels, they would often come back to visit. It always intrigued me to hear what they remembered from class. They would recall the stories I would tell—stories about the ordeal of the Donner Party or about the letters young soldiers wrote home in the Civil War. They never forgot the time I came dressed up as Thomas Jefferson or when we volunteered as a class to help a family in need in our neighborhood. I have heard many other teachers comment in a similar vein about what their students remember from years passed. This is certainly why Mr. Dornan's students remember his lesson on the Aztecs' religion. If we reflect on the school experiences we have retained over long periods of time, invariably they will have strong emotional components.

Understanding that long-term memory is tied to emotional content, just as it is tied to practice and figuring things out, it is incumbent upon us to bring emotion into our teaching. A few experiences that the students remember with joy or excitement are worth far more than weeks and months of bland and lifeless worksheets and drill. What sorts of experiences might yield this sort of emotional response from the early adolescent? One example would be the fifth-grade teacher from Georgia who encouraged her students to put Goldilocks on trial for "breaking and entering." Still another example would be the seventh-grade life-science teacher from British Columbia whose students were studying a unit on tropical rain forests. Through the Internet, she contacted a teacher in Nigeria. Her students then prepared a video demonstrating their understanding of the tropical environment, while her counterpart's students developed a video that represented their understanding of a midlatitude forest environment. The students exchanged videos and sent one another critiques of the other's video. In each of these lessons, there is a strong probability that the material being studied and the learning experience itself will be remembered. The memory forms because of the energy the student invests in projects like these but also because there is a measure of the emotion of joy involved in doing them. Emotion solidifies memory.

To summarize, early adolescents thrive with teachers who invest in developing positive relationships with them. They love novelty and situations that encourage their curiosity and their desire to figure things out. Active learning and learning that connects to their world are necessities for these young people. Thus, for the early adolescent to retain learning in long-term memory, there must be strong, hopefully positive emotional components to the learning. They will usually remember the special projects we structure for them. Let's see how we might pull these principles together in a teaching unit.

WHERE WOULD YOU PUT YOUR CASTLE? A POTENTIAL-IGNITING TEACHING UNIT

While it is challenging to capture all of these adolescent-friendly components in one instructional sequence, the following unit from a middle school classroom in Gunnison, Colorado, illustrates many of the key applications. In the interdisciplinary "Castle Project," World History teacher Mark High at Gunnison Middle School begins by giving his students an imaginary scenario that allows them to connect their knowledge of their own community and local environment with Europe in the high Middle Ages. They are told that the year is 1300 and that their village is a growing trade center. The "Lord" of Gunnison needs their help. There are tribes of barbarians in the vicinity that threaten their community. In order to maintain control of this area, their king, who lives in a distant place, has ordered the Lord of Gunnison to build a castle that will provide military protection for their valley and thus allow trade to be carried on without interruption. Mr. High then divides the class into mixed-ability cooperative groups and equips each group with a topographic quadrangle of their community.

Their task includes several problems. First, they must research the locational factors for castles in Europe in the high Middle Ages. In this, they use both Web-based and conventional library sources. Then they make a locational decision as if the Gunnison Valley were Europe at the beginning of the fourteenth century. They must then design their castle and make an oral presentation as if they were defending their location decision and castle design to their king. Then each group constructs a model of its castle using salt and flour or clay. They must show not only how it will be defended, but where merchants will gather to trade, since a major function of these castles will be to facilitate the exchange of goods.

When the students have completed their model and made their presentations, Mr. High connects the project back to their personal lives at school and in their community by introducing a study of medieval chivalry. The class researches the principles and customs of knighthood. They learn about the qualities that were idealized in this culture, and then they consider what those principles would look like if they were instituted in their own lives. Mr. High sets up a system whereby the students can work toward their own knighthood by collecting points for bravery, courtesy, honor, or gallantry. The acts for which they earn points must be attested to by another student or adult, but virtually the entire school gets into the spirit of being chivalrous. There is great ceremony when a student reaches the levels of "page" or "squire" and finally "knight." Each successive level carries both more privilege and more responsibility. Remarkably, the outcomes of this unit carry far beyond the actual time when chivalry is studied in Mr. High's classroom. The faculty at Gunnison Middle School feel the climate of their school is impacted for the entire school year because of this unit. The kids are just a little bit more mannerly than usual.

The castle project is adolescent-friendly for several reasons. First, the tasks given to these middle-level students are novel. They have never considered or tried to figure out where a castle might be located in their community. The novelty of the task, if developmentally appropriate, holds the brain's attention and in this case connects the brain's present knowledge structure to new material. The students understand the environment and situation of their community and have something to which to attach the learning about European feudalism.

The use of a group problem-solving process in this activity brings energy, curiosity, and a social dimension to the learning environment that might facilitate the development of dendrites in the students' cerebral cortex.

It is also important that the uniqueness of each child is addressed by the variety of tasks that the teams must undertake in the castle project. Even within the initial research the students do, there are varied intellectual undertakings with both Web-based and conventional library searches. Then each group must synthesize that historic location information with an aerial view and their knowledge of their valley, and decide where to situate the castle. They then encounter another, more creative task to design their fortress so that it is both a functional trade center and fortification against the imagined roving barbarians.

In this complex problem-solving activity, students utilize many different regions of the brain and potentially create neuron circuitry that facilitates both transfer of the knowledge learned and better retention of that knowledge. Because of the multifaceted tasks the students have been given to consider, the information they are working with must be considered from many vantage points. They encounter it in the initial research, again in the decision about locating the castle, and once more in their oral defense of their decision. These varied encounters are not the equivalent of going over material in the same repetitious way. The fact that these students input the same ideas through different channels means the brain has more ways to retrieve this information. They will know it more flexibly and apply it more readily than if their teacher imparted the material and reviewed it in the way it was imparted.

Complex tasks like the castle project show that other recognized cognitive theories are in agreement with what we are understanding about how our brains learn. Certainly the project honors Gardner's multiple intelligence theory. Gardner and others argue that there is more than one way to learn and be intelligent. Wherever possible, we should help students learn by supporting their unique strengths. In this one project, the students within each group have opportunities to utilize at least five of these eight autonomous intelligences. They utilize "linguistic" intelligence in researching and discussing where castles were built in medieval Europe. They use "logical" intelligence in applying those locational factors to their decision about where their castle might be situated and "spatial" intelligence in taking into account their county topography. They are problem solving continuously in groups, so there are many opportunities for "interpersonal" intelligence. They physically build a model of their castle from salt and flour or modeling clay so there is genuine "kinesthetic" application.[24] There is a good likelihood that this sort of project will result in a positive amygdala experience because of its creative, imaginative, and hands-on aspects.

AN ACRONYM TO HELP US REMEMBER THESE STRATEGIES

Here is an acronym to synthesize some of the most applicable instructional principles in working with the early adolescent learner. The acronym is ASIA-U$A. The first *A* is for *active* learning. Clearly, when the learner is actively engaged, experientially making decisions, and figuring out how to do complex meaningful projects, there is more likely to be dendritic growth. The *S* reminds us that well-functioning, on-task *social* learning is brain-friendly. The *I* is for *investigative* learning. This is a way to remember the importance of providing inquiry or problem-solving opportunities for our early adolescent students. The second *A* stands for *adventuresome* learning. When we provide novel circumstances in our classroom, we find our students to be more attentive and often more creative. The *U* stands for *useful*. The human brain searches for meaning and personal relevance. This is one of our most difficult challenges in teaching adolescents. They need to understand how any concept that they are learning relates directly to their lives. The second *S* has a slash through it to remind us of the negative issues associated with creating high *stress* situations in our classrooms. The third *A* is a reminder of the *amygdala* and the importance of positive emotional experiences. ASIA-U$\!\!\!/$SA is a simple way to remember how we might teach middle-level students in a brain-friendly manner.

THE EARLY ADOLESCENT NEEDS A UNIQUELY SKILLED, COMPASSIONATE TEACHER

Early teens might be the most challenging of all students to teach. They possess enormous potential, but it often remains untapped. They might be sensitive and vulnerable while, at the same time, challenging and sniping at authority. They are inherently mercurial, being up and enthusiastic one minute and sullen and gloomy the next. This often unstable teen will only flourish with an exceptional teacher. The ideal middle school/junior high teacher is, first of all, secure in who she is and what she is about. She can provide the stability this young person needs as well as the enthusiasm, spark, and creativity that bring out the teen's best effort. This teacher, though caring and relationally oriented, is tough when he needs to be. He knows how to provide the consistent rules and discipline that give the teen security and structure. But he also understands how to make the classroom a warm, safe, and mutually respectful place to be. He also knows how to challenge and inspire. These teachers can have compassion for their students, even when it is not deserved, and can be compassionate to themselves because, no matter how talented they are, they will not succeed with their students every day.

Outside of the classroom, these exceptional middle school/junior high teachers are "learning sponges." In the back of their mind when they listen to the news or read a book, there is a "receptor" that continually monitors, "How can I use this idea or illustration with my students?" I have known teachers who keep a videotape running in their VCR anytime they are watching television. They will often pick up an idea from an advertisement or even a conversation in a comedy that will help them bring a fresh and creative illustration to their classroom.

These unique middle-level teachers are also involved in building alliances with parents. They realize that as teachers, they "control" their students' brains only a quarter of any school day or less than 15 percent of the time in a school year. If dendrites can be developed in school, they certainly will be developed by what a teen is focused on and thinking about outside of school. This wise teacher understands that partnerships with parents are essential to the healthy development of their students' brains and in the development of their students' potential. Chapter 10 deals more fully with how this special teacher can best be developed and trained.

NOTES

1. Herman-Giddens, M. E., Slora, E. J., & Wasserman, R. C. (1997). Secondary sexual characteristics and menses in young girls seen in office practice. *Pediatrics, 99*, 505–512.

2. Academy eBriefings. (2003). Adolescent brain development: Vulnerabilities and opportunities. Retrieved January 2004 from www.nyas.org

3. The Media Project. (2002, October). *Child and adolescent development*. Retrieved January 2004 from www.themediaproject.com/facts/development

4. Dahl, R. E. (2004, June). Adolescent brain development: Vulnerabilities and opportunities. *Annals of the New York Academy of Sciences, 1024*.

5. Herman-Giddens, M. E., et al. (1997), p. 507.

6. Carnegie Council on Adolescent Development. (1989). *Turning points*. New York: Author, p. 22.

7. Bucholz, T. J. (2003). Michigan Youth Risk Behavior Survey, 2003. Retrieved June 11, 2006, from www.emc.cmich.edu/yrbs

8. Bumpass, L. L., Roley, R. K., & Sweet, J. A. (1995). The changing character of step families. *Demography, 32*, 425–436.

9. Bumpass, L. L., et al. (1995), p. 429.

10. Niolon, R. (2003). Consequences of parental divorce. Retrieved June 11, 2006, from www.psychpage.com/family/divorce/amato.booth.html

11. Bumpass, L. L., et al. (1995), p. 431.

12. Berger, R. (2003). *An ethic of excellence*. Portsmouth, NH: Heinemann, p. 8.

13. Diamond, M., & Hobson, J. (1998). *Magic trees of the mind*. New York: Plume.

14. Quoted in Jensen, E. (1996). *Brain based learning*. Del Mar, CA: Turning Point, p. 145.

15. Diamond, M., & Hobson, J. (1998), p. 256.

16. Scheibel, A. (1994, November). You can continuously improve your mind and your memory. *BoHum Line Personal*, p. 9.

17. Diamond, M., & Hobson, J. (1998), p. 260.

18. Margulies, S. (1990). *The effect of chess on reading scores: District 9 Chess Program, second year report*. New York: The American Chess Foundation.

19. Scardamalia, M., & Bereiter, C. (1992). Test-based and knowledge-based questioning by children. *Cognition and Instruction, 9*(3), 177.

20. Quoted in Jensen, E. (1996), p. 174.

21. Richburg, R., Nelson, B., & Tochterman, S. (2002, January). Gender inequity: A world geography lesson plan. *The Social Studies, 93*(1), 24.

22. Smilkstein, R. (1993, Winter). The natural human learning process. *Journal of Developmental Education, 17*(2), 4.

23. Eisenberg, L. (1995, November). The social construction of the human brain. *American Journal of Psychiatry, 152*(11), 1563–1574.

24. Gardner, H. (1997). Integrating learning styles and multiple intelligences. *Educational Leadership, 55*(1), 22–27.

7

What Keeps Satellites Above Earth?

Scientific Investigations for Teenage Learners

The focus of this chapter is late teenage years, the last few years of high school or the two or three years after leaving school, and the scientific problems we will look at are perfectly suited to these ages. Many of the skills involved in the methods of science are acquired in the elementary and junior high years so, by the ages of 16 or 17, students are ready to tackle the challenges of making decisions and judgments about more complex scientific problems.

TEENAGE INTELLECTUAL ABILITIES

Jean Piaget, in his analysis of intellectual growth in young people, decided that their brains were fully equipped to think rationally, to do what he called formal operations, at the age of 12. Implicit in this kind of thinking was the assumption that the human brain had reached its zenith of development at 12, and that everything thereafter would be just experience, utilizing the intellectual skills that were assumed to be available. We now know that babies are also able to think rationally, as discussed in Chapter 3, so that the difference between what babies think and what adults think is only the difference between the quantity and quality of their experiences. In other words, the difference in their brains between what children and adults know is the difference between their neural networks.

According to the constructivist definition of learning, as explained in Chapters 2 and 3, teenagers' brains can be fully developed, and their cortexes grow at any age as their dendrites and neural networks develop from experience. However, for the average North American teenager, largely because of the lack of responsible experience and critical and creative thinking, the story may be very different. Dr. Jay Giedd of the brain imaging division of the National Institute of Mental Health is one of many researchers who has studied the late adolescent brain. Over a period of 13 years, he measured the changes in the brains of a thousand teenagers using a powerful magnetic imaging machine known as an MRI. He found that the adolescent brain undergoes extensive structural changes at the age of 18 and often at 20 years of age. These changes are the biggest that young people experience in the course of their lives. A trimming of neural networks occurs in the frontal lobe of the cortex, getting rid of the least-used pathways so that the most useful links can be maintained and the brain can therefore be enabled to operate more efficiently. Why are these changes in the frontal lobe significant? It is because this area of the brain, just behind the forehead, is where the highest mental functions are performed. It is here that decisions are made about goals and priorities, and where good judgment is exercised on things that have high emotional content. It is often referred to as the CEO of the brain.

LEARNING TO USE SCIENTIFIC METHODS

Learning to use scientific methods in complex situations is the kind of activity that grows students' dendrites and enables them thereby to make mature judgments. Scientific methods are quite different from the kind of brain-compatible learning involved in other subjects, such as studying different cultures around the world or analyzing the meaning of a poem. In these studies, students are encouraged to be subjective, to express opinions and feelings along with the factual information. In scientific work, students are required to be like research scientists, completely objective, putting aside data that have not been verified by repeated experiments. This kind of thinking is not always easy because no one is completely free from personal opinions or biases. It is therefore very important that students in the end years of secondary education, because of their need to exercise mature judgment at that stage of life, have experience in the kind of rigorous thinking that scientific work demands.

Where do scientific problems come from? People wonder why things are the way they are. Albert Einstein once said that identifying a problem is more important than solving it because it calls for good observation and creative imagination. The best scientific investigations are those that arise in the students' own minds when they encounter a problem that stimulates their curiosity. There are times when information is presented in the public media as being scientifically accurate and the challenge to readers is to decide whether the claims are justified. Take for example the following newspaper report from Eastern Europe:

> The Russian chess champion Nikolai Gudkov was competing against a supercomputer for a world title. He had won three games and was involved in his fourth and final one when a surge of electricity touched the chessboard and he was killed. Computer experts had already concluded that the computer against which he was competing was so intelligent that it was capable of thinking independently. They examined all the circuits and found them to be in order. Their conclusion was that the machine must have been so angry at losing to Gudkov that it diverted the flow of electricity from its brain to the chessboard. Some legal authorities say that the computer must be charged with murder.

Students should first be left to sort out this report with no help from the teacher in order to discover their initial reactions. Then, if they have not already provided the kind of investigative questions that ought to be asked about a report of this kind, the teacher should raise them. Newspapers and magazines frequently carry accounts of scientific discoveries, and an essential part of scientific thinking is learning to ask the right questions about each one, questions like the following: Are there other accounts of it? What is known about the people who made the discovery? Did the writer of the article give a description of the research that led to the discovery? Where can one read about it?

Some scientific problems could not be resolved when they were first studied. The answers had to wait for later discoveries. Delayed solutions of this kind are good ways of developing maturity. Our fast-paced society wants quick resolutions to problems, and there is frustration when they do not come quickly. One problem that we will study later in this chapter, the behavior of gravity, took more than a thousand years to be resolved. We will begin with one that needed only a little over a hundred years for a solution. It concerns certain sea animals known as corals. They live in warm, shallow ocean water with temperatures of 70 degrees Fahrenheit or more, so very large numbers of them can be found in the tropical areas of the Pacific Ocean. Corals have hard, limestone skeletons that, after they die, become coral reefs near land. The Great Barrier Reef off the coast of Australia is the largest coral reef in the world. It is more than 1,200 miles long.

CORAL ATOLLS

Charles Darwin, while sailing in the south Pacific in the 1820s, was fascinated by what he called the lagoon islands, what we now know as coral atolls. These are the rings of coral that surround a shallow area of sea known as lagoons. Darwin asked the questions, "Why are these islands usually ring-shaped, and why do they contain a lagoon?" He was always interested in scientific problems, and this was the one he posed. Like all good scientists, he and the others who were with him offered some hypotheses, that is to say, best guesses for answers to the questions he posed. Students can be asked for their hypotheses before they are told about Darwin's, and it is possible that some of them will come up with excellent possible explanations, better ones that Darwin could possibly have suggested. The reason for this is because they have access to scientific data that did not exist in 1820. They may even be able to respond quickly to the two hypotheses proposed by Darwin: (1) that coral rock had built up above sea level on the rims of volcanoes that had emerged from the sea floor and were now below sea level; (2) that coral rock had built up on the edges of sea floor elevations.

With the combined hypotheses of the students and Darwin, ask the question: how do we find out which one is the right one and which ones can be shown to be false? As the problem is being tackled, remind students that the crew of Darwin's time did not have any of the sophisticated instruments or oceanic knowledge of today. Record class proposals for testing the hypotheses. Darwin's crew began the test by measuring the depth of the water on the ocean side of the atoll. They found that the land dropped off quickly and was soon well below the level of the lagoon. Down as far as 180 feet below sea level, they first found almost all coral, then mixtures of coral and other material. Beyond 180 feet, there was no coral of any kind. That discovery proved that coral reefs could not have been built up from the ocean floor, so one hypothesis had to be dropped. What about the other one? Darwin was sure that a volcanic mountain had risen from the ocean floor and rose above sea level. Coral ridges then formed on its edges, and later it gradually sank beneath the level of the sea. As it sank, coral kept forming on the edges until the atolls reached their present form.

Darwin was partly satisfied with his explanation, but he would have liked to see deeper borings made from the lagoon to confirm that volcanic rock existed all the way down to the ocean floor. Other scientists were less convinced. At this stage, the class can be asked again if this is a satisfactory confirmation of the second hypothesis, and their answer, following class discussions, should be recorded. Many years after Darwin's lifetime, borings were made in atolls in the same area that he had investigated. This time, the borings went down through 4,000 feet of limestone and then on through volcanic rock to the ocean floor. The surprise data that emerged was the presence of coral very far below the surface. Knowing that corals cannot live in cold deep water, could there possibly be other explanations? That is always the way of good science, assessing and reassessing what is known in the light of new discoveries, being ready to throw out existing theories if new information proves them to be wrong. In fact, more than one new discovery affected subsequent thinking about atolls. One was the effects of the last ice age on the level of the ocean. All over the world, it dropped about 300 feet during glaciation. These changes did not happen suddenly. They developed over hundreds of thousands of years, and during that time, coral ridge formation could have kept up with sea level changes.

The second discovery that finally resolved the problem of the atolls did not come until about 1970. It was the new and revolutionary awareness that the ocean floor all over the world is constantly in motion in the form of several huge tectonic plates. These plates move along above the molten magma that lies deep down below them, and occasionally a hot spot occurs, a weakness beneath one of these plates that allows huge amounts of magma to escape and build up to the surface of the sea and beyond it to heights of thousands of feet above sea level. As the tectonic plate moves away from the hot spot, it carries away with it this new mountain. A new one then begins to appear above the hot spot, and the older one, now being carried away from the source of heat, begins to cool down. As it cools, it gains weight and sinks. Not until scientists understood the nature of this new phenomenon did they realize that they were dealing with masses of volcanic rock far greater than anything they had seen before. The total weight, say, of the volcanoes that form the islands of Hawaii, which were built up over a hot spot, was so great that as they sank, they depressed the ocean floor by more than a thousand feet. The process was very slow, and the coral animals were able to maintain their ridges during the entire process of the volcanoes' slowly cooling and sinking.

Thus, while the changes in sea level may well have affected the formation of atolls, the main causes were the hot spots and the movements of tectonic plates. So, almost 150 years after his initial investigation, Darwin's scientific problem was finally solved. There is plenty of information on tectonic plates and coral atolls, and teachers may wish to pose additional questions about them and have students develop and test the hypotheses they advance. Teachers can ask questions about how we know that tectonic plates move all the time. Students can be asked to figure out some way of measuring them. They can be reminded that we use GPS (the Global Positioning System) in our cars to check out where we are, and the potential of this system can then be explained. Can we not also use it to tell us where the tectonic plates are at any given time and how fast they are moving?

Figure 7.1 Galileo Used a Pendulum Like This in His Experiments

PENDULUM CLOCKS

Earlier in this chapter, it was pointed out that it took more than a thousand years to find a theory that would explain gravity. The person who first proposed this theory was Galileo, and his ideas will be examined later in this chapter. Galileo lived about 400 years ago and, while his ideas about gravity are the ones that are best known about him, his first important discovery, which concerned pendulum clocks, was just as important. One Sunday in 1583, at a church service in the cathedral of Pisa, his hometown,

Galileo became fascinated with a lamp above his head that kept swinging backward and forward. Sometimes the swings were small, at other times quite big, but it seemed to him that each swing always took the same amount of time. There were no instruments in existence at that time to measure small changes of time, so the only measure he could use was his blood pulse. This he did, and so, during the long sermon to which he had to listen, he discovered that 60 beats of his pulse always coincided with the same number of swings. The length of the swings did not seem to affect the result.

Soon afterward, Galileo designed a pendulum and began to conduct experiments to see if his conclusions were correct. He used different weights, different lengths of rope, and different lengths of swings for each change in the other two variables. The result of these experiments confirmed his first discovery and added two more: (1) the time taken is always the same whether a pendulum swings in a small arc or a big one; (2) changing weights at the end of the pendulum makes no difference in the time as long as the length remains the same; (3) changing the length of the pendulum rope changes the time of the swing. Later, exact measurements were made to determine how different lengths of rope determined the time of swings. For the first time in history, there was now an instrument that could measure small changes of time. It was not long before a pendulum with a one-second swing was designed and used as the standard measure of that unit of time.

Pendulum study provides one of the simplest yet most valuable experiences of the experimental method in science. Students can be given the generalized task of designing a pendulum that will have a one-second swing time, and that the length of the pendulum must be one foot. They can even have the added task of how to find out if temperature changes affect the time. Questions can be raised by the teacher as needed. Playground swings can be employed for the experimental work if students think they will help.

Once the influences of the various variables are understood, students should be presented with one of the great problems from Galileo's time that affected travel and trade around the world. Portuguese sailors had been exploring the Atlantic, Indian, and Pacific oceans for the previous century, but they had a major, unsolved problem as soon as they were very far from land. They could tell their latitude using a sextant or similar instrument, but only an accurate measurement of time could tell them their longitude, that is to say, the distance from their port of departure. Some explanation of latitude and longitude may be needed here.

As long as they sailed around Africa and kept close to land, they could go as far as India or the islands we now know as Indonesia. It was much more difficult for Columbus on the long voyage to America, but he succeeded because he followed a well-known ocean current that led to North America. It was not so easy for Magellan, who sailed around South

America and had great difficulty crossing the Pacific Ocean. A large sum of money was offered as a prize to anyone who could invent a clock that would provide time for ships, and Galileo proposed using a pendulum clock to meet this need. Although his proposal was not accepted in his lifetime, many people subsequently tried to use his idea in different kinds of pendulum clocks. None of them succeeded. A very different type of clock finally won the prize more than 200 years after Galileo's death. Have students figure out why the pendulum clock failed. Have them also read the book *Longitude* to find out the kind of clock that did work and why it took so long to invent it.

GRAVITY

Understanding gravity, as was pointed out above, took a long time, more than a thousand years. The Greek philosopher Aristotle, who lived more than 2,000 years ago, was quite sure that he knew certain things about gravity, but he based them on what he called common sense, or personal judgment. Aristotle was a philosopher, not a scientist, but his ideas were widely accepted. Then, around the year 1600, Galileo became convinced that Aristotle's ideas about gravity, namely that heavier objects fall to earth quicker than lighter ones, were quite wrong. He set about proving his convictions experimentally. It should be explained to students that the prevailing view of the universe at this time was that the earth did not move in any way, either on its axis or around the sun. The stars, sun, moon, and planets, it was claimed, all moved around the earth, but the earth stayed in one place all the time.

Once again, students can be given the two viewpoints and asked to design an experiment that will prove which one is right before being told what others had done. Galileo said that if he dropped two objects—one light, like a feather, and another quite heavy, like a brick—from the top of the tower of Pisa, both would reach the ground at the same time. He also said that both objects would probably fall behind the tower rather than in front of it. Very few people believed him. It is not clear if Galileo actually carried out the experiment, but he insisted he was right on both points. One or two did try to conduct his experiment, but the objects did not reach the ground at exactly the same time. Why was this, and why did Galileo say that the objects would fall behind the tower rather than in front of it? This is a good starter for the subject of gravity. The class can be asked if Galileo was right on the two points of view he held. They can also be asked to explain the second point. Why do you suppose no one believed him when he made the two claims about the falling objects? The answer is that from a high point like the top of the tower of Pisa, any object would be displaced from a vertical drop by the rotation of the earth on its axis.

Figure 7.2 The 184-Foot-High Leaning Tower of Pisa

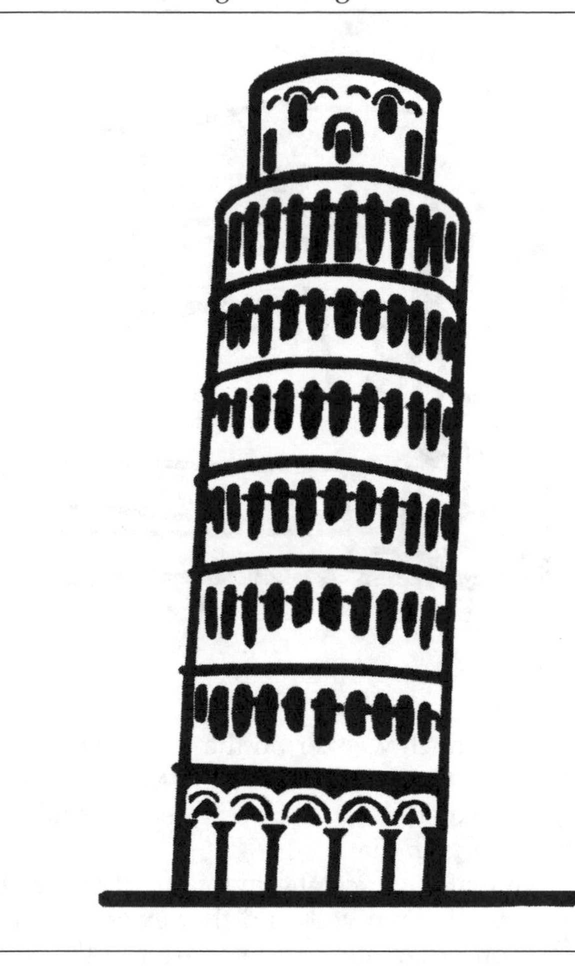

Almost 400 years after the time of Galileo, the subject of who was right about the action of gravity was still being asked. So, when David Scott and Jim Irwin walked on the moon during the *Apollo 15* mission in the summer of 1971, they were asked to conduct an experiment about it. With cameras recording the event, David Scott, with a feather in his left hand and a geologic hammer in his right, dropped the two objects simultaneously. They reached the ground at the same time. Students can be told that the strength of gravity on the moon is one sixth that of the earth, and asked if that was why the experiment worked there. If not, then what? The answer is that there was no air resistance. However, the fact of the lesser gravity having no effect needs to be pursued. Let students figure it out for themselves even if it takes a lot of time. The record of the moon demonstration is available today from NASA or via the Internet. Does gravity always have the

Figure 7.3 Astronaut Jim Irwin of *Apollo 15* Saluting Beside the Flag

same power? Why is it so much weaker on the moon compared with the earth? How would living on the moon be different from life here? The class can be asked to design an experiment to show the same result as Scott's on the moon. Let students work on that.

They can also be told that the force of gravity is determined by distance and the masses of the objects involved, and that every object exercises a force of gravity. The moon's diameter is one quarter of the earth's, yet its gravity is one sixth of the earth's. Why is it not a quarter? When I am walking or skiing, do I push the earth away from me each time I move? Acceleration of falling objects is another major idea in gravity. If I drop a stone from the 10th floor and it takes three seconds to reach the ground, how long will it take if I drop it from the 20th or 30th floor? How can I find out? How far do I have to go from the earth to escape the effect of its gravity? Is there any place in the universe where gravity is zero? Why doesn't the moon fall to the earth? NASA is concerned about people being in space for long periods of time and feeling weightless during that time. Why? Are they really weightless? For a possible trip to Mars, this is especially important, so NASA is conducting an experiment at present, putting mice into orbit for an extended period of time in a capsule that has the same gravity as Mars. How do they design such a capsule?

Students at the upper high school level should be left to sort out all of these problems on their own. They have access to computers and libraries and they can do their own research. There are numerous data banks available on the Internet, and a glance at the Google site illustrates the variety that exists. A science teacher in Colorado conducted all of his high school science classes in the way being recommended here, namely, letting students do all the work themselves. The teacher was a consultant to whom they could address questions when they encountered an impasse. It was both a popular and a successful approach. Outstanding achievements were the outcomes year after year.

This approach to teaching is not common because it requires a change of attitude on the part of students as well as teachers. After years of listening to lectures, it is easy to think that this is the proper way to learn anything. At the University of British Columbia, Canada, future high school science teachers enter the Faculty of Education with a science degree and take courses in methods of teaching science. A few years ago, one such class was taught by a professor who wanted to use in class the same method he wanted his students to employ in schools. It was the same approach that the Colorado teacher used. He said nothing as the class met, but he had organized his lab into a series of displays and questions. This went on for several days, and gradually a wave of resentment built up among the students. They felt they were not learning anything and they decided that the lecturer was either incompetent or just lazy. At the end of the second week of classes, they launched a formal protest to the dean, stating that nothing had been taught by their lecturer in their first six class sessions and requesting a change of lecturer. It took considerable efforts by the dean and other faculty members to convince them that they were being given the best possible methods for teaching science.

SATELLITES

This chapter is titled "What Keeps Satellites Above Earth?" It is a question that raises a number of additional aspects of gravity and, as before, they can be understood by students as a result of their own efforts. Nothing keeps satellites above earth. In fact, they are always falling back toward earth in what is called *free fall*, a condition in which gravity is not being resisted by anything so there is a feeling of weightlessness. Gravity is only felt when something resists it. The resistance can be a chair on which I sit, or my feet, which press against the surface of the earth. A person on a roller coaster can have the same experience of weightlessness as an astronaut if he or she is temporarily lifted off a seat and the resistance of the seat is removed. It is difficult for students to understand that there is only one force operating on things in the air and that force is gravity. If an object is tossed into the air at the right speed, it will follow a path that matches the curvature of the earth, but it will be steadily falling to earth all the time it is in the air. However, the earth is curving away from it because it is always rotating on its axis, so the object stays at a distance above the earth even as it keeps falling. What speed is necessary, then, to make this happen?

The earth's surface curves downward by approximately 5 meters for every 8,000 meters of its surface. Students can stay with the metric figures or change them into feet and yards. So for an object to orbit the earth, it must travel horizontally a distance of 8,000 meters for every 5 meters of vertical fall. It so happens that the vertical distance that a horizontally launched object would fall in its first second is approximately 5 meters, so its speed must be 8,000 meters per second. As it travels a distance of 8,000 meters in one second, it will drop approximately 5 meters towards the earth, yet it will remain the same distance above the earth because the earth curves at the same rate that the object falls. If the object is sent out at a speed greater than 8,000 meters per second, it would orbit the earth in an elliptical path. A shuttle at 200 miles above the earth has to travel at more than 17,000 miles per hour. This takes it around the earth in 1.5 hours. A satellite, 22,000 miles above earth, has a speed half that of the shuttle and, because it takes 24 hours to circle the earth, it seems to be in the same place all the time because the earth is rotating at the same speed.

There are some questions that can be asked to help clarify the fundamental facts about feeling weightless. They are useful summary activities for class discussions: Are astronauts free of the influence of gravity? You are in a plane that is out of control and is in free fall toward the ground. You go to pick up your parachute, but it is located behind a two-ton box. What should you do? Space is a vacuum and has no air resistance, so there cannot be any gravity in it. Astronauts are far from the earth's surface, so the influence of gravity on them is minimal.

RELATIVITY

There is one more aspect of gravity that should be included. It is relativity, a view of gravity made famous by the work of Albert Einstein. Only the basic idea behind it need be included here as a subject for discussion. The theory of relativity says that nothing in the entire universe is absolutely stationary. Everything is constantly moving. Einstein introduced his ideas about relativity through two very simple stories. In the first, he described a man who was busy in his lab measuring gravity by sliding weights down an inclined plane and recording what happened each time he changed the angle of the plane. Unknown to him, a trickster had entered his lab when he was not there and installed a mechanism beneath the floor, enabling him to make the entire lab rotate at a fast rate around a point in the middle of the room. When this mechanism was switched on during an experiment, the researcher saw his weights slide off to one side while he himself felt a strange force pushing him against the wall. His measurements became useless. What is the relevance of this story? It represented to some extent the earth's movements around the sun, which affect the accuracy of measurements that we might make on earth. As long as the researcher worked in an isolated spot and ignored the fact that his lab was speeding through space at more than 20,000 miles an hour, his findings might seem to be accurate. In reality, they were not, because the earth's movements change any value of gravity that he might have calculated.

Einstein's second story imagined a few people sitting in an elevator at the top of a very tall building. There are no windows in the elevator. Suddenly the supporting cable breaks, but it happens so gently that the occupants are unaware that they are hurtling down to the ground. For them, the rules of gravity do not seem to exist. An observer outside the elevator sees a very different condition. In Einstein's mind, the transfer of this story to satellites and planets is a simple one, and it shows the basic fact of everything being relative, accurate within a defined range, inside the elevator, but always relative to other events when looked at by someone outside the elevator. Einstein did not live to see space travel. He died in 1955, two years before the first Russian-manned satellite, Sputnik, went up. However, Einstein knew all about space travel because so much of his work was related to action in space. In this imaginary story of the elevator, he says that we can think of the elevator as a satellite flying through space with people living in it all the time. Is that a good way to live, assuming that the satellite carried all the things we need? They would never know any other kind of gravity than the one they experienced. It would be a gravity that is completely different from the one seen by observers outside their elevator.

Returning to the elevator story above, the subject of the chapter can be concluded with several questions: If someone drops a handkerchief or a watch, what happens to them? If one person pushes another, what happens? What weight would show if someone stood on a bathroom scale in the elevator?

REFERENCES

Dewey, J. (1916). *Democracy and education*. New York: Macmillan.

Matthews, M. R. (2000). *Time for science education*. New York: Kluwer Academic.

Sobel, D. (1996). *Longitude: The true story of a lone genius who solved the greatest scientific problem of his time*. New York: Penguin Books.

Zee, A. (1989). *Einstein's universe: Gravity at work and play*. Oxford, UK: Oxford University Press.

PART III

Teacher Skills

Learning Communities

8

Falling Empire and Rising Democracy

LEARNING COMMUNITIES

> *The demand is clear. . . . [L]ife requires knowledge and thinking skills that transcend the traditional disciplines. Such understanding demands that we draw on multiple sources of expertise to capture multi-dimensional phenomena, to produce complex explanations, or to solve intricate problems. The educational corollary of this condition is that preparing young adults to be full participants in contemporary society demands that we foster their capacity to draw on multiple sources of knowledge to build deep understanding.*[1]

How will students learn to participate responsibly in a vigorous, authentic democracy if they do not have an opportunity to practice doing it, to grow their dendrites, synapses, and neural networks for doing it? Academic learning communities provide this opportunity.

What is a learning community? It can be any group, small or large, that learns together. Why learn together? Many research studies have found significant academic and social benefits for students who study, think, problem solve, create, and reflect together. Compared with students not in learning communities, their retention is higher, persistence is higher, achievement is greater, and satisfaction is stronger.[2]

Many schools (K–12) and colleges have students work together in learning communities to help their students better accomplish their academic goals (to be successful and confident learners) and their personal goals (to make friends at school or on campus and have a social life connected to the school or campus). Learning communities can provide rich academic and social benefits for students in K–12 as well as for students in higher education. Older students also benefit from learning communities.[3]

A Falling Empire

The traditional system of education, which is based on instructor-centered, stand-alone courses of unrelated subjects and students working alone, might be an empire that needs to fall. Instead, a democracy invites educators and students to do what the research finds is necessary for deep learning, for creative and critical thinking, and for igniting the innate motivation of the human brain and the potential of every student: Everyone needs to be an active participant.

In 1995, John Tagg and Robert Barr introduced the "learning paradigm" to replace the traditional "instruction paradigm."[4] The learning paradigm is a learning community paradigm. Since a learning community is more likely to ignite students' potential than the traditional classroom, perhaps we should think about having more learning communities throughout our educational institutions, from kindergarten through graduate school.

Unlike in the traditional classroom, learning communities focus on student engagement. This is essential because engagement seems to be the best predictor of student success.

MODELS OF LEARNING COMMUNITIES

Taking learning communities to a higher level, some high schools and colleges are offering learning community courses. The guiding concepts across all learning community course models are that students are actively engaged in working collaboratively and in interrelating different subjects. The models vary; how faculty prepare for and conduct them vary; and how institutions select, organize, and advertise them vary. Seminal work by Faith Gabelnick, Jean MacGregor, Roberta S. Matthews, and Barbara Smith and further work by Gillies Malnarich and Emily Lardner detail these variations and guide newcomers through the process of learning-community course development.[5]

Linked or Clustered Courses

One model is to have two separate courses, for example, a U.S. history course and a communication course, offered as "linked courses." Taking these classes together gives students the opportunity to know their classmates better than if they had only one class together. Further, the two teachers coordinate their assignments, for example, examining the relationship between intercultural communication and the civil rights or immigration movements in the United States. When three or more courses are linked in this way, they are called a "cluster." A third course that might be added to this cluster could be an economics course.

Freshman Interest Groups

In this variation, usually at the college level, three or more courses are linked and advertised as a Freshman Interest Group (FIG), but all the students do not need to co-register for all the courses, and the instructors do not coordinate their subjects. The purpose is to help students, as they begin high school or college, to be part of a community, which has a positive emotional effect and also gives the students the important opportunity to study and learn together. For example, the smaller cohort that does co-register for all the courses in the FIG has one or more separate meetings a week, led by an instructor or an experienced student. These meetings, sometimes called seminars, give that cohort, as a community, the opportunity to focus intentionally on interrelating or integrating the linked subjects more deeply and also to experience a richer social environment than if the students studied alone.

Coordinated Studies Programs

In this team-taught model, two or more teachers create a multicourse program. Students register for the whole program, which might be the full load for both the faculty and students. For example, at a college with a quarter system, a full load for both faculty and students might be 15 credits (three 5-credit courses). The teachers, from three different disciplines, will team teach. Because this is their full load, they will all be present in every class. In the previous term, they will have planned the integration of the subjects and figured out who will do what when. Of course, these plans can change during the term.

In another configuration, there might be only two courses in a two-person team-taught coordinated studies program. Both the teachers and the students would, then, also have other, stand-alone courses to complete their schedules.

Coordinated studies programs are organized around a theme. For example, a literature and history coordinated studies course had this theme: "Created Equal: Civil Rights in the United States."

Students are actively involved in critical- and creative-thinking projects, conduct and present research together, and participate in seminars (student-led discussions on specific topics and readings). There can also be "fishbowl seminars" in which, while students observe and listen, the faculty reflect on and discuss their thinking about the course theme. Sometimes a small group of students do the fishbowl seminar while the faculty and the other students observe and listen. There is a discussion session after each fishbowl seminar to deepen the learning.

Moreover, team teaching is an extremely effective faculty development opportunity in that faculty observe each other teaching, can give each other feedback, and, in general, can be mentors and coaches for each other. Faculty schedule time to do this feedback and coaching interactivity, as well as have private, non-fishbowl discussions in their self-scheduled out-of-class meetings. This is one of the most—if not *the* most—productive and intellectually satisfying forms of faculty development.

For information about this and other models, see the Washington Center for Improving the Quality of Undergraduate Education Web site.[6]

Other Research

The Interdisciplinary Studies Project is a research project at Project Zero at the Harvard Graduate School of Education and is led by Howard Gardner. The researchers are studying both high school and college interdisciplinary education and are examining pedagogical and curriculum design challenges and opportunities. Information about their research is on their Web site at http://www.pz.harvard.edu/Research/GoodWorkIS.htm.

There is also currently in progress a study by V. Tinto and C. Engstrom for the Lumina Foundation of Education on underprepared college students.

Student Feedback

In feedback sessions with outside researchers, students in learning community programs have talked about their experiences in these programs.

1. "There's time for students to talk with each other to figure things out and solve problems."
2. "There's time for reflection. There's no time in 50-minute classes."
3. "You retain more. It's richer."
4. "It's easier for students who heard something from the teacher to explain it to someone else in class because they are at the same level."
5. "Learning and discovering together produces deeper learning."
6. "In an integrated [linked] class, my mind is stimulated by thinking of, and connecting to, what's going on in the other class."

7. "Conversation is great. Listening to teachers talking to each other [in their fishbowl seminar] I learned more that day than any other day."
8. "Even just having the opportunity to turn to a neighbor and see what that person thinks helps you retain and understand."
9. "It's a safe place where you feel secure enough to share your unique self and ideas."
10. Quoting someone else, a student said, "The point of education is not that every topic is touched but that every student is touched."

Feedback From Students in One Coordinated Studies Program

A coordinated studies learning community program at North Seattle Community, taught by Jane Lister Reis (communications) and Carol Hamilton (English), had the theme of "Rememberings: The Roots of Our Voices." The course focused on "Learning Activities That Supported the Development of an Authentic and Inclusive Voice." Students read six books, wrote three papers, and had weekly seminars and seminar papers, relational learning activities (e.g., "Families as Our First Cultural School" and "Listening Quiz"), a final portfolio (which asked students to "write reflectively about voice, interdisciplinary learning, etc."), and a final discussion with questions generated by the students (e.g., "How could sexism or racism affect listening and communication? What about indirect racism?" "What is one contiguous factor shared between all the main characters in our books which is a main foundation of their voice and why?").

The following are some excerpts from the students' final portfolios:

1. The environment of our class was very safe. It felt like a family, who was caring, respectful, understanding, and not judgmental. It's easier to speak one's mind in a safe environment. As I got better at critical reading of our text and analysis, my confidence grew in seminars. I also became more active in seminars. But the active participation in seminars would not have grown if I hadn't felt safe in expressing my opinions. Due to this safe environment my skills as a speaker in class also improved. Now I tend to speak up in my other classes as well. The culture of this class was composed of caring and respecting one another. (Manpreet)

2. I have said many times that these classes [learning communities] are a real representation of how the real world works. In our personal and professional lives, we must be able to interact with diversity and see value in all people involved. This style teaches us to be better communicators in all areas not only a few. (Dave)

3. I feel like I entered the class with a locked compartment of thoughts and ideas I didn't really know how to get to, and the seminar discussions provided the key. Once my opinions were freed, the thoughts and insights

of my classmates provided the stimuli I needed to develop those thoughts and ideas of mine, blend them with the insights of others, and turn my new thoughts into verbal and written expressions. The seminars allowed me to not only listen to others' voices but to have my voice listened to as well. It was truly a freeing experience.

I feel I didn't just acquire knowledge; I experienced learning. And that experience spilled over into my essay writing, which gave me a chance to really reflect on my voice in the midst of these other voices and allow new insights and perceptions to emerge from the process.

The learning experience has changed my thought process about school and my direction insofar as I am now considering an interdisciplinary studies program. Just the interdisciplinary [aspect] seems a much more honest approach to learning, for isn't that what life is all about? It's not as if we can isolate each facet of our lives from touching the others. And hopefully when things do touch—be they experiences, struggles, ideas, or even people—understanding is expanded. If life is about connecting, then it seems things should be connected. It's a concept I see now as important in learning as it is in living. (Beth)

"The role learning communities can play in the high stakes endeavor of preparing students for an education of quality—if these efforts are scaled up and become an initiative embraced by an entire institution—is a conversation worth pursuing and a practice worth doing. . . . It is our work to figure out how we can support and challenge students—and ourselves—so they can meet our greater expectations while realizing their own."[7]

THE "ASK THEM" METHOD FOR ASSESSMENT AND ENGAGED LEARNING

This section shows how assessment, faculty collaboration, and student participation work in a coordinated studies learning community program. (See Chapter 9 for more details about, and examples of, assessment.)[8]

A number of years ago, a *Shoe* cartoon showed, in the first frame, an older man in a suit at a lunch counter with pen in hand ready to write on a sheet of paper. Addressing the woman behind the counter, he says, "Let me get that recipe." She responds, "Sure, it's easy. . . . First you boil water." In the second frame he interrupts her by holding up his hand and saying, "Whoa," to which she answers, "Okay. . . ." In the last frame he is writing down what she is saying: "1. Put water in pan. 2. Put pan on burner. 3. Turn burner on high."

The term for where students are, for what they already know and can understand, is *ceiling level*. Like Shoe, we need to start with "1. Put water in pan . . ." if that's where the students are. The challenge is that some students are below the ceiling level at which we've decided to start, and some are above it. If they don't tell us "Whoa," or "Giddy up," then what?

Usually when we find a great range of ceiling levels in a class, we have a problem meeting the needs of all the students, especially those at the top and bottom ends. Needless to say, in a coordinated studies learning community program with many more students than in a regular stand-alone course, this range and this problem are exacerbated. But the assessment-teaching method described here not only lets us know what the range is, it also, by its very nature and function, mitigates the problem.

How can we find out where they are? We can ask them. It's not only educationally sound to ask, it also creates a democratic environment that is opposite to the one in the traditional classroom empire in which students are not invited to do their own creative and critical thinking. It's also invigorating and engaging for the teachers as well as for the students.

"Ask Them": Assessment in a Coordinated Studies Learning Community Program, "The Fall of Empires"

Here is an example of using the "Ask Them" assessment approach in a coordinated studies program that was the full load for four faculty and 95 students. This assessment method, however, can be used in any classroom, in any subject, at any level; and whenever and wherever it is used, the students actively participate and collaborate. Faculty can also use the "Ask Them" approach for teaching as well as for assessment, as explained below.

In the fall of 1991, three faculty members at North Seattle Community College—Jim Harnish (history), Tom Kerns (philosophy), and myself (English)—were scheduled to team teach a coordinated studies program, "The Fall of Empires," focusing on the Roman empire and the Soviet empire (then in the process of falling), with implications for the United States. We taught with York Wong, a guest faculty member (history) from The Evergreen State College in Olympia, Washington, a leading institution in the coordinated studies movement. Before the term began, we thought about what the students' levels of knowledge, their different ceiling levels, might be. We didn't have any idea how much, if anything, they knew about Rome and the then-falling USSR. We didn't want to direct the course above their ceiling level or below it, either. We wanted to use a constructivist approach, starting where they were and then constructing from there. We thought we would know how to proceed if we asked them what they knew.

We wanted to raise the activity, interactivity, and contribution level to a high pitch. We wanted to spread a wide net and catch everything that was there. So, after the pleasantries and program business, on the first day of class, a three-hour session—since it was everyone's full load, we had our own schedule—we wrote on the chalkboard, "What do you know about the Roman empire?" We asked them to write individually for a few minutes so they could consult their own mind-store of knowledge. Then we asked them to get together with two or three other students, introduce themselves, and share their ideas. In small groups, everyone can actively participate in a short period of time. In the meanwhile, Tom readied a Mac with an LCD (a machine that projects what's on the computer monitor onto a screen for class viewing). We asked how many groups had finished sharing their ideas and, when most had, we asked the class, "What did you come up with?" As they called out their responses, Tom recorded them verbatim, until a list of 38 items appeared on the screen, including "brought an enforced peace on other cultures," "two distinct classes of people, aristocracy and slaves? [sic]," "excelled in administration and engineering," and "ruled with a military dictatorship." We felt excitement stirring in the class.

The key to their excited and ever-increasing participation was our accepting every contribution as they gave it—even those we considered incorrect. We included those just as we included those we believed were correct. We were not teaching during this activity; we were assessing. We were also acting on our belief that merely telling students correct answers wouldn't produce authentic, internalized understanding and learning; for that they must actively participate and do their own figuring out and thinking. The students would have many opportunities to correct their own mistakes during the course, whereas our prematurely critiquing, correcting, and co-opting their contributions, before they had the opportunity to go through the learning process, would shut them up, cause them to disengage. A study at McGill University Lifelong Learning Institute in Montreal, Canada, concluded, "A knowledgeable [teacher] may dominate the discourse, unintentionally overwhelming [students] with information and inhibit further discussion."[9] This study was of older students, but it is, of course, just as true for younger students.

However, if one student disagreed with another, we put a question mark next to that contribution and let it stand. For example, when one student said all of Western civilization is based on the Roman culture but others disagreed, we told the students that during the course that point would be clarified. This approach validates both the contributor and the critic (either or neither of whom might be right) and demonstrates that the program is all about deepening our study with respect for every person and with open-minded consideration of every idea. We were modeling community learning.

The next question was, "What do you know about the Soviet Union?" Same process: individual writing, small-group sharing, large-group collating. This time they had 57 items, including "we have a limited history background of Russia/Stalin/Lenin," "tremendous inefficiency in agriculture and industry," "there is a cultural revolution going on now," "much of Eastern Europe was gained in WWII or by invasion." Now the excitement and energy were even more palpable. Next, after making those initial personal connections at whatever ceiling level each student had, we asked one of the program's key questions: "What characterizes a society that is in decline?" Same process. At the end, they had 29 dynamite characteristics, including "economic problems," "dissension leading to revolt," "military heavy-handedness, overextension, not welcome, invasive," "the ruling class/government oppresses society." By this time, the three of us were congratulating ourselves for having made this such a wonderful class. But all we had done was ask them what they knew and invited them to figure it out themselves.

What had happened through this process was that the students had given themselves and each other pretty much the content of a lecture that, otherwise, we would have had to deliver. We liked this better: a class full of students heated to the chase of knowledge and teachers doing a good job of standing out of their way. Not that everything they said was true nor did they include everything we thought was important. But the ideas were seminal—and the community building was powerful. As noted above, they would be able, as we went along, to correct any errors or resolve any disagreements.

Now they were ready to make the connection between what they already knew and the new things they were going to learn. We were also going to invite them to collaborate in shaping the course. The final question that day was, "What questions do you have about all this?" Our intention was to have them answer all their questions by the end of the program. They had 21 questions, including "Where are WE headed?" "Who specifically suffers in a decline?" "Who prospers in a decline?" "Is there a set pattern in decline?" "What rises from decline?" "What can we do in our incline to prevent a decline?" And one wag asked, "Where can we go to live if we have a decline?"

By the end of the term, the students had answered their initial questions and many more besides and had constructed an authentic and deep understanding of why and how empires fall.

Side Benefits

The side benefits of this assessment method are many. Asking students what they know tells us where they are as a class and the range of their knowledge or ceiling levels. It also tells them we respect what they know. Moreover, it helps students tell each other what they know, in the end raising everyone's ceiling level. In addition, this assessment method sets the tone of the class as one of community and collaboration, tolerance of others, and open-minded inquiry. It unleashes students' energy and intelligence. We always knew they were energetic and smart—but did we know they were *that* energetic and smart? It motivates students to search for more knowledge and understanding. It also makes the faculty very happy because we see our students enthusiastically engaged in learning.

These benefits and more are reflected in the feedback from students in other learning communities (pages 152–154).

Pitfalls and Troubleshooting

Does the approach always work this well? Yes, it does—if certain pitfalls are avoided. One potential pitfall already noted is disputes between students. Troubleshooting advice is to accept every student's contribution without criticism or co-option and without allowing, at this initial point in the course, prolonged disputes between students. A way to cut off such disputes is to say that this question will be explored during the course; and, of course, then everyone's curiosity is aroused about what the answer will be.

Another potential pitfall is that students may be at very different ceiling levels. What if some students who are advanced in their knowledge contribute lots more—or more sophisticated—answers? What if they contribute their knowledge with haughty superiority, not in the spirit of community and collaboration? What if some advanced students, throwing in their answers with naively high and eager spirit, dominate the discussion? Students with less knowledge and/or less confidence might feel intimidated. What do we do with these disparities?

Remember that, at each step in the process, students begin with individual writing so that each student can collect his or her thoughts; then they proceed to small-group discussions before the whole-group debriefing. The intent of the small groups is, first, to give everyone the opportunity to be as active as possible and, second, to have the group members teach and learn from each other. Also, small groups are effective for peer tutoring, which is a powerful way for students to learn.

Furthermore, it is important for students to know that by participating in small-group interaction they are developing skills and qualities that are the most sought after by employers, including communication skills, interpersonal skills, and teamwork skills.

Small groups of three or four give faculty the opportunity to make relatively unobtrusive but helpful corrections before the whole-group discussion. Thus, while the students are discussing in their small groups, we are able to circulate and politely intrude ("Is it okay if I sit in for a bit?"). If we observe someone dominating, we have the opportunity to ask whether everyone has had a chance to talk since there are only x minutes left. We can, if the situation seems seriously out of control, even go around the small group and ask each person to tell us, because we're curious and interested (and we really are), what he or she thinks. We might not be able to give every group such full attention; but if we scan the groups quickly, we can usually identify those with a dominating member and can intervene in those groups first.

Another benefit of small-group discussion is that students might hear some new and interesting ideas from their group mates. As a result, during the whole-group discussion, we can call on students to contribute either their own ideas *or* ideas they heard from others in their small group. Thus, everyone can contribute an interesting point, minimizing a potentially intimidating contrast between those with many or advanced ideas and those with few or undeveloped ideas. Moreover, as another side benefit, whenever I've called on specific students and asked for either their own idea or another idea they heard in their small group, they almost invariably, after their first experience of having their contribution accepted and written on the board without criticism, become active participants in class discussion.

This approach reveals the wide and deep array of what students know and understand, but it does not provide a specific measurement or accounting of what each individual student knows. This is not individual assessment. This approach assesses the class as a whole. Thus, its aim is not to identify which student knows what, but to assess the general level of knowledge. We want to assess where they are after having learned from each other. We want to assess their collective and collaborative community-constructed knowledge.

This approach is also a useful pretest/posttest assessment. After the first day of the course, we printed and distributed the four lists they had come up with on that first day, and we often referred to the items on these lists during the term. At the end, we pointed out that if we asked these same questions again, they would now have such long lists it wouldn't be feasible to write them down. They pulled out their lists and read them over. By reflecting on where they were at the start and where they were now, the initial assessment then became part of their final self-evaluation. Assessing the knowledge students bring with them into a course reaps a gold mine of benefits. This assessment approach helps create a learning community and, as a part of the course, is a vital, enriching process.

Evaluation

Throughout, there are opportunities to evaluate each student by whatever methods the faculty prefer. For example, there can be tests, papers, projects, and/or reports. The method we used was created by Jim Harnish. A week before the test, students brought in test questions, which was an engaging and effective review activity. In class, they discussed and synthesized their questions in small groups. We collected their synthesized questions, synthesized the questions from all the groups, and added whatever we thought was missing. All the questions were listed on a study sheet for the students, and they knew that the test would be composed only of selected questions from the study sheet. They then had a week to study together. In studying all the questions, they were doing a full review of the course. We also used some class time to answer questions they had about the test and about any items on the study sheet. For the test, we selected several questions from the study sheet and let them use their notes and books. After the tests were graded, students could retake the whole test or parts of it.

Yes, everyone could get an A or a B. In other words, everyone could increase his or her learning and test-taking skills. This approach helps every student get on a more level playing field by giving all students an opportunity to fulfill their potential as learners and test takers.

This approach can be used in any and every class, whether a stand-alone or a learning community class; and it never fails to motivate students to study because they know, especially those who have not been successful test takers, that they have it in their power to succeed.

Making a First Connection

One other point needs consideration. What if the subject or theme of the course is something we think is sufficiently misunderstood or unfamiliar or new that assessment of what the students initially know would probably not lead to rich feedback or information? In this case, it would be more important to prepare students to learn something new than to assess their current knowledge. In this case, the question needs to stimulate each student to think about a related personal base (an idea, feeling, experience) and to bring that into the classroom. As discussed and exemplified on pages 71–72, "No-Fail First-Stage Learning Tasks," having a personal base (neural structure) upon which to construct the new learning is a critical first step in learning.

IGNITING STUDENT POTENTIAL

As the natural learning research (Chapter 2), brain research (Chapter 3), and the four chapters in Part II seem to show, the most galvanizing force for learning is already inside the students—a natural, innate ability and motivation to think, figure things out, discover, explore, and create. Moreover, as the student feedback (pages 152–154) also seems to show, their potential as learners is actualized most productively and satisfyingly in a community of learners. The invitation to participate in an active and interactive learning community in any and every classroom, whether in a stand-alone class or in an integrated program, gives students the opportunity to fulfill their potential to be thinkers and learners. This experience is even richer when students have the opportunity to participate in an interdisciplinary environment.

NOTES

1. Mansilla, V. B. (2005, January/February). Assessing student work at disciplinary crossroads. *Change, 37*(1), 14–21.

2. Harvard Graduate School of Education. (2006). Interdisciplinary Studies Project, Project Zero. Retrieved July 6, 2006, from http://www.pz.harvard.edu/Research/GoodWorkIS.htm

MacGregor, J., & Smith, B. L. (2005, May/June). Where are learning communities now? National leaders take stock. *About Campus, 10*(2), 8.

Learning Communities National Resource Center. (2006). Retrieved July 6, 2006, from http://learningcommons.evergreen.edu

Taylor, K., Moore, W. S., MacGregor, J., & Lindblad, J. (2003). *Learning community research and assessment: What we know now*. National Learning Communities Project Monograph Series. Olympia, WA: The Evergreen State College, Washington Center for Improving the Quality of Undergraduate Education, in cooperation with the American Association for Higher Education.

3. Brady, E. M., Holt, S. R., & Welt, B. (2003). Peer teaching in lifelong learning institutes. *Educational Gerontology: An International Journal, 29*(10), 851–868.

4. Barr, R. B., & Tagg, J. (1995, November/December). From teaching to learning: A new paradigm for undergraduate education. *Change, 27*, 12–25.

5. Gabelnick, F., MacGregor, J. L., Matthews, R. S., & Smith, B. L. (1990). Learning communities: Creating connections among students, faculty and disciplines. In *New directions for teaching and learning* (Vol. 41). San Francisco: Jossey-Bass.

Malnarich, G., & Lardner, E. D. (2003, Winter). *Designing integrated learning for students: A heuristic for teaching, assessment, and curriculum design*. (Washington Center for Improving the Quality of Undergraduate Education Occasional Paper No. 1). Olympia, WA: The Washington Center for Improving the Quality of Undergraduate Education.

6. Learning Communities National Resource Center. (2006). Retrieved July 6, 2006, from http://learningcommons.evergreen.edu

7. Malnarich, G. (2005). *The pedagogy of possibilities: Developmental education, college-level students, and learning communities*. National Learning Communities Project Monograph Series. Olympia, WA: The Evergreen State College, Washington Center for Improving the Quality of Undergraduate Education, in cooperation with the American Association for Higher Education, p. 67.

8. Adapted from "Ask them," Learning Communities National Resource Center. (2006). Retrieved July 6, 2006, from http://learningcommons.evergreen.edu

9. Brady, E. M., et al. (2003).

REFERENCES

Barr, R. B., & Tagg, J. (1995, November/December). From teaching to learning: A new paradigm for undergraduate education. *Change, 27*, 12–25.

Brady, E. M., Holt, S. R., & Welt, B. (2003). Peer teaching in lifelong learning institutes. *Educational Gerontology: An International Journal, 29*(10), 851–868.

Brookfield, S. D., & Preskill, S. (1999). *Discussion as a way of teaching: Tools and techniques for democratic classrooms*. San Francisco: Jossey-Bass.

Cross, K. P. (1998, July/August). Why learning communities? Why now? *About Campus, 3*(3), 4–11.

Davis, J. R. (1995). *Interdisciplinary courses and team teaching: New arrangements for learning*. Phoenix, AZ: American Council on Education and Oryx Press.

Gabelnick, F., MacGregor, J. L., Matthews, L. R., & Smith, B. L. (1990). Learning communities: Creating connections among students, faculty and disciplines. *New directions for teaching and learning* (Vol. 41). San Francisco: Jossey-Bass.

Goodsell, A., & Tinto, V. (1994). Freshman interest groups and the first year experience: Constructing student communities in a large university. *Journal of the Freshman Year Experience, 6*(1), 7–28.

Harvard Graduate School of Education. (2006). Interdisciplinary Studies Project, Project Zero. Retrieved July 6, 2006, from http://www.pz.harvard.edu/Research/GoodWorkIS.htm

MacGregor J. L. (1991). What differences do learning communities make? *Washington Center News, 6*(1).

MacGregor, J. L. (Ed.). (1993). Student self-evaluation: Fostering reflective learning. In *New directions in teaching and learning* (Vol. 56). San Francisco: Jossey-Bass.

MacGregor, J. L., Cooper, J. L., Smith, K. A., & Robinson, P. (2000). Strategies for energizing large classes: From small groups to learning communities. *New Directions in Teaching and Learning* (Vol. 81). San Francisco: Jossey-Bass.

MacGregor, J., & Smith, B. L. (2005, May/June). Where are learning communities now? National leaders take stock. *About Campus, 10*(2), 8.

Malnarich, G. (2005). *The pedagogy of possibilities: Developmental education, college-level students, and learning communities*. National Learning Communities Project Monograph Series. Olympia, WA: The Evergreen State College, Washington Center for Improving the Quality of Undergraduate Education, in cooperation with the American Association for Higher Education, p. 67.

Malnarich, G., & Lardner, E. D. (2003, Winter). *Designing integrated learning for students: A heuristic for teaching, assessment, and curriculum design* (Washington Center for Improving the Quality of Undergraduate Education Occasional Paper No. 1). Olympia, WA: The Washington Center for Improving the Quality of Undergraduate Education.

Mansilla, V. B. (2005, January/February). Assessing student work at disciplinary crossroads. *Change, 37*(1), 14–21.

Millis, B. J., & Cottell, P. G., Jr. (1998). *Cooperative learning for higher education faculty*. American Council on Education Series on Higher Education. Phoenix, AZ: Oryx Press.

Learning Communities National Resource Center. Retrieved July 6, 2006, from http://learningcommons.evergreen.edu

Palmer, P. (1988). *The courage to teach: Exploring the inner landscape of a teacher's life*. San Francisco: Jossey-Bass.

Shapiro, N. S., & Levine, J. H. (1999). *Creating learning communities: A practical guide to winning support, organizing for change, and implementing programs*. San Francisco: Jossey-Bass.

Smith, B. L. (1994). Team teaching. In K. Prichard & B. M. Sawyer (Eds.), *Handbook of college teaching*. Westport, CT: Greenwood Press.

Smith, B. L. (2001, Summer/Fall). The challenge of learning communities as a growing national movement. *Peer Review, 3/4*(4/1), 22.

Smith, B. L., & MacGregor, J. T. (1992). What is collaborative learning? In A. S. Goodsell, M. R. Maher, & V. Tinto (Eds.), *Collaborative learning: A sourcebook for higher education* (National Center on Postsecondary Teaching, Learning, and Assessment). University Park, PA: Syracuse University.

Smith, B. L., MacGregor, J. T., Matthews, R. S., & Gabelnick, F. (2004). *Learning communities: Reforming undergraduate education.* San Francisco: Jossey-Bass.

Smith, B. L., & McCann, J. (2001). *Reinventing ourselves: Interdisciplinary education, collaborative learning, and experimentation in higher education.* Bolton, MA: Anker.

Taylor, K., Moore, W. S., MacGregor, J., & Lindblad, J. (2003). *Learning community research and assessment: What we know now.* National Learning Communities Project Monograph Series. Olympia, WA: The Evergreen State College, Washington Center for Improving the Quality of Undergraduate Education, in cooperation with the American Association for Higher Education.

Tinto, V. (1997). Classrooms as communities: Exploring the educational character of student persistence. *Journal of Higher Education, 68*(6), 599–623.

9 Assessment Strategies That Promote Learning and Ignite Student Potential

Evaluation and grading can be the heart and core of learning. Its purpose is to provide feedback to both the student and the teacher. The teacher uses the process to assess the result of his/her instructional efforts in order to make adjustments. . . . It informs the students of what they know well and what they need to learn better within a time frame that provides feedback on deficiencies before it is too late for correction.

—Benjamin Bloom[1]

Humans are said to be unique among all the species on Earth in our persistent quest for information about how we are performing. We see this in virtually every human endeavor. In our vocations, we are alert for indicators of whether we are doing our work adequately or not. When we play, we typically measure our performance against some standard, like "par," or against the performance of another competitor. Even in the simplest human interactions, we may find ourselves looking for visual or auditory cues about how well we are communicating. We might ask ourselves questions like, "Is this person understanding me?" and "Am I connecting?"

In our desire for feedback, we expect that it will be rendered sensitively and with regard to criteria that are appropriate for the circumstance. If our supervisor evaluated our performance as a salesperson on the basis of how neatly we kept our desk or whether we could recall the early history of the company we work for, we would be indignant. We would not only feel an injustice had been done, but we would have received no information that would help us do our job better. We would be similarly indignant if our supervisor didn't inform us about the criteria we were going to be assessed on but instead, after some period of time, merely handed us a statement that said our performance was "unsatisfactory." Such unfair treatment would undoubtedly impact our attitude toward our work and could certainly affect our subsequent performance. It is doubtful that, thereafter, we would be as productive and positive an employee.

Injustices like these occur in classrooms across North America every day, with similar effects on the attitudes and productivity of young people. Often students are not told in advance the criteria that will be used to assess their performance. "What will be on the test, Mrs. Jones?" is really a question that shouldn't have to be asked. Students should know with some precision at the beginning of each class and unit of study what they will be asked to know and how they will be asked to demonstrate that knowledge or skill.

A second sort of classroom injustice occurs when student performances are assessed on criteria that are not representative of what the real objective of the learning is. A teacher may intend to teach her students to be better critical thinkers but then measure their abilities at this by asking them to define critical thinking. The assessment doesn't match the intended learning. A better approach would be to give the class an opportunity to think critically that parallels the instruction they have received.

An even more common injustice occurs when our students are given information about their performance at a point in time when it is too late for them to use that feedback to improve. Teachers have an often overwhelming job of evaluating perhaps 150 student papers in a week, but when written assignments that record evidence about student understanding are returned, opportunities to clarify misunderstandings are lost. Each of these situations hinders immediate learning and affects student attitudes and subsequent performance in a negative way.

This chapter will explore what can or should be assessed in the classroom situations that have been described in other chapters in this book. If our goal is to instruct in a way that enhances our students' potential, how would we measure learning? What would we measure and when and how would we collect that information? As important as these "what" and "how" questions are, we also need to look at how this information can be turned back to both the learner and the teacher in order to enable both of them to perform their jobs more effectively. First, let's look at this critical idea of how we use feedback.

The notion that the primary purpose of measuring learning is to improve the learner's opportunity to learn is not a new idea. It has been espoused in generations of literature on evaluation. Robert Marzano quotes John Hattie's review of 8,000 studies, concluding that the most powerful single modification that a teacher can make in the classroom in order to improve student achievement is the effective use of feedback to the learner.[2] Unfortunately, while lip service is given to the use of feedback to genuinely improve learning, the reality is that teachers rarely do this with any consistency.

Below are descriptions of two instructional sequences. Each one utilizes feedback processes, but the strategies and purposes differ. As you read, look for differences in the ways assessments are used and their intended purposes. Also, note where assessments take place in the instructional sequence.

INSTRUCTIONAL SEQUENCE: CASE 1

Mary is a sixth-grade Language Arts teacher at Prairie View Middle School. Every week, Mary has a list of 25 spelling words that she wants her students to learn to spell from hearing the words pronounced. She begins on Monday by writing the words on the board and pronouncing them for her students. She points out a few letter combinations that will help in spelling the words correctly.

Thursday in class, she reminds the students that the spelling test is Friday and that it will count for 50 points toward their six-week grade. On Friday, she dictates the words, has the students correct each others' lists, and records a letter grade. Those with 24 or 25 correct (96% or more) receive an A. Those with 20 to 23 correct (80% to 92%) receive a B. Those with 18 to 19 (72% to 76%) receive a C, those with 15 to 17 receive a D, and those with below 15 receive an F.

INSTRUCTIONAL SEQUENCE: CASE 2

Juan teaches seventh-grade World Geography at Stanford Middle School. He begins his unit on France by having a brainstorming session in which he invites the students to share what they already know about the nation. He asks questions like, "What comes to your mind when you think about France?" "Who has been there?" "What have you heard about this country?" He also uses an interest-assessment technique to measure their feelings about this nation before he actually begins to teach the unit (see

Appendix A on page 181). He records whether they think it is an interesting place, a friendly place, a place they would like to visit. He saves this information.

Next, Juan explains what the objectives are for the unit and on what basis the students will receive a grade. He posts the unit objectives in large print on one wall of the classroom. One of his objectives is that students will be able to explain several ways that the natural resources of France have influenced the behavior of the French people. Another objective is that the students will learn to work more collaboratively in groups. A third objective is that the students will appreciate the contributions that France and the French people have made to the world and be more likely to want to learn more about this fascinating nation. If the students identify things that they would like to learn about France, Juan incorporates those in a prominent place among the unit's objectives. Periodically, he reminds students about each of these objectives so they know what they are to learn.

At the end of each class period, Juan uses different strategies to find out whether the students are learning what he wants them to learn and to help them review and reinforce those learnings. One day, he distributes a note card to each individual and asks everyone to write three questions, the answers to which summarize the most important things each one had learned that day. Then he directs the students to write answers to their own questions on the back of the card. They put their name on their card and he collects them. He doesn't grade the cards, but rather he reviews them quickly to check on what the class is learning from his instruction. At the start of the next class period, he distributes the cards, pairs up his students, and has them alternately ask and answer one another's questions. This leads to a discussion of ideas from the preceding day that they are still not clear about and which, in turn, leads right into the lesson he has for that day.

Other days, he varies this routine for ending the class by giving his students the task of writing one or two test questions that would measure the key learnings of that day. Again, he uses those to review at the beginning of the next class period. He also saves the best ones for the end-of-the-unit test. In this manner, the students develop their own final exam.

One of the topics in Juan's unit deals with the natural resources of France. When they have discussed the principal mining regions of northeastern and southeastern France, Juan arranges his students in groups of three and distributes the map of a hypothetical place called *Eporue* (see Appendix B on page 182). He asks his students, "I want to find out if you have understood what we have been learning about France. You are to decide in your groups which city in Eporue would be most like the city of Strasbourg and why." Juan then tells them he will be evaluating them not only on how well they are able to solve the problem he has given them but also on how effectively they work in their groups. As the class works on the task he has given them, he circulates, listening to their group interactions and recording his assessments on a rating form he has constructed (see Appendix C). When they have made their group decision and reported it to the whole class, Juan shares with them what he observed in watching their groups work. He mentions specific positive behaviors he saw as well as behaviors that did not help a group work well together.

When Juan is convinced the students are ready for a unit test, he uses class time to refocus his students' attention on the unit objectives as well as on each day's objectives, and they review from these. He is careful to have the students do the mental work of the review by asking and answering, in their groups, questions that they anticipate from the topics they have been studying. Then they take the unit test, which is a compilation of the test items the students themselves have constructed over the course of the unit.

Juan adds a question or two to assess major learnings the students might not have come up with in their test-item activity. One of these questions involves the students' solving a problem that parallels the problem they had worked on about the hypothetical place Eporue.

When the students have completed taking the test, Juan schedules an opportunity to give the class feedback in a timely manner. If there is time the day they take the test, he uses that; otherwise, he will do it the next class. He won't have the tests read by then, but he goes over the answers with the students, getting them to talk through what they think the answers are and why. He adds and corrects as needed.

When Juan is reading the unit tests, he uses a rubric for the open-ended questions so he knows what he is looking for in a good or not-so-good performance and has point values to award for each. Before he returns the tests to the students, he looks for items that may have confused students and is ready to drop them from consideration of the grade.

For the unit grade, Juan records a grade for each student on the test, along with grades for their group work, how well they have solved the problems he has given them over the course of the unit, and any other assignments. He also measures, but doesn't grade, the students' attitudes and feelings about their study of France. How do they now feel about France? Would they be more or less interested in visiting there? How interesting is France as a topic to learn about? These measures he uses to compare with the data he collected at the beginning of the unit.

WHAT ARE THE DIFFERENCES BETWEEN JUAN'S AND MARY'S APPROACHES TO ASSESSMENT?

There are many differences between Mary's and Juan's approaches to assessing classroom learning. Juan's unit is quite a bit longer and more involved than Mary's, but both of them want to develop information that is useful feedback. Significantly, they use this feedback for different purposes and to some extent for different audiences. Mary's approach will generate a weekly grade for spelling. That grade, along with the knowledge of which words each student spelled correctly and incorrectly, is good information for her as she might consider reteaching or reviewing the words that were most often misspelled. It is certainly good information for the student, and these results might be shared with parents as a strategy to enlist their help with their child's spelling in the future. To a limited extent, Mary's feedback actually benefits learning. Hopefully, the students have revisited the spelling words they missed so, if they are assessed again, they might do better, but in this sequence, the grade indicating their performance has already been recorded.

In Juan's classroom, there is a wider range of learning being assessed, and the assessments are used before, during, and after instruction both to document that learning and, more importantly, to improve the learner's opportunity to learn before a final grade is awarded. Many years ago, Benjamin Bloom espoused a philosophic position that the learning process itself is much more important than the giving of a grade. He took the position that, given adequate time, appropriate support, and motivation, a very high percentage of students could achieve the levels of accomplishment associated with the grade of A.[3] Many of our evaluative schemes force a pattern of discrimination so that our grades fit the normal curve. We sometimes act like it is desirable or rigorous to have a certain percent of students earn C's, D's, or F's. Wouldn't it be interesting if we had a situation where we had all or almost all "legitimate" A's?

We see Bloom's philosophy borne out in the way Juan uses assessments in his classroom. His activities at the end of each class period helped his students go over the most important learnings of that day so that they were reviewing and receiving feedback from their teacher about how they were doing in the learning process. "Steering" their learning in this way increases the likelihood that they will be successful when they take the unit test. Each day, Juan finds out what his students are learning and can begin the next day straightening out any misunderstandings the class might have. This sort of strategy creates for students a security that is brain-friendly. Finally, when there is a knowledge assessment that counts for a grade, there will be a high probability that the students' grades will be high. When these students feel successful and receive high grades, their motivation is likely to improve. Success breeds success, as the saying goes. Mager,[4] Richburg,[5] and others have posited a close relationship between such measures and the likelihood that learners will desire to actively continue to study a subject. When interest improves, the learner will usually want to pursue that subject further. On the other hand, if interest in a subject declines over the course of a unit, this negative result is both unfortunate and predictive. If the unit has lessened their interest, it is doubtful that they will seek out opportunities to learn about France in the future.

Juan has used assessments in other ways as well. He began his unit with a discussion in which he asked his students what they already knew about France. Even though this is simply a discussion, it is also an important assessment. It compels the learners to retrieve from their memory what they can about this new topic. It also tells the teacher about the level of understanding that a group of students have initially. This gives the teacher a clearer picture of where to begin his instruction. Without this pre-assessment, Juan is more likely either to teach things the students already understand and bore them or to begin at too sophisticated a level and confuse them. When handled effectively, simple pre-assessments, like Juan used, are definitely brain-friendly because they enable the learner to locate and draw upon the neural networks that hold the knowledge they already possess. Thus, teachers receive information that allows them to orient the instruction to the understandings based in those networks. This simple process creates a readiness that sets the learner up to successfully connect the new knowledge to what is already known and, from there, to construct a higher-level, richer neural network of knowledge and understanding of this topic.

There have been many studies that show how student achievement can be boosted through the use of pre-assessments like Juan has done in this example. If the assessment is an actual test, it doesn't even have to be graded to be effective. It is the act of taking it that promotes the learning because the learner is made ready through the test, used here as a pretest for the instruction that follows.[6]

Juan used still another type of assessment when he used a simple attitudinal measure before and after his unit on France. By collecting group attitudinal data, he has quantifiable information about how his instruction impacted their feelings about a subject of study, which he can show to the "audiences" he has who are concerned about accountability. If Mager and others are correct, attitude toward the subject being studied might be more important than are results on achievement tests. Parents, the principal, the school board, and even taxpayers would find it valuable to know that a teacher is increasing student interest and improving their attitude toward the topics being studied in the curriculum. (Appendix D explains how to set up and interpret this sort of measure.)

In the way Juan administered and graded his unit test, we see still other strategies to improve the likelihood that students will be successful learners. He doesn't schedule the test until he is as sure as possible that the students are ready for it. He bases the test on objectives that have been visually a part of the classroom since the beginning of the unit. He also utilized test items that the students themselves have submitted. He will edit and clarify ambiguous parts of these items, but much of the ownership of the test is clearly the students'.

Juan also uses a rubric to assess learning on open-ended or problem-solving components of his test. This enables him to be fairer and more objective in awarding points. Open-ended responses are especially vulnerable to subjective teacher reactions, and while rubrics take time to create, they reduce any bias or prejudice that might creep into the grading process.

Finally, Juan has provided immediate feedback to his students regarding the test. He might not have their papers to return for several days, but he has gone over the correct answers to it as soon as he is able to. Research is clear that going over a test in a timely way, with careful explanations about why particular answers are correct or incorrect, elevates student learning.[7]

In Juan's approach to the assessment of learning, we see him collecting a wide variety of information that will help his learners be successful and will help him teach more effectively. While Mary's primary goal in gathering assessment data is to provide a grade that reflects students' performance, Juan collects feedback initially to focus his teaching, then to guide the learner through the learning process, and finally to provide evidence of learning for audiences who have an interest in knowing what is happening in his classroom.

Without any doubt, Juan's approach to teaching will take longer than a usual coverage of his subject. If he does similar things with each unit, he certainly will not get to all parts of the world in his geography class. With the explosion of knowledge that characterizes the world today, this is an issue that confronts every teacher. Should I teach for depth and genuine learning so the students really know and retain a body of content, or do I utilize a more superficial approach whereby students end up with an awareness of some pieces of knowledge but really don't learn them in a way that will enable retention or real understanding to take place? From my perspective, the answer is obvious: going slow and promoting genuine learning for the learner and the realization that they are being successful is the only approach that makes sense.

INFORMAL FEEDBACK

Some educational thinkers would argue that the most helpful feedback for learners is moment-by-moment planned assistance given every day in class. An acquaintance of mine who teaches writing in a rural junior high school obtains excellent results with his **"F.A.R.M."** method of providing his students with feedback in class. He will give them a writing task and tell them they will have about 20 minutes to develop a draft. He waits a few minutes to allow them to get a good start and then uses a set regimen that allows him to provide quick feedback to each student individually three or more times in 15 minutes.

Here's how F.A.R.M. works. As he circulates, he disciplines himself to spend no more than 20 seconds at a time with each student. First, he *focuses* on or studies their writing. That's the *F*. Then he finds something specific to *affirm* or complement them on. That's the *A*. He points out a *rethink*, something that they might consider doing differently. That's the *R*. Then he *moves* on. That's the *M*. He's off to another student, where he begins "farming" again. He has the opportunity to work with every student at least three times in the class period. The students get immediate feedback and encouragement while they are in the formative stages of their writing. This instructor is convinced that his students' writing is much improved since he began this process. He also says he has much less to do when he evaluates their completed work.

MAKING CERTAIN WE ARE MEASURING WHAT OUR STUDENTS ARE LEARNING

In Chapter 6, we saw a middle school teaching unit focused on locating and building castles in the Middle Ages. What would this teacher measure that would be evidence of his students' learning? The initial task that the teacher gives to the students in this interdisciplinary project is to determine where in their own community they would locate a castle as if a feudal lord had ordered them to do so in the Middle Ages. To make this decision, they have to research castle locations in Europe both by Web and by library research. They must consider economic factors as well as defensive military considerations. They must be able to gather information from a topographic map, work in cooperative groups and make group decisions, and finally make an oral presentation in which they effectively defend their locational decision. The teacher also adds a character-building aspect to his unit by incorporating chivalry in his intended learnings. He wants his students to learn and practice the ideals of care and respect for others, especially those in challenging circumstances. Finally, much of what the students do in the learning activities of the unit depends on their using initiative and being able to work without his direct supervision. Having his students learn and be successful at this was one of his goals as he developed his unit.

He then breaks down the complex task he has given his students, in order to determine both the relative importance of each of the components and then also the fairest way to measure students' actual learning of these components. The determination of the relative importance of these sub-learnings allows him to weight his grading rubric appropriately. For example, he might determine that the content and delivery of the oral presentation of their project are three times the value of the research component. He might also determine that the consensus-building skills that each group utilizes in reaching a decision are twice as important as their knowledge of Middle Age terminology like *fief* and *vassal*. These weightings will be communicated to the students in advance so they are clear about what they will be graded on as well as the relative importance of the different components of their assignment. This reduces the ambiguity that is present in so many classrooms in which the student must try to read the teacher's mind about how grades will be assigned. When students are clear about what the specific learning objectives are and how their learning will be assessed (see Figure 9.1), achievement and motivation improve. This simple step would greatly enhance learning in our schools.

This teacher might determine that some learnings, like practicing chivalry, while important, shouldn't be graded. He will assess students in this regard but not include this in his grading scheme. By taking this type of attitudinal learning out of his grading rubric, he is hoping that his students will practice these behaviors for stronger reasons than merely to receive a grade. Instead of grading, in keeping with the reality they are studying, he creates levels of chivalric achievement to which students can aspire. They could become a "page" with so many chivalric points for small or great kindnesses they have performed, a "squire" with more points, or even a "knight of the round table" with more yet. A committee of the class decides on the number of points to be awarded for each behavior submitted for their consideration. Wisely, the teacher has the students keep track of the points they have earned. He organizes great celebrations when students move from one level to the next. The names of those reaching knight status are announced and posted for all to see in the classroom. All of this promotes the learning this teacher wants but is not included in his grading.

Other objectives, like effort and the ability to work without direct supervision, might involve the students in evaluating themselves and each other. In this situation, the teacher would give the class a simple rubric like the one shown in Figure 9.2 on page 176.

Once the teacher has determined the relative weightings of the learning components, he or she must decide how to assess the learning of those components. There is more strategy to this than many of us realize. Wherever possible, the assessment should mimic the learning. For example, a key learning activity in this castle project involves the learners' using a topographic map to decide where their castle would be best located if the considerations are economic and military ones, as they were in Europe in the Middle Ages. Clearly, the fairest assessment of what they learned from this activity would be to give students another topographic quadrangle from a community that they are familiar with and then ask them to make a similar locational decision. Then, to parallel the initial activity, the teacher would ask them to defend in an essay the decision that they had made. While this would be a comparable task to the one in which learning initially occurred, and therefore a fair assessment, the teacher would have created a very time-consuming job grading the open-ended

Figure 9.1 Castle Project Grading Rubric

Group Members: ____________________

Library/Web Research

1	2	3	4	5	× 1 = ______
Only a few sources		Some good sources of information		Many high-quality references	

Quality of Castle Drawing

1	2	3	4	5	× 2 = ______
Poor quality, few features		Some interesting features, generally neatly done		All required features included, neatly done	

Content of Oral Presentation

1	2	3	4	5	× 3 = ______
More information needed/Inaccuracies		Sufficient information/ Few mistakes		Plenty of accurate info about castles	
Neither design nor location described		Design or location not described		Both design and location well described	

Process of Oral Presentation

1	2	3	4	5	× 3 = ______
One person dominated		Unbalanced participation		Everyone made significant contributions	
Read notes		Occasional eye contact		Rarely referred to notes; good eye contact	
Mumbling				Excitement, as though group was trying to sell their castle's location	
No introduction or conclusion		Brief introduction or conclusion		Rich introduction and conclusion	

Castle Location Decision

1	2	3	4	5	× 2 = ______
Neither military nor commercial factors considered		Good for either factor, but not both		Strong location considerations, commercially and militarily	

(Continued)

Figure 9.1 (Continued)

Use of Terminology

1	2	3	4	5	× 1 = ________
None of the required terms used/Did not use castle terms/ Inaccurate terms		About half of the required terms used/Some accurate castle terms		Many accurate castle terms used	

Required terms:

— feudalism/feudal

— knight

— vassal

— fief

Total for Project = ________

Total Points Possible = ___60___

Figure 9.2 How Would You Assess Your Own Effort in Doing This Project?

How would you assess your own effort in doing this project?

1	2	3	4	5
I put very little effort into this project		I put some effort into the project, but I could have done more		I worked hard and completed all aspects of the project

How would you assess the effort of your whole group on the project?

1	2	3	4	5
As a group we didn't work very hard		We put some effort into the project, but we could have worked harder		We worked hard and completed all aspects of the project

responses. If a teacher has five or six classes each taking this assessment, she would now have an entire weekend of work ahead to grade their responses. Open-ended or essay responses might better capture thinking or problem-solving skills that students have utilized in a learning situation, but the format creates a formidable amount of work.

Figure 9.3 Map A and Map B

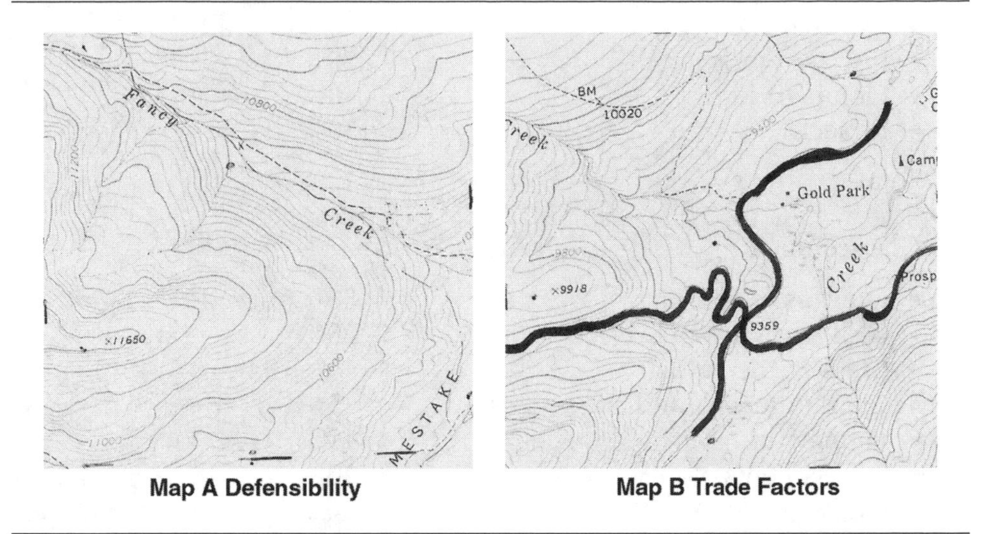

Map A Defensibility **Map B Trade Factors**

Fortunately, problem-solving skills such as these can be assessed in more close-ended fashion to save teacher grading time. This takes some creativity and time in advance of the assessment itself. To do this, the teacher might reproduce two segments of a topographic quadrangle, like those shown in Maps A and B in Figure 9.3. In one, as on the left, she might identify four locations (A, B, C, and D) and ask which would be the best location for a castle in 1300 if defensibility was most important. Then, she would ask which one on the right would be the best location if trade factors were the most important consideration. In both cases, students might also be asked to explain why those locations are the best by filling in the blank with no more than one sentence: "I think this is the best location because ________."

In an easy-to-grade multiple-choice format, with or without an additional sentence, this teacher can readily determine the students' ability to transfer the factors learned in one context to a similar problem in a different context.

TEST CONSIDERATIONS VERSUS PROJECTS

Teachers who want to maximize the development of their students' potential must consider grading systems that give students the best opportunity to be successful. Look at the following grading schemes. Ask yourself which gives students the best chance to succeed, Classroom A or Classroom B?

Classroom A

• Quizzes and tests	50% of grade
• In-class work	30%
• Homework	10%
• Projects	10%
Total	100%

Classroom B

• Quizzes and tests	30% of grade
• Oral and written projects	20%
• Class participation	15%
• Class notebook and class notes	15%
• Homework	10%
• Assessments of group work	10%
Total	100%

The issue here is not which approach is "easier" for the student but rather which gives the learner the best opportunity to show his or her capabilities. While there might be circumstances in which either of these grading schemes would be appropriate, Classroom B has many advantages. Not all young people are equally proficient test takers. Because tests count less, test anxiety would likely be lower in Classroom B. The diversity of assessments also acknowledges that there are different learning styles and that young people are intelligent in many different ways. This understanding certainly helps the majority of students.

In our classrooms, the messages we give our students by way of feedback and grades are profoundly important to the development of their capabilities. Some of these messages encourage and inspire our students, and some unwittingly might stunt their development and even crush their spirit. In each of the instances below, individuals received evaluative feedback that communicated a strong negative message about their capabilities.

- Enrico Caruso's music teacher told him, "You can't sing! You have no voice at all!"
- Verner von Braun, father of modern rocketry, flunked ninth-grade algebra.
- Louisa May Alcott was told by an editor that she was incapable of writing anything that had popular appeal.
- Louis Pasteur was rated as "mediocre" in chemistry when he attended the Sorbonne.
- Beethoven's music teacher once said of him, "As a composer, you are hopeless."
- Winston Churchill, who was later to author 50 books, flunked remedial English three times.

Fortunately, this feedback didn't permanently scar or destroy these individuals. They went on to achieve great things in their respective fields. There is another group, however, of whom we have no record because they achieved no such acclamation. This group includes the many talented young people who are turned away from a budding talent by negative or insensitive feedback from their instructors. There is no more important role that a teacher plays than that of being a reviewer and evaluator of their students' work. But this role, because of the power inherent in it, must be carried out with great care. Bloom put it this way, "Evaluation is a two-edged sword which can enhance student learning and personality development or be destructive to student learning and personality development."[8] We must be enhancers, not destroyers.

NOTES

1. Bloom, B. S. (1981). *All our children learning*. New York: McGraw-Hill.
2. Marzano, R. J. (2003). *What works in schools*. Alexandria, VA: Association for Supervision and Curriculum Development, p. 37.
3. Bloom, B. S., Madans, G. F., & Hastings, J. T. (1981). *Evaluation to improve instruction*. New York: McGraw-Hill.
4. Mager, R. F. (1968). *Developing attitude toward learning*. Belmont, CA: Fearon Press.
5. Richburg, R. W. (1970). *Using evaluation to improve instruction*. Boulder, CO: Association of American Geographers.
6. Howard, P. J. (2002). *The owner's manual for the brain*. Austin, TX: Bard Press, p. 473.
7. Marzano, R. J. (2003), p. 37.
8. Bloom, B. S., et al. (1981), p. 236.

Appendix A

INTEREST INVENTORY

Assess Topics 1–5 according to your own opinion. There are no right or wrong answers. Use the lettered scale at the left to assess the topics.

How would you rate the following topics in terms of how interesting you think they would be to study?

Assessment Scale	Topics
A. dull	___ 1. The people of France
B. generally uninteresting	___ 2. The resources of France
C. generally interesting	___ 3. The cities of France
D. very interesting	___ 4. The history of France
	___ 5. What it would be like to live in France

Appendix B

EPORUE

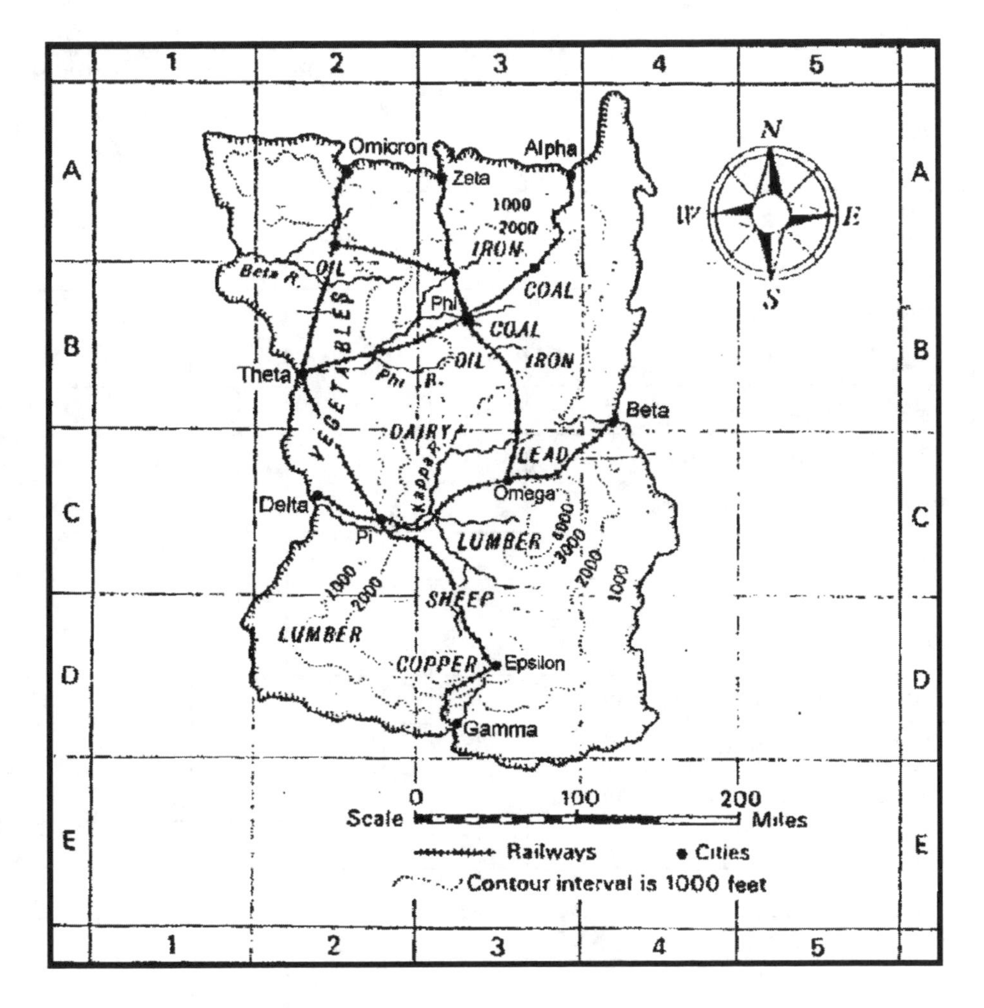

Appendix C

JUAN'S CLASSROOM

Teacher Observation Form for Assessing Group Collaboration Skills

	Group 1 Names					Group 2 Names					
Facilitation skills											
Initiating ideas											
Careful listening											
Encouraging others											
Being willing to compromise											
Establishing rules											
Drawing others into the discussion											
Negative group behaviors											
Not paying attention											
Blocking											
Withdrawing from group											
Holding private conversations											
Putting others down											
Being unwilling to compromise											
Griping											
Other											
Helpful behaviors											
Setting group goals											
Asking for information or opinions											
Giving information or opinions											
Clarifying and elaborating others' ideas											
Asking about group progress											
Summarizing											
Self-evaluating											

Appendix D

USING JUAN'S INTEREST INVENTORY TO SHOW GROUP ATTITUDE CHANGE

Juan's simple Interest Inventory can yield valuable group attitude change information if administered before and after an instructional unit.

The following is hypothetical data for Juan's class of 25 students. When he gives them the pre-assessment (done anonymously) for the topics about France, he gets these results.

Topic 1. The people of France

A. dull (4 responses)
B. generally uninteresting (10 responses)
C. generally interesting (8 responses)
D. very interesting (3 responses)

By giving each response A–D a point value, 1 for each A response, 2 for each B response, 3 for each C response, and 4 for each D response, he can generate quickly a weighted mean for each topic. The above data would look like this:

4 (A's) × 1 = 4

10 (B's) × 2 = 20

8 (C's) × 3 = 24

3 (D's) × 4 = 12

He sums these values and gets a total of 60, which he divides by the number of students responding and gets a 2.40 average.

What if, then, for the post-assessment, this topic's average is 3.10? He has evidence that his group's interest in studying about the people of France has improved. If the post-assessment for the topic were a 2.00, he would also have valuable evidence that something in the unit turned off his students.

This same sort of scale can be used profitably at the beginning and ending of a course or for assessing interest change as a result of a specific assignment or course component like a service-learning assignment.

10

Developing Teachers Who Inspire Their Students

If we are hoping to inspire learning and draw out the latent talents in each student, that hope will only be realized if we are unflinchingly determined to select and educate an exceptional caliber of teacher. It may be surprising to some, but highly effective teaching involves the most complex skill set of any profession. Certainly, the knowledge and skills needed to practice law, engineering, or medicine are challenging to learn, but consider how they compare to teaching. My son, at the time a social studies teacher in Minnesota, was visited in his classroom by a prominent orthopedic surgeon. After a couple of class periods, the doctor observed:

> In my job, I only work on shoulders or knees. Every shoulder or knee is very much like every other one. I only work with one patient at a time and I rarely do more than five or six surgeries in a week. I always have nurses and other specialists, anesthesiologists and the like, available to take care of parts of the process so that I can focus on my specialty. In between the two or three days a week that I do surgery, I have relatively low key days of removing stitches and casts and developing rehabilitative programs for my patients. After a while the entire surgical procedure is fairly routine. From what I have seen, I don't think days are ever routine for a teacher.[1]

Each day, the average classroom teacher works with from 30 to 180 learners, depending upon grade level. Unlike knees or shoulders, each learner has a unique brain formed by different home backgrounds, life experiences, and opportunities. Fortunately, some come eager and ready to learn, but many others come with serious needs and pathologies that stifle their ability even to concentrate. Each learner requires a different prescription, but teachers rarely get to work with their students one at a time.

While this surgeon has a more or less set approach to his patients, a teacher's approach is inevitably contextual. There are certain skills all teachers use in virtually all situations, but the manner in which they apply these skills will depend on the circumstances of a particular situation. An algebra teacher in a small rural community must have skills to control and manage her classroom, plan challenging lessons, and make up appropriate assessments just like her urban or suburban counterpart, but there will be enough uniqueness in their contexts that the applications of these skills might look dramatically different. Similarly, the teacher who teaches the same course in the first and last hour of the day will rarely use the same strategies or apply her teaching skills in the same way in both classes.

To identify all the skills and dispositions that a new or experienced teacher needs in order to teach effectively in these largely different circumstances is well beyond the scope of this chapter. Instead, I will address some of the special and less obvious teaching skills that are needed for a teacher to teach in concert with the natural way the brain learns. If, when we teach, we can bring our approaches in concert with the way the human brain most naturally learns, we have the optimal circumstance to help a young person develop to his or her potential. That is our goal. Later in the chapter, I will describe the sort of training programs that would be most effective in assisting preservice and experienced teachers to learn these skills.

WHAT IS DIFFERENT ABOUT INSTRUCTION THAT ALLOWS THE BRAIN TO LEARN IN ITS MOST NATURAL WAY?

Teachers who would utilize the power of the brain's natural learning processes will want to try some unconventional strategies. Instead of simply giving or feeding their students information as in a lecture, they will want to develop ways to involve students in actively "figuring out" the knowledge to be learned. There are many versions of this and many names used to describe the process, but in its essence this instruction allows the learner to learn by solving problems. The lesson materials that follow might help illustrate how this would work in a junior high social studies classroom. It might also help to identify the special teacher skills needed to teach in this way.

The following data sheet is a compilation of information about a European nation that might be the subject of study in a middle-level World

Figure 10.1 Data Sheet

What can you tell about this nation from the data below?

Do you have any hypotheses about what country it is?

Nation X is a European nation.

	Area in Square Miles	Population (millions)	Wheat Production (millions of metric tons)	Number of Mechanized Harvestors	Total No. of Computers (PCs) (millions)	Number of Internet Users	Fishing Production (thousands of metric tons)	Coal Production (millions of metric tons)	Iron Ore (million of metric tons)	Bauxite (aluminum) (millions of metric tons)	Life Expectancy (Years)	% of GNP Spent on Education	Primary Religions and Denominations
Nation X	211,000	60.1	15,000	153,000	9.5	18.7 Million	850	23,600	15,500	3,150	77.6	6.8	88% RC* 10% M**
Italy	116,305	57.4	9,000	27,000	6.4	17.0 Million	528	None	277	32	74.3	5.7	93% RC*
Turkey	301,380	71.3	11,000	10,800	0.1	4.9 Million	595	5,000	1,262	57	60.6	3.1	99.8% M**
Democratic Republic of the Congo, Zaire	905,560	52.7	734	680	0.03	6,000	208	90	40	160	47.2	2.2	50% RC* 20% P*** 10% M**
Japan	145,800	127.6	241	130,000	17.4	57.0 Million	5,521	10,000	326	21	78.1	4.9	84% B**** & Shinto
U.S.A.	3,717,000	294	58,000	900,000	91.5	155 Million	5,400	539,000	40,000	2,190	75.9	6.6	56% P*** 28% RC* 2% J*****

* Roman Catholic ** Muslim *** Protestant **** Buddhist ***** Jewish

Geography class. The data is carefully chosen to reveal important insights about the nation so that when the students are determining what this nation is like, they are focused on the sorts of learnings that the curriculum (and standards) will expect them to understand, such as the nation's location, means of economic livelihood, and cultural characteristics. The learnings from this activity are in no way a sufficient discussion of this nation, but rather, it is expected that the activity will open up other avenues of investigation that will enable other concepts and information to be brought into the discussion.

The data sheet is set up to give the students "cues" as to the nature of this nation because it provides important comparisons with background and information the learner might already have. They might not know what "6.8 percent of GNP spent on education" means, but they can see that it is more than the United States spends and can make conclusions from that. Similarly, they can see the number of mechanized harvesters in comparison with Turkey or Italy or Zaire and realize that this is a highly developed nation with a modern agricultural economy.

The crucial teacher skill in putting a data sheet like this together is the ability to capture the natural curiosity of the learners, but yet for the learners to have sense of "efficacy"—that they can figure out the puzzle. The teacher has to be able to structure a puzzling circumstance and yet convey just enough clues that the learner won't either give up because it is too hard or solve it too quickly because the answer is obvious. The first time I utilized this activity sheet, I included information on wine production in the nation. There was no challenge to the problem because the students knew which nations in Europe are major wine producers. It took the students 30 seconds to determine which nation this was, and they then lost interest in pursuing other insights about the nature of its geography. It would be equally uninteresting if there was not sufficient information to which the students could relate. They would simply give up as many of us do with a crossword puzzle in the newspaper that is "over our head."

> *"Let your learner know nothing (or as little as possible) because you told him or her, and everything (or as much as possible) because they figured it out for themselves."*
>
> Barry Beyer[2]

The lesson plan that utilizes this data sheet is quite simple. The teacher initially conveys to the class that she has a mystery for them to solve that will compel them to use their best skills as geographers. "What do you think this mystery nation is like?" She then organizes her students in groups of two or three with one copy of the data sheet per group and lets them brainstorm what they can figure out about this place.

The teacher then moves around the room listening to their conversations about this mystery nation. As the teacher circulates, she will hear correct and incorrect inferences being made. Her approach is simply to ask additional questions, but not give direct answers. When a group is stuck, she directs them toward a particular piece of data that might give them clues that makes it possible for them to continue. The students will almost automatically try to figure out which European nation this is. While that is natural, the teacher will keep focusing them on describing the country because it is from figuring this out that the rich understandings will develop.

When the students have had enough time to develop some conclusions about Nation X (about 10 minutes), the teacher calls the class back together. She then asks them to share their hypotheses about the nation. They will typically determine that Nation X is a developed nation that values education and that it has a prosperous, varied economy characterized by a modern farming sector, fishing, and mining. The mining leads them to consider that it probably has mountainous regions. The fishing industry of Nation X, though not as productive as in some nations they can compare it to, leads them to infer that this might be a coastal nation. The number of mechanized harvesters will lead some to wonder if there aren't large regions that are relatively flat and conducive to large-scale farming. No one student will know all of these pieces. However, when they pool their insights, they know a considerable amount, and the knowledge has been constructed by their own efforts by working with the data and their fellow students. Typically, this will have been an enjoyable task because they became curious about this place. The activity concludes with the teacher leading a summarizing discussion. The point here is to bring the inquiry to conclusions that students can register in their notes for future reference. This is a simple, but essential, part of the process.

After the students have generated as much as they are able to about the nature of Nation X, the teacher must help consolidate their insights. Here again, the students should do the mental work, but the teacher must be skilled in guiding the culminating discussion and focusing on the key insights. She might ask a question like, "So what have we learned about this nation (France) from this activity? Let's get the key things we have learned down in our notebooks." The students will again generate some of the key points that they discovered earlier, but there will usually be important ideas they have omitted. Again, the teacher will use "cuing" questions like, "What do you remember about the general topography of France?" The teacher can certainly embellish their answers, but must be careful not to take over or communicate in any way that the students weren't the ones who figured out the problem.

> *"The method employed by the majority of the teachers in the public schools of the U.S. is that of 'giving out' knowledge. Seventy-five percent of all instructional time involves teachers telling students facts and information. . . . Less than one percent of instructional time involves teachers inviting open responses from students or posing problems with multiple possible answers."*
>
> Ken Sirotnik[3]

WHY DOES THIS APPROACH WORK?

This same material could certainly be "presented" in a lecture by the teacher and, if done with visuals and stories, might attract student interest. There would, however, be much less likelihood that the brain would be able to commit the outcomes to long-term memory. Here is why. The Nation X activity creates in students a motivation to learn because they want to see what they can figure out about this place. Curiosity sustains the mental effort that they must put forth in order to solve the problem and learn the material. Mental effort must occur for the brain to store new material in long-term memory, but in conventional teaching the curiosity is not usually present to promote that effort.

> *"Connected learning is a physiological imperative. Dendrites don't grow from nothing. Dendrites grow from lower dendrites."*
>
> Rita Smilkstein[4]

The way that students must approach this problem also advantages learning and long-term memory. In order to determine what the characteristics of Nation X are, they must make comparisons with geography they are more familiar with—that of the United States. The data about the number of computers in Nation X makes sense to them only as they consider what they know about their own nation. In this pattern of instruction, they begin from what they already know and, because of the way the activity is conducted, each student's knowledge supplements that of every other student. What the whole class knows becomes the knowledge base for solving the problem. Each shared new insight or inference adds to what the whole class has available to solve the problem. In Rita Smilkstein's conceptualization, the preexisting knowledge represents "the lower dendrites" in each learner's brain. As the learners make comparisons and generate additions to what they know, they are changing those dendritic patterns and adding to their long-term memory. As Pierce Howard puts it: "Knowledge is the pattern of connectivity and 'learning' is the change in the pattern of this connectivity, a result of the growth of new dendrites."[6]

> *"When we mentally process something—reflect upon it—take it apart—reassemble it in new ways—we are learning more than just the information we are working with. By relating it to our present structure of knowledge, we make it mean something to us and* we will retain it far better."
>
> Barry Beyer[5]

Compare this to a more traditional instructional approach in which the teacher tries to promote learning by giving the students conclusions about a topic in a lecture or teacher-centered strategy. The teacher might understand how this new information connects to the learning that some students already have, but the knowledge base of each student is unique. All the teacher can do is make a general appraisal of that base of knowledge. As he or she lectures or explains, the brain of the student might seek to make connections with what it already knows, but if it cannot match the teacher's pronouncements with its own knowledge base, it cannot commit this knowledge to long-term memory. The information also comes too quickly in a lecture, and if the brain cannot make the match, there is no way for it to really learn. It is even doubtful that the learner can capture very complete representations of the lecture material in class notes since the average teacher speaks five or six times faster than the average student writes. This makes even short-term memory difficult.

> *". . . activation of prior knowledge facilitates the subsequent processing of new information. Consequently, in education, explicit attention should be paid to students' existing knowledge. The activation of this knowledge provides a framework for new learning."*
>
> William Gijselaers[7]

There are certainly many other ways for teachers to conduct problem-posing teaching without using data sheets. In Chapter 6, a junior high history teacher utilized a hypothetical problem in which students had to figure out where in their own community they would locate a castle as if they lived in Medieval Europe. In Chapter 7, we saw how a high school science teacher utilized a puzzle that Galileo faced in order to help the students learn gravitational principles.

These look like different strategies and they might go by differing terms—inquiry, discovery, constructivism—but they all operate in concert with how the brain learns best. In each situation, the learner learns by figuring things out and making his or her own meaning.

If we abstract the process, it looks like this:

Figure 10.2

The students are given a generalized question or problem to solve. ⇨

Students interact with "data"* and other students to solve the problem. (The teacher asks questions to focus attention on cues to solve problem.) ⇨

The teacher poses interpretive questions to clarify what was learned. ⇨

The students make notes or register learnings to refer to as needed later.

**Data* simply means un-interpreted information, the raw material of knowledge. It can be tabled information, as in the "Nation X" activity, but it might also be pictures or evidence from a laboratory experiment, a passage of literature, a diary account of an event, etc.

The problem or question posed in this process is a key to the success of the lesson. It should create some measure of intrigue for the learner. Every discipline has mysteries that the researchers of that subject have found puzzling. In history, we wonder what happened to the lost colony on Roanoke Island or how the Egyptians built those remarkably complex pyramids. In science, we can pose "wonderment questions" like, "How are salmon able to find their way back from the sea to their birthplace to spawn when the journey might be over 2,000 miles?"

Sometimes the stimulus for problem-solving lessons isn't even a question. A startling fact can generate as much intrigue as a question and might just as certainly lead to problem solving. Here are a few examples:

- "Eighty-one percent of the world's executions took place in three countries, China, Iran, and the United States."
- "One out of five of the world's people lives on less than $1 a day."
- "There are 27 million slaves in the world today."[8]

Inevitably, curiosity will lead students to want to know more about the fact, and they will generate their own problem to solve. "Why?" is the most obvious question, but other questions will also emerge.

The materials or data that we provide for this sort of problem-solving learning is also a key. We can have students research in order to find the information for their inquiry, but that will lengthen the process and sometimes reduce the thinking level involved. In the Nation X activity, for example, it is an option for the teacher not to provide any data at all and instead have students find their own sources of information to determine what the characteristics of France are. While this can be an effective way to learn, summarizing the conclusions from a secondary source probably doesn't generate curiosity or compellingly motivate the students to do their own critical thinking and deep learning that this sort of inquiry will do.

HOW DO TEACHER SKILLS DIFFER IN PROBLEM-SOLVING INSTRUCTION?

Let's look at the teacher dispositions and skills needed to teach in this manner. First, as surprising as it may seem, instructors must know the content they are working with even better than if they were delivering that content in a more traditional lecture mode. Here's why. Using the geography example from our lesson plan above, a teacher giving a presentational overview of France, rather than taking a figuring-it-out or problem-solving approach, has to a larger degree complete control over where the lesson goes. He or she chooses what features, such as topography, climate, and economic or cultural characteristics, to focus on. The students might ask questions, but the questions will most probably only be to clarify points made by the instructor. Only rarely will the questions students ask take the instructor into areas for which the instructor hasn't been prepared. He or she controls the transaction and can usually steer the discussion so it doesn't go into "uncharted waters."

In the problem-solving approach illustrated by the Nation X example, the teacher must more thoroughly understand the geography of France in order to determine what data to include in the stimulus or data sheet the students work with. Look again at the illustration. The author has carefully included economic information like "number of mechanized harvesters" and "percent of GNP spent on education" to lead the students to consider whether this is a developed or not-so-developed nation. Also, the information included on fishing very subtly suggests that this is likely to be a coastal nation because it would be unlikely for fishing production to be as great from a landlocked nation or even a nation like Poland with a relatively short coastline. Similarly, the inclusion of the data on iron ore and bauxite production is selected because it leads to student inferences about the likelihood that this is a nation with significant mountain ranges. (The uplifting forces that create mountains expose veins of minerals that facilitate mining activity.) Without these understandings and knowledge of how this information would compare with places that differ from Nation X, a teacher can't readily structure this sort of problem-solving activity.

Additionally, in the conduct of the activity, the problem-posing instructor really doesn't know where students will go with their inferences, so he or she must thoroughly know the geography of Europe. Sometimes the students will be led astray and believe, because it is a developed nation that values education, that it might be a Scandinavian nation. Norway, Sweden, or Finland might seem like logical possibilities because they're also bounded by oceans and have strong fishing industries. The instructor would have to be comfortable enough with his content knowledge and skilled enough to ask the students headed in this direction to consider whether these Scandinavian nations, being as far north as they are, would be likely to have the agricultural productivity that Nation X has. The teacher using this style of teaching must thoroughly understand where she wants the students to end up in their problem solving and how to read the misperceptions they might express so she will be able to steer the students toward more correct understandings.

Some other skills that the teacher who would teach in concert with the way the brain learns are the following:

1. The teacher must have the ability to develop an environment in the classroom that allows students to "take risks" and make guesses or

hypotheses without fear that they will be criticized by either the teacher or their fellow classmates.

2. While the students are in the problem-solving mode, the teacher must be able to act like the Peter Falk character Columbo. In the television mystery series, Columbo would always act like he didn't know what was going on. He would seem clueless and keep asking his suspects for help even though he knew exactly what was happening. In the same way, teachers in this style of teaching act like they have no idea what the answer to the problem is. Like Columbo, they answer student questions with many versions of, "Gee, I don't know, what do you think?" They just keep asking questions and looking for the responses that indicate the students are moving toward the insights that are desired.

3. Along with the Columbo style of asking questions without giving too much information is the process of turning student responses back to other students. When a student offers a hypothesis about the nature of Nation X, this teacher doesn't just accept the response at face value. In order to produce greater depth in the student's thinking and more participation from the class, the teacher turns the response back (either to that student or to the class as a whole). This sort of deflection is always done in a way that reinforces the students and makes them feel safe, but that also surfaces additional ideas or refines their thinking. These teacher responses might sound like this: "I like that idea; is there anything else you conclude about this?" or "That's an interesting insight; what do you think about that, class?"

4. Teachers who would teach in keeping with the natural way the brain learns must be able to recognize and develop stimulus materials that can be used for this type of problem solving. These materials are abundant but not always readily recognized. The general idea is that they represent interesting but uninterpreted information, which upon study can lead to an understanding of an important concept. Articles from the newspaper like "Historians Rank Top Presidents in History" work well because the task of determining who should or should not make the list is intriguing. Similarly, excerpts from a diary or pictures of a scene with visual information might lead the student to want to figure out where the scene takes place. A dollar bill with the Great Seal of the United States is an excellent data source for understanding the vision that our nation's forefathers had for the United States in the late eighteenth century. An article from *Popular Science* that describes the movement of the tectonic plates under the Pacific Ocean will lead students to wonder about the recent earthquakes and tsunamis in that region. The issue is that while data sources for problem solving are plentiful, the brain-compatible teacher must learn what makes a good one and sees them where others might not.

A MODEL PRESERVICE TEACHER TRAINING PROGRAM: TRAINING TEACHERS TO TEACH WITH THE BRAIN'S NATURAL WAY OF LEARNING

Ironically, at a time when we are beginning to understand how complex the human brain is and how intricate the skills of inspirational teaching are, the trends in teacher licensure are toward easier paths for candidates to become "qualified" to teach. In an effort to recruit more teachers, many states have adopted "alternative" licensure policies whereby a candidate can be licensed simply by possessing a bachelor's degree and passing a content knowledge exam. No training in pedagogy or even minimum college course work standards are required in these "deprofessionalized" approaches. Linda Darling-Hammond's research indicates that there are at least two serious problems with these minimally trained or not-at-all-trained new teachers. First, they drop out of teaching at a disproportionately higher rate than fully qualified teachers do. Second, and even more seriously, their students do not achieve at as high a rate as the students of well-trained teachers do.[9]

There is an accumulating body of research that says the preparation and expertise of the teacher are the most important predictors of student achievement. In a review of 65 studies of K–12 student achievement, Darling-Hammond found "consistently positive relationships between students' achievement in science and math and their teacher's background in both education courses and their content course work. The better prepared math and science teachers—both in their subject matter and their expertise in pedagogy—the more successful their students are."[10] Additionally, she found that the effects of solid teacher preparation are particularly strong when measures of student achievement are focused on higher-order thinking tasks such as problem solving. Clearly, the teacher who would promote learning in the way that the brain learns best must be very well trained.

> *"Teaching has not improved because teacher educators, frankly, are limited in their pedagogical abilities, and no major pressures exist (in colleges and universities) to change the nature of their teaching."*
>
> The National Commission on Teaching and America's Future[11]

So, what would a really strong teacher prep program look like? First and foremost, a model program would be staffed with master teachers who have recent K–12 public school experience. They must be strongly invested in the art and craft of teaching and able and willing to model all aspects of high-quality instruction. They must be enthusiastically able to live the life of a "model teacher" in front of their candidates. Talking about how to teach without modeling it simply doesn't work in teacher training.

The candidates will never believe the proposed skills are important if they don't see their instructors using them on a regular basis.

CANDIDATE SELECTION PROCESS

It is essential that the program be thoughtfully selective. Even in times of serious teacher shortages, there will be significant numbers of applicants to teacher training programs who should not become teachers. Beyond the obvious issues of moral character, there are many potential candidates who should be selected out because of having rigid personalities or lack of drive and commitment necessary to be an excellent teacher or the basic warmth and caring that will enable them to be effective with young people.

Grade point average can be a selection factor, but it is not a good predictor of future teacher success. I have trained teachers for more than three decades and have found virtually no correlation between overall GPA and the performance of candidates as teachers.[12] Sometimes, candidates who have struggled themselves in learning the content they will teach can be wonderful teachers because they know how to help the students in their classes who also struggle. By the same token, candidates with high GPAs might be impatient with learners who do not learn as quickly as they did. On the other hand, many high-GPA candidates also make outstanding teachers. There simply is no pattern, so we must be careful about weighing GPA too heavily in selection decisions.

The team of instructors who will be working most closely with the candidates in the training process should conduct the selection interviews. They should develop a series of interview questions that all candidates answer so there is some standardization, but follow-up questions that delve more deeply into a candidate's initial response are also a part of a good interview session. The members of the interview team should keep their own rating and comments sheet private and divulge their evaluations only after everyone in the candidate pool has been interviewed. This will keep the process more objective.

There are many important questions to ask potential teacher candidates. One of the often-asked and insightful questions for prospective teacher candidates is simply, "Why do you want to be a teacher?" Another is, "What would I see if I were to visit your classroom when you are a teacher?" Still a third would be, "Tell us about an incident when you helped someone learn something." Each of these sorts of open-ended questions gives the candidates an opportunity to display crucial attitudes about teaching. Listen carefully to whether they focus on helping students develop their potential or simply on conveying the course content. Are their first comments about themselves as teachers or about their students as learners? Do they understand the "process" orientation of teaching or is their mission simply to deliver information? The teacher who is focused on the unique learning needs of each student and who consciously relates their instruction to these needs will be far more likely to be successful in drawing out the capabilities of their students.

PROGRAM STRUCTURE

Well-designed cohort teacher-training programs are especially effective because they provide a structure for support and nurturance that enables the candidate to develop more fully. One effective model that has been used successfully brings a cohort of about 20 students together with a faculty cohort of two to three faculty and a graduate teaching assistant or part-time additional instructor.[13] In this model, all of the course work and student teaching supervision for the 20 students is delivered by the three- to four-member faculty cohort. The faculty must be versatile and intensely committed, but the dividends, because of the continuity of this approach, are powerful. There is also much more accountability in this model as compared with a more traditional model whereby any one faculty member sees a candidate for only a single course in the training program. In the cohort model, the same instructors follow the candidates through the entire program. There is ample opportunity to remediate problems that a candidate might have, and there is no passing the buck about who is responsible if a candidate is not a strong teacher by the end of the program.[14]

Several other structural elements of traditional teacher education programs should be challenged. We must break with the traditions of teacher education in how we sequence programs. Typically, we focus on the most abstract concepts first. Teacher licensure students in most university programs complete three to nine credits in so-called 'foundations' course work as the first phase of their training program. In these courses, they study educational philosophy, the history of education, and the like. While the understandings in these courses are ultimately important for the candidate, these subjects have little to do with the essential issues of life in the classroom and, therefore, often turn off perspective candidates because they are not ready for them. It works better to hold these "foundations" until after the candidate has actually had significant classroom experience. After the candidate has experience in the classroom teaching, he or she will be more ready for these abstract concepts. A better approach might be to begin with an emphasis on more concrete elements like teaching strategies, effective lesson planning, and techniques for classroom management. There will be a readiness for these components well before there will be a readiness for more philosophical concepts.

THE TEACHER EDUCATION CLASSROOM AS A LABORATORY

The optimal program structure will utilize the actual instructional experiences that the instructors and students are having in each class as a significant part of the candidate learning. For example, when the teacher educators post their behavioral objectives for a class or use an "anticipatory set," they might ask their candidates what the reasoning was for taking these steps and how these strategies would promote learning. Before a class ends, the instructor might distribute his or her lesson plan and lead a critique of that day's lesson: "What worked and what didn't and why?" In this way, every bit of instruction can count doubly. There are the materials or skills that are the content focus of the lesson, but there is also the discussion of the processes of learning that the candidates experienced that day.

Student Teaching

The final student teaching experience is the make-or-break part of a teacher preparation program. All too often, it is a very negative experience for teacher candidates, and it might not allow them to develop the skills they will need once they are certified. In traditional programs, there is only a single culminating student teaching experience during which the candidates must practice and show proficiency in the myriad skills of teaching under great pressure. Since the whole experience typically lasts only 12 to 14 weeks, they must become quickly acclimated to a school they might never have been in before and adapt to the system and personality of a mentor teacher they have never met, build instant relationships with 150 or more students, and then demonstrate literally thousands of skills they have been introduced to in theory but have not practiced in any real setting before. If the candidate isn't a perfect match with the style of the mentor teacher or the representative from the university who oversees student teaching, the situation becomes even more difficult.

The emergence of professional development schools (PDSs) is a step in the right direction because teacher candidates in this context get at least some classroom experience before they face student teaching. The way PDSs are structured, candidates are usually assigned as aides in a classroom and in the school where they will eventually student teach. This happens a full semester before the actual student teaching is to take place. This experience does give candidates a feel for the philosophy of the teacher they will student teach with. Also, they get to know the students they will teach. Unfortunately, despite these advantages, PDSs don't acquaint the teacher candidate with the contextual issues of teaching, so the candidates might complete their program not realizing that each teaching situation they will find themselves in will be unique. Teaching in junior high school is much different from teaching in senior high, for example, and teaching in an urban elementary school will be a much different experience from teaching in suburban or rural ones, and teaching high school in one community will be different from teaching high school in a different community.

Imagine a program intended to train high-quality physicians that only provided their candidates with a single opportunity to practice their medical skills. The results would be scary. There would be simply too many skills to master in that single all-important experience. Fortunately, medical schools are too wise to do this, and schools of education should be too.

A MORE EFFECTIVE APPROACH TO THE PRESERVICE EDUCATION OF TEACHERS

Universities willing to commit the resources to make student teaching work better for their candidates are adopting a multiple approach to student teaching that is like the system of rotations in a medical or veterinary school. Teaching is too complex to give teachers-in-training all the theory they will need to be effective and then have them try to practice it in a single student-teaching experience. It is much better to give them a few specific skills and understandings and then let them go into a classroom and practice those. Besides classroom management skills, they might be given question-asking and discussion skills and some simple lesson-planning strategies. Then, let them actually teach with close supervision from their teacher training faculty. They will then come back to campus and process their experience working with those skills before looking at additional skills.

I am familiar with one teacher licensure program in which there are four actual student-teaching experiences. The shortest involves only about 25 hours of actual teaching, but those hours enable the prospective teacher to try specific skills and return to the campus or teacher training site with questions and concerns. Having four separate experiences also allows the student teacher to see and become aware of the contextual nature of teaching. In this particular program, which prepares secondary-level teachers, the students-in-training teach for a week in a rural classroom, then nine weeks in a middle school or junior high school, another week in an urban classroom, and finally nine weeks in a senior high school. These experiences are carefully supervised, and they are spread throughout their program with theory and other "foundations" courses presented between each.[15] Mass theory first and then mass practice simply is not a brain-friendly sequence. Moreover, programs that offer these contextual experiences can reveal the potential in student teachers that might not otherwise be realized.

In addition to learning the sophisticated skill set needed to be effective in a classroom, candidates must also learn the skills and dispositions to be agents of change after they graduate. Regardless of how competent they are or how forward looking their training program is, their knowledge and skills will be to some degree obsolete in a relatively short period of time as they enter the teaching profession. They must emerge from their university or college training understanding the need for and being committed to continuous personal and professional growth. Even more of a challenge, they must understand how to work collaboratively to promote program improvement and innovation in a complex organization like a school.

THE ONGOING PROFESSIONAL DEVELOPMENT OF TEACHERS

John Goodlad referred to the ideal for teacher development as being a "seamless web."[16] Preservice training ought to flow in a natural, uninterrupted way right into the training that practicing classroom teachers receive through their school or district. The well-being and achievement of young people depend on the quality of ongoing learning available to their teachers. If the teachers' need for their own learning is met, there is a far greater likelihood that their students will be enthusiastic learners. The National Commission on Teaching and America's Future put it this way:

> Ultimately, the quality of teaching depends not only on the qualifications of the individuals who enter teaching but also on how schools structure teaching work and teachers' learning opportunities.[17]

Unfortunately, the seamless web ideal is rarely realized. New teachers, typically fresh from their preservice training, sign their first contract and enter their own classroom only to find very meager learning opportunities available in their building and district. There is usually a "new teacher inservice" that focuses on district policies, insurance, sick leave, and the like. They will be assigned a mentor teacher who is to assist them in learning their new craft, but seldom are they or their mentor provided enough time away from their teaching responsibilities to meet for genuine learning or mentoring opportunities. There will be a day or so in the fall and spring when their district offers some form of professional development, but these sessions are often diluted with presentations about security proceedings, building lockdowns, or policies on absenteeism. At the time when new teachers need the most help and have the greatest desire to be learners, what they receive is often inadequate and unstimulating.

For most school districts, the lack of adequate professional development is due to the twin problems of lack of resources and the ignorance of the public. Teacher learning that is done well is expensive. The National Staff Development Council advocates that a school system dedicate at least 10 percent of its budget and 25 percent of its educators' work time to learning. In actuality, very few school systems commit even 1 percent of their budgets to professional growth, and a day a week of professional learning opportunity is unheard of anyplace in our nation.[18]

This lack of resources is related to the ignorance of large numbers of the American public. Many Americans fail to understand the extent and intensity of a teacher's workweek. The average elementary and secondary teachers in the United States are in front of their students 25 to 30 hours a week. This does not count lesson preparation time or time to confer with colleagues, time to evaluate student work, and time to take care of all the administrative detail for which every teacher is responsible. In other nations of the developed world, against which our students' achievement is compared—Japan, France, Germany, etc.—the hours of formal teacher instruction number about half the weekly total for teachers in the United States.

This fact is relevant because the public becomes irritated when schools announce that students are not to be at school because it is a professional development day or even professional development hour. Some parents will have to find child care coverage, and this is expensive for them. Schools can buy teacher time outside of contract hours, on Saturdays or in the summer, to carry on professional learning, but this is very expensive and it becomes an issue of available resources.

IF THE RESOURCES WERE AVAILABLE, WHAT WOULD A MODEL PROFESSIONAL DEVELOPMENT PROGRAM LOOK LIKE?

Some professional development activities in a building or district will inevitably be reactive. If a curriculum committee adopts a new textbook, procedure, or technology, teachers will need to be helped to understand how to effectively incorporate the innovation into their teaching. The research of Bruce Joyce and Beverly Showers makes it clear that the innovation will not end up being utilized without far more training time and effort than educators have previously assumed were necessary. Even with many demonstrations and opportunities for the teacher to try the innovations and be videotaped and critiqued, the new approach still won't be adopted without a peer coaching process.[19] When teachers have time and a nonthreatening process like peer coaching, innovation and change occur far more certainly and rapidly. One of the keys to an effective professional development program is making the investment to incorporate a peer coaching program in a school.

The degree to which teachers are involved in visioning and carrying out their own professional development is another key to inspiring classroom learning. Chapter 8 details several approaches to building learning communities in the classroom. In these approaches, the learning process is energized because the instructor creates an environment where much of the control and responsibility for the learning is given to the student. In the same spirit, schools may become professional learning communities when teachers are provided the resources and opportunity to plan and implement their own learning around the agreed upon goals of their school and district. In some of these communities, teachers are forming their own study groups to look at their classroom achievement test data and to develop plans to improve the results. In other schools, small groups of faculty organize themselves to read and discuss articles and books about effective teaching. Some of these even develop "accountability partnerships" to commit themselves to experiment with strategies and ideas they encounter in their study.

LESSON STUDY: ANOTHER PROFESSIONAL DEVELOPMENT STRATEGY

An exciting tool for teacher development that operates in the spirit of a learning community has been brought to the United States recently from Japan. Referred to as "lesson study," this innovation provides a structure and process to assist teachers in deepening their understanding of teaching. The process works in cycles. Small groups of teachers, usually having a similar teaching assignment, form with a commitment to think at a deeper level about the teaching of a particular piece of content. They collaborate in searching diagnostically for weak areas in their curriculum. Then they think through and plan a lesson or series of lessons related to these identified areas of need. Ultimately they will all teach these special lessons in a rotating manner. The ongoing dialogue about the development of the lesson in which different perspectives and understandings are brought in is one of the keys to this process. The isolation that so many American teachers experience is lessened, and each teacher benefits from the creativity of the others.[20]

When the special lesson has been developed, one of the teachers teaches it in his or her classroom with the other teachers observing carefully. During the conduct of the lesson, the observers are gathering evidence about student learning. What parts of the lesson really seem to capture student attention? Which students are involved and which are not?

At the conclusion of the lesson, the team discusses the evidence gathered by the observers about what worked well and what didn't. These observations are then used to revise and improve the lesson, which is then taught again by another team member in his or her classroom. As before, careful observations are made and then discussed, and the lesson is thought through and revised again. If desired, it may be taught yet a third time. Lesson study is credited with enabling Japanese science teachers to make dramatic shifts in their teaching from lecture-oriented approaches to those that promote genuine student involvement and understanding.[21]

EDUCARE

New understandings about how the brain most naturally learns are causing educators to rethink the skill sets teachers need in order to be effective and inspirational. The Latin verb *educare,* from which we get our word *education,* describes an approach to instruction that fits what we are coming to understand about the way the brain learns best. *Educare* means "to draw out from." It implies that the learner already possesses the ingredients for any new understanding. It simply must be drawn out. The drawing-out approach utilizes the curiosity as well as the innate problem-solving abilities that are inherent in all learners. It is centered on challenging questions or puzzlements that engage the learner in seeking and finding answers. The teacher's role in this *educare* is to be a question finder, problem poser, clarifier, orchestrator of full student participation, and guide.

The contrast between the *educare* approach and current practice is significant. The most prevalent instructional approach today might be best described with the Latin verb *ponere,* which means "to put in." Researchers who observe classrooms, especially at the secondary level, see a prevalence of what is sometimes termed "direct instruction." In this approach, which certainly also has a place—though limited—in our classrooms, the teacher is the information giver, lecturer, and question answerer. The student is the recipient of knowledge but spends little energy attempting to acquire it. Unfortunately, as David Sousa has said, "Passive learning is an oxymoron."[22]

If we aspire to have more *educare* in our classrooms, we will need different approaches to teacher training, both preservice and inservice. The preservice component is especially critical because students on university or college campuses who wish to enter the teaching profession have been fed throughout their secondary and college careers with a full diet of teacher-centered instruction. At the collegiate level, that is virtually all they will have experienced. It will take more extensive and intensive training to help these candidates understand and practice other and more brain-friendly ways of teaching.

Already-practicing teachers also need new approaches to their ongoing training that are different from what is typically done in our schools today. They will have had little instruction in lesson study strategies or in understanding how the brain learns. They will need to experience and learn how to use problem-solving strategies and methodologies that enable the learner to learn without being placed in a passive mode. They will need opportunities to practice the drawing-out skills within the safe environment of a peer coaching process. They will flourish in learning these new skills, especially if they come, even gradually, to control and direct their own professional development programs.

CONCLUSION

As teachers experience the power of the *educare* approaches in their own training, we will see a greater commitment to constructivist approaches to learning in their classrooms. When their learners, in turn, become more active and confident in building more of their own knowledge, they will experience greater degrees of academic success. The process spirals upward. Each incidence where the learners have learned something important by their own energies reinforces their skills and desires to learn. They are realizing more of their potential. The success of students energizes teachers to use more of these strategies. Success not only breeds success but also facilitates change as new patterns evolve in the classroom.

NOTES

1. Conversation between Andrew Richburg and Dr. Paul Wicklund, Minneapolis, MN. (1996, Spring).
2. Beyer, B. K. (1971). *Inquiry in the social studies classroom*. Columbus, OH: Merrill.
3. Sirotnik, K. A. (1983, February). What you see is what you get: Consistency, persistency and mediocrity in the classrooms. *Harvard Educational Review, 53*(1), 16–31.
4. Smilkstein, R. (1993). The natural human learning process. *Journal of Developmental Education, 17*(2), 2–10.
5. Beyer, B. K. (1971).
6. Howard, P. (2002). *The owner's manual for the brain*. Atlanta, GA: Bard Press, p. 44.
7. Wilkerson, L., & Gijselaers, W. H. (1996). *Bringing problem-based learning to higher education*. San Francisco: Jossey-Bass.
8. Williams, J. (2004). *Fifty facts that should change the world*. Icon Books.
9. Darling-Hammond, L. (2002). Teacher quality and student achievement: A review of state policy evidence. *Education Policy Analysis Archives, 8*, 1.
10. Darling-Hammond, L. (2002), p. 18.
11. National Commission on Teaching and America's Future. (1996). *What matters most: Teaching for America's future*. New York: Carnegie.
12. Richburg, R. W., & Knox, K. (1996, Spring). Adding power to our ability to develop outstanding new teachers. *The Teacher Educator, 3*(4), 259–270.
13. Richburg, R. W., & Knox, K. (1996).
14. Richburg, R. W., Penna, C. J. , McWhorter, B. A., Paccione, A. V., & Knox, K. A. (1996, November 5). *Can universities afford to train world class teachers: A cost benefit study*. Paper presented to International Council for Innovation in Higher Education, Vancouver, Canada.
15. Richburg, R. W., et al. (1996).

16. Goodlad, J. I. (1994). *Teachers for our nation's schools*. San Francisco: Jossey-Bass.

17. National Commission on Teaching and America's Future. (1996), p. 189.

18. National Staff Development Council Resolutions. (2005). Retrieved July 6, 2006, from www.nsdc.org

19. Interview with Bruce Joyce. (1998, Fall). *Journal of Staff Development, 19*(4), 33–35.

20. Lewis, C. C. (2002, November/December). What are the essential elements of lesson study? *The California Science Project Connection*, 2(6), 1.

21. Lewis, C. C., & Tsuchida, I. (1998, Winter). A lesson is like a swiftly flowing river. *American Educator, 23*, pp.12–17, 50–52.

22. Sousa, D. A. (2001). *How the brain learns*. Thousand Oaks, CA: Corwin Press.

Index

Academy eBriefings, 112
Acceleration, 142
Accountability, 8
Active learning, 124–125
Adolescents. *See* Early adolescent learners; Teenage learners
Adults:
  creativity, lack of, 59
  early adolescents and, 113
Age, 112, 113–114
Air travel class, 94
Alcohol, 74, 113
Alzheimer's disease, 74–75
American public, 201
Amrein, A., 10
Amygdala, 127, 130
Anderson, J., 36
Aptitude, 40, 66
Aristotle, 140
ASIA-U$A acronym, 130–131
"Ask them" method, 154–160
Assessment:
  "ask them" method for, 154–160
  testing obsession, 8–10
Assessment strategies:
  approaches to, 169–172
  informal feedback, 172–173
  instructional sequences, 167–168
  measuring what students are learning, 173–177
  overview of, 165–167
  tests *vs.* projects, 177–179
Atlas of Canada Web site, 102
Attention, 117
Attitude, 7
Attitudinal measures, 171
Axon, 53, 57
Barr, R., 150, 154
Beliefs:
  neural network changes and, 71
  teacher beliefs about students, 19–28, 69
Bereiter, C., 124
Berger, R., 116
Berliner, D., 9, 14
Beyer, B., 188, 190
Bloom, B. S.:
  early learning environment findings, 85
  on student assessment, 165, 170, 179
Boredom, 121–123
Boys, 112, 113
Brady, E. M., 150
Brain:
  active learning/problem solving, 124–125
  of adolescents, 63–65, 133–134
  ASIA-U$A acronym, 130
  boredom's effects on, 121
  brain-friendly learning environment, 85–88
  complexity of, 56, 58
  connected learning, 125–126
  early adolescent, physical changes in, 112–114
  emotion and learning, 127–128
  environment for learning, 118–119
  feeding, 75
  growth from experiences, 83–84
  learning of preadolescents, 98–99
  multiple intelligences, 92–93
  plasticity of, 70–71
  of preadolescents, 97
  problem solving and, 129–130
  social learning, 126–127
  stress and, 123

Brain, learning process of:
  Alzheimer's disease, 74–75
  complexity of brain, 56, 58
  constructivism, 60–63
  creativity, 59
  drugs/alcohol and, 74
  emotions, fight or flight, 59–60
  feeding the brain, 75
  first-stage learning tasks, 71–74
  knowledge about, 47
  metacognitive knowledge of, 52–53
  motivation, 58–59, 63–69
  neural networks, 53–56, 57
  neurons, 53
  plasticity of brain, 70–71
  rote learning, 56
  seven magic words, 48–52
  students' potential, opportunities for, 75–76
Brain cells, 53–56
"Branches and twigs" metaphor, 52–53
Bransford, J. D.:
  on constructivism, 60, 61, 68
  on learning and brain structure, 56
  on shaping of brain, 64
Brown, A. L.:
  on constructivism, 60, 61
  on learning and brain structure, 56
  on shaping of brain, 64, 68
Brownlee, C., 75
Bullying, 97
Bumpass, L. L., 113

Cambridge Bay, Canada:
  Inuit of, examination of, 101–108
  Inuit society today, 108–109
Candidate selection process, 196–197
Carnegie Council on Adolescent Development, 112, 113
Carper, J., 75
Castle Project:
  description of, 128–130
  student assessment and, 172–177
Ceiling level:
  coordinated studies programs and, 158
  learning, 39–40
  neural networks and, 62
Character building, 173
Checkley, K., 34
Chemicals, 59–60
Chess, 123
Child Study Center, University of British Columbia, 86–87
Children:
  brain's learning and experience, 83–84
  creativity of, 59
  See also Elementary learners; Students
Chivalry, medieval, 129
Churchill, W., 10–13, 15
Classroom:
  as community, 14
  environment, 193–194
  injustices, performance and, 165–166
  math for early learners, 83–95
  math learning outside, 93–95
  math-friendly environment, 85–88
  playful, 15–17
  teacher training, as laboratory, 198–199
"Climb the ladder" game, 88
Climograph, 102
Clocks, pendulum, 138–140
Clustered courses, 151
Cocking, R. R.:
  on constructivism, 60, 61
  on learning and brain structure, 56
  on shaping of brain, 64, 68
Cohort. *See* Group learning
Colburn, E.:
  Justin Matott and, 114–115
  relationships with students, 116–118
  teaching characteristics of, 115–116
Columbus, C., 139
Combs, A., 13
Community, classroom as, 14
Compassion, 130
Computers, 85
Connected learning, 125–126
Connection:
  connected learning, 125–126
  in coordinated studies programs, 160
  first-stage learning tasks for, 71–74
  students who can't connect, 68–69
Constructivism:
  brain's learning process and, 60–63
  building on incomplete knowledge, 68
  constructivist learning of preadolescents, 98–99
  learning about the past, 99–101
  math curricula, 34
Content, 6–7
Contract grading systems, 118
Contrasts, 98
Control, student, 117–118
Conversation:
  for social learning, 126–127
  speech of children, 84–85
Cookie making, 88

Coordinated studies programs:
in learning communities, 151–152
student feedback from, 153–154
Coral atolls, 135–137
Cortex, 63–65
Cortisol, 60, 123
Courses:
linked/clustered, 151
multicourse programs, 151–152
stand-alone, 150
teacher training, natural learning, 197
Creativity, 59
Critical thinking:
coordinated studies programs and, 152
Criticism, of students, 13
Curiosity, natural:
memory and, 190
problem-solving instruction and, 192
student, capturing, 188
Curriculum:
bloated, 6–7
math content for early grades, 88–92
teacher's curriculum goals, 116

Dahl, R., 112
Darling-Hammond, L., 195
Darwin, C., 136–137
Data sheet, 186–189
Delpit, L., 69
Dendrites:
of adolescent brain, 63, 64
brain's learning process and, 52
"branches and twigs" metaphor for, 52–53
connected learning and, 126
constructivist learning, 61
environment and growth of, 119
growth from experiences, 83–84
growth of, 53, 55
in neural network, 57
plasticity of brain, 70, 71
student connection to learning, 69
Denny, M., 124
Denny, T., 16
Dewey, J., 84, 94
Dialogue, 126–127
Diamond, M.:
environment study of, 118–119, 121
Magic Trees of the Mind, 87
Diary, 86
Differentiation, 42, 71–72
Direct instruction, 203–204
Discussion, group, 152, 158–159
Disney, W., 12
Disputes, student, 158
Distant place:
examination of, 101–108
state in today's world, 108–109
Divorce, 113–114
Domination, group, 158
Dornan, Mr., 120
Drinking, 74, 113
Drinking Fountain Joe (Matott), 115
Dropout rates, 10
Dropouts, 31
Drugs, 74, 113
Dweck, C., 35

Early adolescent learners:
active learning, problem solving, 124–125
ASIA-U$A acronym, 130–131
boredom, solutions for, 121–123
Castle Project, 128–130
connected learning, 125–126
emotion, importance of, 127–128
environment for, 118–121
family situations of, 113–114
physical changes, 112–113
play, importance of, 123
relationship with teacher, 116–118
social learning, 126–127
stress and learning, 123
teachers for, 131–132
teaching, 114–116
transformations in early adolescence, 111–112
Earth:
gravity and, 140–142
relativity and, 144–145
satellites and, 143–144
Educare, 203–204
Education:
classroom as community, 14
creativity, lack of, 59
life-altering teachers, 12–13
Maginot Line, moral of, 3–5
misdirection of, 5–10
Educators. *See* Teachers
Einstein, A.:
on identification of problem, 134–135
as student, 12
theory of relativity, 144–145
Eisenberg, L., 126
Elementary learners:
distant place examination, Cambridge Bay, 101–108
Inuit society today, 108–109

natural learning of, 97
past, discovery of, 98–99
past unit, beginning, 99–101
real-world math for early learners, 83–95
Emotions:
brain and, 59–60
of early adolescents, 112–113
emotional barriers to math, 87–88
importance of, 127–128
Empowerment:
brain's learning process and, 52–53
emotions and, 60
seven magic words and brain, 48
student control in instruction, 117–118
students figuring it out themselves, 48–52
Engaged learning, 154–160
English literature class, 72–73
"Entity theory", 35
Environment:
boredom, solutions for, 121–122
for early adolescents learners, 118–121
family situations of early adolescents, 113–114
learning and, 83–84
math learning outside classroom, 93–95
math-friendly, 85–88
supporting risk-taking, 193–194
Estimating, 89
Eton College, 12–13
Europe, 3–5
Evaluation:
of brain-compatible teaching, 95
in coordinated studies programs, 159–160
See also Assessment strategies
Experience, 87

Faculty collaboration, 154
Faculty development activity, 23, 74
Failure, fear of, 67
Family:
of early adolescents, 113–114
life in the past project and, 99–100
See also Parents
F.A.R.M. method, 172–173
Fate:
nature *vs.* nurture, 35–37
of students, 34–35
Fear, of success, 65, 67–68
Feedback:
assessment and, 169–172
capabilities development and, 177–179
informal, 172–173
on learning communities, 152–154
methodology, 169–170
performance and, 165–167
Fight or flight, 59–60
FIGs (Freshman Interest Groups), 151
Figuring it out:
active learning/problem solving, 124–125
creativity, 59
learning through, 191–192
in NHLP pedagogy, 42
no-fail first stage learning tasks, 71
seven magic words for brain, 48–52
student participation in, 156
First connection, 160
First-stage learning tasks, 71–74
Fishbowl seminars, 152
Food, for brain, 75
Fractions, 88–89
France, 3–5
Free fall, 143
Freedom, 86, 97
Freshman Interest Groups (FIGs), 151

Gabelnick, F., 150, 154
Gabriel, J. G., 22
Galilei, G., 138–140
Games:
"Climb the ladder", 88
for evaluation, 95
"I Spy" game, 94
for math learning, 91–92
for multiple intelligences, 92–93
"mystery contest", 121–122
"People bag" presentations, 117
"People scavenger hunt", 117
seal hunt game, 106–107
"Weird Things That Hardly Anyone Knows Contest", 122–123
Gardner, H., 130, 152
Geehan, W., 90
Gender:
age of puberty, 112
children of divorce and, 113–114
nature *vs.* nurture and, 37
women, treatment of, 125
Geometry, 90–91
Germany, 3–5
Giedd, J., 134
Gijselaers, W. H., 191
Girls, 112, 113–114
Glucose, 75

Goals, 116
Goethe, J. W., 3
Goodlad, J., 200
Grade point average (GPA), 196
Grading:
  alternative approaches to, 174
  contract grading systems, 118
  open-ended test components, 174–175
  rubric, Castle Project, 175–176
  tests *vs.* projects, 177–179
Gravity:
  Galileo's theory of, 138
  relativity, 144–145
  satellites and, 143–144
  scientific investigation of, 140–143
Great Barrier Reef, 135
Group discussions, 152, 158–159
Group learning:
  interest inventory for, 183
  student assessment and, 168–169, 172
  Teacher Observation Form for, 182
  in teacher training program, 197
Gudkov, N., 135
Gunn, A. M.:
  elementary learners, learning about the past, 97–109
  real-world math for early learners, 83–95
  scientific investigation for teenage learners, 133–145
Gunnison Middle School, Colorado, 128–130

Hamilton, C., 153–154
Hamlet (Shakespeare), 73
Harder, B., 75
Harnish, J.
  coordinated studies program, 155, 159
  "The Russians as People" course, 48–51
Harvard Graduate School of Education, Interdisciplinary Studies Project, 149–150, 152
Harvard Medical School, 64
Hattie, J., 167
Healy, J. M., 51
Heath, S. B., 69
Herman-Giddens, M. E., 112, 113
High, M., 128–130
High school dropouts, 31
"High Score Education: Games, Not School, Are Teaching Kids to Think" (McGee), 58
Hobson, J., 119
Holt, S. R., 150
Home:
  of early adolescents, 113–114
  student transition to school, 84–85
House construction metaphor, 98–99
Howard, P. J., 171, 190
Howell, Mr., 120–121

"I Spy" game, 94
Ideas, 159
Identical twins, 35–36
Igloos, 105–106
Illinois Valedictorian Project, 16
"Incremental theory", 35
Individual/Small Group/Whole Group (I/SG/WG):
  for cognitive construction, 99, 100
  for first-stage learning tasks, 72
  NHLP pedagogy, 42–43
Informal feedback, 172–173
Initiative, student, 174
Injustices, classroom, 165–166
Instruction, natural-learning style, 186–189
Instruction paradigm, 150
Instructional sequences, 167–168
Intellectual abilities, 133–134
Intelligence. *See* Multiple intelligences
Interdisciplinary Studies Project, 149–150, 152
Interest, in learning, 41
Interest inventory, 179, 183
Internet, 102, 142–143
Interpersonal intelligence, 130
Inuit:
  of Cambridge Bay, Canada, 101–108
  society today, 108–109
Inuktitut, 107
Irwin, J., 141–142

Jacobs, B., 61
Japan, 202–203
Jensen, E., 119
Jesus, 84
Joyce, B., 201

Kerns, T., 155
Kinesthetic intelligence, 130
Knowledge:
  of brain's learning process, 47
  constructivism, 60–63
  curriculum bloat and, 6
  experience and, 83–84
  house construction metaphor for, 98–99

metacognitive, benefits of, 38–41
See also Metacognitive knowledge
Knox, K., 195, 197
Koerger, A., 53
KWL technique, 118

Laboratory, teacher training, 198–199
Ladson-Billing, G., 69
Land, G., 59
Lardner, E. D., 150, 156
Latitude, 139
Lazar, S., 64
Leakey, M., 12
Leaning tower of Pisa, 140–141
Learners, 66
See also Early adolescent learners; Elementary learners; Teenage learners
Learning:
active learning, 124–125
brain cells and, 53
connected learning, 125–126
engaged, 154–160
environment for, 85–88
learners' levels of ability, 66
measuring, 173–177
misdirection of education, 5–10
as organic process, 76
play and, 15–17
social learning, 126–127
See also Natural human learning process; natural learning
Learning communities:
"ask them" method, 154–160
"lesson study" and, 202–203
models of, 150–154
overview of, 149–150
student potential, 160
traditional system *vs.*, 150
Learning Communities National Resource Center, 150
Learning community models:
coordinated studies programs, 151–152
FIGs, 151
Interdisciplinary Studies Project, 152
linked/clustered courses, 151
overview of, 150
student feedback, 152–154
Learning disability, students with, 65
Learning paradigm, 150
Learning process:
classroom example, 19–28
fate, nature *vs.* nurture, 35–37
NHLP in math, 33–34
NHLP pedagogy, 42–43
NHLP research/metacognitive knowledge, benefits of, 38–41
potential, motivation of students, 41–42
research on NHLP, 28–33
students, different fates of, 34–35
students as natural learners, 19
students' self-understanding, 37–38
See also Brain, learning process of
Learning tasks, first-stage, 71–74
Lecture, 7, 190
"Lesson study", 202–203
Levine, M., 65
Lewis, C. C., 203
Licensure policies, compromised, 195
Life preparation goals, 6–7
Lindblad, J., 150
Linguistic intelligence, 130
Linked courses, 151
Logical intelligence, 130
Longitude, 139–140
Long-term memory:
emotions and, 127–128
natural learning and, 190–191

MacGregor, J., 150, 154
Magellan, 139–140
Magic Trees of the Mind (Diamond), 87
Magic words, seven, 48–52, 58, 72
Maginot, A., 3–4
Maginot Line, 3–5
Malnarich, G., 150, 156
Manchester, W., 12
Mann, D., 15
Mansilla, V. B., 149
Mantle, M., 120
Map sample, 181
Mapes, L. V., 34
Margulies, S., 123
Marshall, G., 12
Marzano, R. J., 167, 171
Mastery, 58
Materials, stimulus, 194
Math:
Mickey Mantle's home run exercise, 120
multiple intelligences and, 92
neural networks of students and, 69
NHLP in, 33–34
Math, real-world math for early learners:
brain development and experience, 83–84
evaluation, 95
learning outside classroom, 93–95

math content, 88–92
math-friendly environment, 85–88
multiple intelligences, student potential, 92–93
transition from home to school, 84–85
Matott, J., 114–115
Matthews, R. S., 150, 154
Mayo, C. H. P., 11, 15
Maze, 93
McGee, J. P., 58, 61
McGill University Lifelong Learning Institute, 155
McLaren, J., 7
McPhail, C. J., 69
McPhail, I. P., 69
McWhorter, B. A., 197
Measurement, 89–90
The Media Project, 112
Meditation, 64
Memory:
emotions and, 127–128
lecture and, 7, 190
long-term memory, 190–191
tests and, 60
Menarche, 112
Menstruation, 112
Mental effort, 190
Mentoring, teacher, 200
Metacognitive knowledge:
benefits of, 38–41
of brain's learning process, 52–58
on emotions and brain, 60
as resource, 68
Metaphors:
for brain concepts, 52–53
for knowledge, 98–99
Mid-Continent Regional Educational Laboratory, 6
Middle Ages:
castle placement question, 124
"Castle Project", 128–130
Model professional development program, 201–202
Models. *See* Learning community models
Montgomery, Mrs., 15–16
Mood swings, 112
Moon, 141–142
Moore, W. S., 150
Moriarity, Mr., 11
Motivation:
brain's learning process and, 58–59
to learn, 48
reasons for lack of, 63–69
self-motivation, 87
of students to learn, 41–42
Movement, 86
Multiple intelligences:
Castle Project and, 130
student potential and, 92–93
Multiple-choice test format, 177
Musical talent, 92
Mystery contest, 121–122

Naiman, L., 59
National Aeronautics and Space Administration (NASA), 141–142
National Commission on Teaching and America's Future, 195, 200
National Council of Teachers of Mathematics (NCTM), 33–34, 69
National Staff Development Council, 200–201
National Staff Development Council Resolutions, 201
Natural human learning process (NHLP):
ceiling level and neural networks, 62
classroom example, 19–28
fate, nature *vs.* nurture, 35–37
fate of students, 34–35
in math, 33–34
pedagogy, 42–43
potential, motivation of students, 41–42
of preadolescents, 98–101
research on, 28–33
research/metacognitive knowledge, benefits of, 38–41
students as natural learners, 19
students' self-understanding, 37–38
at upper elementary age, 97
Natural learners, students as, 19–28
Natural learning:
active learning/problem solving, 124–125
advantages of, 186–189
past, discovery of, 98–99
why it works, 190–192
Nature *vs.* nurture, 35–37
NCTM (National Council of Teachers of Mathematics), 33–34, 69
Neill, A. S., 97
Nelson, B., 125
Neural networks:
active learning/problem solving and, 124–125
of adolescents, 63–65, 134
ceiling level and, 62

constructivist learning and, 61
elimination of bad networks, 67–68
growth from experiences, 83–84
illustration of, 57
learners' levels of ability, 66
plasticity of, 70–71
of preadolescents, 97
rote learning and, 56
structure of, 53–56
success, fear of, 65, 67
Neurons:
alcohol and, 74
cortisol and, 60
growth from experiences, 83–84
illustration of, 55
neural networks, 53–56
number of, 56
structure of, 53
Neuroplasticity, 70–71, 119
Neurotransmitters, 53, 59–60
Neuschwander, C., 90
NHLP. *See* Natural human learning process
Niolon, R., 113–114
Noe, B., 36
No-fail first-stage learning tasks, 71–74, 160
North Seattle Community College:
learning community program, 153–154
"The Russians as People" course at, 48–51
Novelty, 119–120, 129
Numbers, 88–89
Nunavut, Territory of, 108–109
Nurture *vs.* nature, 35–37

Ongoing, 200–201
Open-ended test components:
for learning assessment, 170
student assessment and, 171–177
Outdoors, 93–94

Paccione, A. V., 197
Parents:
family situations of early adolescents, 113–114
life in the past project and, 99–100
student achievement and, 16
teacher relationships with, 130–131
Participation, student, 155–158
Past, course for elementary learners:
beginning the unit, 99–101
discovery of past, 98–99
distant place examination, Cambridge Bay, 101–108
Inuit society today, 108–109
natural learning at this age, 97
Patione, B., 64
Patterns, 85, 90–91
PDSs (professional development schools), 198–199
Pedagogy:
for cognitive construction, 98–99, 100
NHLP, 42–43
Pendulum clocks, 138–140
Penna, C. J., 197
"People bag" presentations, 117
"People scavenger hunt", 117
Perceptions, 13
Performance, 165–167
Petain, M., 4
Physical changes, of early adolescents, 112–113
Piaget, J.:
brains of young people, 83
constructivism and, 61
sensorimotor substages of, 32–33
teenage intellectual abilities, 133
Pisa, leaning tower of, 140–141
Pituitary gland, 112
Planning time, 5–6
Planum temporale, 92
Plasticity, of brain, 70–71, 119
Play:
choice of children, 92
in classroom, 15–17
importance of, 123
Potential:
of early adolescents, 111
multiple intelligences and, 92–93
of students, opportunities for, 75–76
students' self-understanding, 37–38
of students to learn, 41–42
See also Student potential
Power, 125–126
Practice:
ceiling level and neural networks, 62
for learning process, 38, 41
learning process ceiling level, 39–40
Preadolescents. *See* Elementary learners
Pre-assessment, 171
Prefrontal cortex, 63–65, 134
Pregnancy, teenage, 114
Preservice education, teacher, 199–200

Preservice Teacher Training Program:
  effective education for, 199–200
  for natural learning, 195–196
Pretest/posttest assessment, 159
Principles and Standards for School Mathematics (National Council of Teachers of Mathematics), 33–34
Problem solving:
  in "Castle Project," 129–130
  of early adolescents, 124–125
Problem-solving instruction:
  natural learning, model for, 195–196
  strategies for, 186–189
  teacher skills and, 192–195
  why it works, 190–192
Problem-solving test components, 171, 176–177
Professional development schools (PDSs), 198–199
Professional development strategy, 202–203
Program structure, 197
Programs:
  coordinated studies, 151–152
  teacher training, natural learning, 195–196
  teacher training selection process, 196–197
  teacher training, structure of, 197
"Project Getting to Know You," 117
Projects, 177–179
Pruning, 70
Pythagorean theorem, 120

Questionnaire, 117
Questions:
  in learning about the past class, 100
  natural learning and, 194

Ratey, J. J., 64, 74
Rational learning activities, 153–154
Rats, 118–119, 121
Reading problems, 52
Reis, J. L., 153–154
Relationships:
  of early adolescents, 113–114
  teacher-student, 14, 114–118
Relativity, 144–145
Religious involvement, 16
"Rememberings: The Roots of Our Voices" course, 153–154
Research:
  on constructivism, 60–63
  on NHLP, 28–33
  on NHLP, benefits of, 38–41
  on the past, 99–102
Resolutions, delayed, 135
Resources, teacher development, 201–202
Respect, 173
Richburg, R. W.:
  on assessment strategies, 165–179
  classroom, playful, 15–17
  classroom as community, 14
  early adolescent learners, potential development in, 111–132
  education, misdirection of, 3–10
  student abilities, cultivation of, 10–12
  on teacher development, 185–204
  teachers, life-altering, 12–13
Rogers, C., 97
Roley, R. K., 113
Roosevelt, T., 7
Rose, M., 38
Rote learning, 56
"The Russians as People" course (North Seattle Community College), 48–51

Satellites, 143–144, 145
Saul, M., 34
Scardamalia, M., 124
Scenarios:
  bad networks, elimination of, 67–68
  figuring it out, 48–51
  of NHLP, 19–28
  students' self-understanding, 37–38
Schall, M., 61
Scheibel, A. B., 61, 119
Schiebinger, L., 36–37
Schmidt, W., 34
School:
  high-stakes testing and, 9
  student transition from home to school, 84–85
  See also Classroom; Education
School trips, 93–95
Scientific investigation for teenage learners:
  coral atolls, 136–137
  gravity, 140–143
  pendulum clocks, 138–140
  relativity, 144–145
  satellites, 143–144
  scientific methods, learning to use, 134–135
  teenage intellectual abilities, 133–134
Scientific methods, 134–135
Scott, D., 141–142

Seal hunt game, 106–107
Seals, Inuit and, 103, 104–105, 108
"Seamless web", 200
"See if you can figure this out", 48–52, 58, 72
Self-empowerment:
  emotions and brain, 60
  knowledge of brain's learning process, 52–53
Self-image:
  of early adolescents, 112–113
  negative, fear of success from, 65, 67–68
  pruning negative self-image network, 70
Self-understanding:
  benefits of, 38–41
  of students, 37–38
Sensorimotor substages, Piaget's, 32–33
SES. *See* Socioeconomic status
Seven magic words, 48–52, 58, 72
Shoe (cartoon), 154
Shopping, 89
Showers, B., 201
Single-parent families, 114
Sir Cumference and the First Round Table (Neuschwander and Geehan), 90
Sirotnik, K., 189
Slora, E. J., 112, 113
Smilkstein, R.:
  on brain's natural learning, 47–76, 124
  on connected learning, 126, 190
  on learning communities, 149–160
  on natural human learning process, 19–43
  We're Born to Learn: Using the Brain's Natural Learning Process to Create Today's Curriculum, 28, 69
Smith, B. L., 150, 154
Snow house, 105–106
Snowden, D., 74
Social learning, 126–127
Socioeconomic status (SES):
  fate and nature *vs.* nurture, 36
  NHLP of students, 28–30
  student test performance and, 9
Socrates, 84
Somervell, R., 12, 15
Sousa, D. A., 203
Spatial intelligence, 92, 130
Speech, 84–85
Spielberg, S., 12
Sputnik satellite, 145
Stand-alone courses, 150
Standardized testing, 8–10
Standards:
  curriculum, 6
  math, 34
Sternberg, R. J., 60–61
Stories:
  geometry learning with, 90
  story-method of brain-compatible learning, 84
  storytelling, 92–93
  of young learners, 87
Stress, 60, 123
Student achievement, 195
Student potential:
  coordinated studies programs and, 160
  learning communities and, 160
  motivation to learn, 41–42
  multiple intelligences and, 92–93
  opportunities for, 75–76
Student teaching, 198–200
Students:
  brain's learning process and, 52–53
  constructivism and, 60–61
  coordinated studies programs and, 155–157
  evaluation of learning, 95
  fate of, 34–35
  feedback on learning communities, 152–154
  figuring it out themselves, 48–52
  first-stage learning tasks, 71–74
  latent abilities, cultivation of, 10–12
  life-altering teachers and, 12–13
  math content for early grades, 88–92
  motivation, brain and, 58–59
  motivation, reasons for lack of, 63–69
  as natural learners, 19
  as natural learners, scenario about, 19–28
  NHLP pedagogy and, 42–43
  NHLP research, 28–31
  NHLP research/metacognitive knowledge, benefits of, 38–41
  playful classroom and, 15–17
  relationships with teachers, 14, 114–118
  self-understanding of, 37–38
  testing of, 9
  transition from home to school, 84–85
  See also Early adolescent learners; Elementary learners; Teenage learners
Sub-learnings, 173–174
Success, 65, 67–68

Suicides, 114
Survival, 58–59
Sweet, J. A., 113
Synapse:
  brain and emotions, 59–60
  brain's learning process
    and, 52, 53, 55
  drugs and, 74
  illustration of, 56
  in neural network, 57

Tadlock, D., 52
Tagg, J.:
  on learning communities, 154
  learning paradigm, 150
  on student motivation, 58
  on students' fate, 35
Talent, 10–12
Taylor, K., 150
Teacher development:
  candidate selection process, 196–197
  educare, 203–204
  instruction, natural-learning style
    of, 186–189
  "lesson study", 201–202
  ongoing, 200–201
  overview of, 185–186
  preservice education,
    teacher, 199–200
  preservice teacher training
    program, 195–196
  problem-solving instruction, 192–194
  professional development
    strategy, 202–203
  program structure, 197
  teacher education classroom as
    laboratory, 198–199
Teacher Observation Form, 182
Teacher skills, 192–195
Teacher-centered teaching strategy,
  190–192
Teachers:
  brain-friendly learning environment
    and, 86–87
  constructivism and, 60–61
  development of, 200–201
  for early adolescent learners, 130–132
  early adolescent learners, teaching,
    114–116
  first-stage learning tasks, 71–74
  as guide, 94
  Japanese, 202–203
  learning as natural process, 84
  learning in house construction
    metaphor and, 98–99
  learning process of, 31
  life-altering, 12–13
  misdirection of education, 5–10
  motivation of students and, 65, 67–69
  natural learning, selection process
    for, 196–197
  NHLP pedagogy, 42–43
  NHLP research/metacognitive
    knowledge, benefits of, 41
  play, importance of, 123
  playful classroom and, 15–17
  preparation, student achievement
    and, 195
  preservice, natural learning training
    for, 195–196
  relationships with students, 14
  social learning and, 126–127
  student abilities, cultivation of, 11–12
  students as natural learners, scenario
    about, 19–28
  teacher-student relationships, 114–118
  understanding and, 15
Teaching:
  early adolescents, 114–118, 124–125
  student, for natural learning, 198–199
  team in coordinated studies programs,
    151–152
  traditional *vs.* educare, 203–204
Team teaching, 151–152
Tectonic plates, 137
Teenage learners:
  coral atolls, 136–137
  gravity, 140–143
  pendulum clocks, 138–140
  relativity, 144–145
  satellites, 143–144
  scientific methods, learning to
    use, 134–135
  teenage intellectual abilities, 133–134
  See also Early adolescent learners
Testing:
  brain and emotions, 59–60
  in coordinated studies programs,
    159–160
  obsession with, 8–10
  projects *vs.*, 177–179
  teacher beliefs about students, 22
  See also Assessment
Third International Math Science Study
  (TIMSS), 9
Tiger Stadium, Detroit, 120

Time:
  ceiling level and neural networks, 62
  for learning process, 38, 41
  learning process ceiling level, 39–40
  planning time for teacher, 5–6
  for testing, 8
Titanic (ship), 120–121
Tochterman, S., 125
Tomlinson, C., 71
Traditional educational system, 150
Training, teacher, 195–196
Transfer, 61, 63
Transformations, 111–113
Tree of knowledge, 61, 76
Trips, school, 93–95
Troubleshooting, coordinated studies programs, 158–159
Tsuchida, I., 202, 203
Tuberculosis, 108
Twins, 35–36

Undiagnosed learning disability, 65
University of British Columbia, Canada, 86–87, 143

Verbal skills, 92
Video games, 58

Wall, Maginot Line, 3–5
Wasserman, R. C., 112, 113
Water, 75
Weather, 102, 104–105
Web sites, 102
Weighting, assessment, 173–174
Weightless, 142, 143, 144
"Weird Things That Hardly Anyone Knows Contest", 122–123
Welt, B., 150
We're Born to Learn: Using the Brain's Natural Learning Process to Create Today's Curriculum (Smilkstein), 28, 69
Wesson, K., 9
Wilkerson, L., 191
Williams, J., 192
Williams, W. M., 60–61
Wind, 104
Wolves, 108
Wonderment:
  environment of, 87
  questions for, 124
  spirit of, 86
Wong, Y., 155
World Geography, 124–125
World War I, 3

The Corwin Press logo—a raven striding across an open book—represents the union of courage and learning. Corwin Press is committed to improving education for all learners by publishing books and other professional development resources for those serving the field of PreK–12 education. By providing practical, hands-on materials, Corwin Press continues to carry out the promise of its motto: **"Helping Educators Do Their Work Better."**